A SUMMER'S DIARY

Inspired by tales of times past in rural Yorkshire, David Wilbourne brings alive the rich tapestry of people and places in the Vale of York in the 1960s, seen through the eyes of a country vicar. It is a thoroughly good read – funny, affectionate and touching, with more than a hint of nostalgia. With an extraordinary ability to turn you from laughter to tears, and back again, Wilbourne celebrates the richness of human life with all its ups and downs.

A SUMMER'S DIARY

A SUMMER'S DIARY

by

David Wilbourne

Magna Large Print Books
Long Preston, North Yorkshire,
BD23 4ND, England.

British Library Cataloguing in Publication Data.

Wilbourne, David
   A summer's diary.

A catalogue record of this book is
available from the British Library

ISBN   0-7505-1811-1

First published in Great Britain in 2001 by
HarperCollins Publishers

Copyright © 2001 David Wilbourne

Cover illustration © Celia Chester by arrangement with
HarperCollins Publishers

David Wilbourne asserts the moral right to be identified as the
author of this work.

Published in Large Print 2002 by arrangement with
HarperCollins Publishers

Magna Large Print is an imprint of Library Magna Books Ltd.

Printed and bound in Great Britain by
T.J. (International) Ltd., Cornwall, PL28 8RW

For Gordon Bates,
Bishop of Whitby 1983-99,
and Betty, his wife.

In thanks for all their care
and the twinkle in their eyes.

CONTENTS

ACKNOWLEDGEMENTS

Once again, I am grateful to Dr David Hope, the Archbishop of York, for originally encouraging this series of books.

To my wife Rachel, for editing and proof-reading the work, and for her good humour in keeping me going.

To my parishioners here at Helmsley, on whom this book is not based.

To my valued colleagues Tim Rowe and Sharon Whittington, for not being Herbert Molescroft.

As 1965 gave way to 1966, David Wilbourne charted a new vicar's first few months, as he settled in to his parish deep in the countryside of the Vale of York. *A Summer's Diary* takes up where *A Vicar's Diary* left off, a fortnight after Easter 1966, and leads us through spring and summer to that year's World Cup final, which made its impact even on the forlorn and faraway Withs...

APRIL 1966

Tuesday 26 April

'Well, you see, Vic-ar, it's all ecc-les-i-as-tic-al,' Bill Everingham pronounced, with the sort of self-satisfied look which I guess Einstein had sported when he'd cracked the Theory of Relativity.

'Ee don't try and dazzle us with your long words.' Doris Harsley retaliated. 'Just spit it out and speak plain English!' I felt that was a bit rich coming from Doris. She had a habit of speaking breathlessly, never pausing to punctuate a single sentence. Her words ran into each other, creating a kind of composite effect with more letters than a Welsh railway station whose nameplate was longer than its platform. And her English was far from plain. Having a conversation with Doris meant that any comment by her was followed by a lag which was positively Transatlantic while you feverishly worked out what she had said before you could phrase your reply.

'Ecc-les-i-as-tic-al means to do with t' Church,' Bill continued, unfazed. He and Doris were Kirkwith born and bred, and had known each other since they were babes in arms. Doris' father had worked on Bill's father's farm and the two men had had an easy working relationship which spilled over into an easy friendship between the two families. A genuine affection between the two children had blossomed, despite Doris teasing Bill for his monosyllables and Bill teasing Doris for her multi-syllables.

'Well, of course it's to do with t' Church,' Ivy Weighton chuckled. 'It is t' church garden party we're talking about, after all.' Ivy was another one who had a childhood in common with Bill, which gave them a licence to bicker with each other without the slightest risk of offence.

I yawned. I was chairing a church council meeting, and they always ended up like this. Conversations which went round and round the table, getting nowhere.

'Punch and Jud-y man can't come un-til t' last Sat-ur-day in Jul-y, cos he's care-tak-er at t' Mins-ter Choir School, and they don't break up till then. We can't have it on first Sat-ur-day in Au-gust, cos that's when they have Trans-fig-ur-at-ion Fayre at Skip-with

16

Church, and we can't afford to lose any of our punt-ers to them. And t' Sat-ur-day aft-er that is t' Feast of Ass-umpt-ion week-end at Thick-ett Priory, when t' nuns open up their house and grounds. You know what nos-ey beggars we are in these parts; no one'll be ab-le to re-sist t'chance to look a-round a place that they're norm-all-y shut out of. And nuns are top o' pops at mo-ment, what with t' *Sound of Mus-ic* show-in' at ev-er-y pict-ure house. Ev-er-y-one would swan off to Thick-ett and our gard-en part-y would be like t' *Mar-ie Cel-este*.'

'Oo don't you just love that *Sound of Music*,' Doris Harsley trilled, going off at a tangent. 'That Julie Andrews her voice is so pure so clear so powerful – Supercala-fragalisticexpialidocius – I don't know how she can get all those words out without taking a breath.' The rest of the meeting suddenly succumbed to a corporate cough-ing fit. 'Mind you it seems a funny song for a nun to be singing,' she continued, her brow furrowed, 'Is it Latin or somert?' She directed her gaze at George Broadhurst.

George, who had moved into Kirkwith just the previous year, was Professor of Classics at the newly established university whose buildings were rapidly mushrooming

17

on the horizon on our side of York. 'I think you'll find that's a different film, Doris. You're thinking of another Julie Andrews film – *Mary Poppins*. "Supercalafragalistlcexpialidocius" is just a nonsense phrase to give you confidence when you're tongue-tied or in a fix.'

'But isn't it sung by a nun?'

'I don't recall a nun,' George replied, his brow furrowed. I admired the air of serious-ness he was able to bring to such a trivial conversation. 'Although it is a few months since I took the children to see the film.' George broke off, suddenly looking pensive as well as serious.

I remembered the occasion well, since I had gone along with them, the first outing George and his brood had had since moving in. Just before the move, George's wife had been killed in a car crash, casting him and his bewildered children into deep and utter grief. *Mary Poppins* had made them all laugh for the first time, a jocund glimmer of light in a bereavement which was so black and heavy, a mere hint of a bright dawn which would eventually dispel death's dark night.

As George brooded on his sorry past, I noticed Pam give his hand a secret squeeze.

She was that bright dawn. A teacher who had given up her career to become the Broadhursts' housekeeper and nanny, and now George's fiancée.

'So thir-ti-eth of Jul-y it'll have to be. I don't see what all fuss is ab-out. You mark my words, this World Cup will be a damp squib. I bet none of you can re-mem-ber who won last time or where it was played.'

'Rome,' chimed in Doris.

'No, that was them Olympics,' corrected Ivy. 'Rome 1960.' Everyone gaped at her. Ivy lived on a farm lit by oil-light, out of touch, yet to be electrified. This detailed knowledge of recent sporting history jarred with her somewhat primitive lifestyle.

'Don't worry, I'm not a *Grandstand* addict,' she explained, detecting our incredulity. 'It's just that we've got a tea-towel commemorating it.' *A* tea-towel seemed a bit of an exaggeration, since it suggested that the Weighton household had others. I had visited their farm frequently, and only ever encountered the one tea-towel, used in season and out of season, put to a plethora of uses, from wiping your hands to drying the pots, from covering food to rubbing down the sheepdogs when they'd rolled into a muddy ditch. Given its grubby state, I wondered when its Olympic message was last visible to the naked eye.

'It was Chile,' George pronounced, the answer suddenly dawning on him.

'No it wasn't,' corrected Doris, 'it was the hottest Roman summer on record.'

'Ay, you're right there,' her husband Sam chipped in. 'Medics warned athletes about the dangers of competing in such sweltering temperatures. It didn't do my brassicas any good, and it's colder up here,' he added, as if it hadn't dawned on us hitherto that the Vale of York had a slightly different climate from the balmy Mediterranean.

'No, you misunderstand me,' George spoke calmly, silencing a babble that would have done justice to Bedlam. 'The last World Cup final was played in Chile in South America. Brazil won.'

'Ay, and one of those South A-mer-ic-an teams will win ag-ain, you mark my words. Ev-er-y-bod-y will be fed up with it by the time it gets to t' final. They'll be glad to have an excuse to get away from tell-y and get out into t' fresh air. T' gard-en party will be a crowd pull-er, you just see. I pro-pose we stay with our trad-it-ion-al date and let t' World Cup go hang.'

'So you won't be my World Cup Willie?'

Ivy Weighton teased, fluttering her eyelids at her old school chum.

'I beg your par-don?'

'Oh you've heard that new song as well Ivy have you? Catchy isn't it?' Doris trilled the tune that was taking the charts by storm: 'We all love him still World Cup Willie ... World Cup Willie's his name and football IS HIS GAME!'

As I hastily closed the meeting with a prayer, I caught George Broadhurst's eye and we smiled at each other. At least Doris hadn't asked him if World Cup Willie was a nun.

Wednesday 27 *April*

The Vicar of Charm had called on me earlier today, and left a generous supply of products from the pig-farming end of his vicarage. A ham now hung from my pantry ceiling, and my fridge was packed with bacon, sausages, black pudding, pork chops, tenderloin... Since it would soon be May they all required pretty quick consumption ('Never eat pork when there's no R in the month', went the rural adage), hence my supper plate was piled high. My sheepdog

Dewi was tucking into a massive repast too, slurping the chitterlings that even I in my enthusiasm couldn't quite bring myself to consume.

'My dear boy, just a small present to mark your engagement,' Stamford Chestnut had boomed, and had thrust into my arms two carrier bags, blood seeping from their soggy base. 'We took the beast to Pocklington for slaughter only last week. Or was it the week before? You know, my memory's a bit foggy these days. But anyway, not long ago. Certainly fresh enough to keep you in supplies for a week or two.

'I'm so pleased for you and Rebecca. My daughter Deirdre has sent a little something just for your good woman.' From the ample pocket of his donkey jacket he extracted a can of hair lacquer, self-consciously trying to wipe off the pig's blood which had transferred itself from carrier bag to his hands to the hairspray. All he achieved was to give an uncharacteristic blush to the imposing lady with the blue-tinted hair staring out at us from the label. Deirdre ran a hairdressing salon in the opposite wing of the vicarage from which her brother ran the pig farm. Posh ladies with tight perms to-ed and fro-ed hourly to her end, jarring somewhat with the dirty animal trucks and the pigs squealing at the other side of the premises. The holy Stamford was sandwiched in between his two children's businesses, setting a nice trend for clerical diversification.

'Oh, do thank Deirdre for her kindness,' I exclaimed, feigning gratitude. My Rebecca, with her natural blonde curls, was the least likely to avail herself of the blue-rinse brigade's props. Still, the stuff would come in handy for a tombola prize sometime.

'Now, now, dear boy, don't overdo all this gratitude lark. Deirdre just wanted to send a token of solidarity from one vicarage woman to another. Personally I wouldn't let that stuff get within a mile of my hair. I use it to spray the teak bench outside me church a couple a times a year. It gives the best all-weather seal I've ever come across. And when your church is perched on top of the only moor in the Vale of York, all weathers come at you from every direction.

'Do you know, I even tried spraying it on me trusty pipe to keep the damp out; it's a devil of a job to relight the thing when one of these Yorkshire squalls is billowing about. Unfortunately it not only kept the damp out, it proved a bit too flammable. It was like having a blowtorch wedged between me molars, proper singed me eyebrows it did. It wouldn't have been so bad if the thing had combusted in the privacy of me own vicarage. I was on a funeral visit at the time, and I was just reassuring the weeping widow that cremation was entirely acceptable and whoosh, a jet of flame that would grace an oil rig shot to the ceiling. I think the old dear thought I was giving her a visual aid. Now I know what they mean when they say smoking's bad for you.'

I laughed so much at Stamford's exploits that I had to dab my eyes with my handkerchief. So much of what he did was pure slapstick, unintentional, without a hint of self-consciousness. The last time we'd had a clergy gathering for breakfast at his house, he'd confused a pack of soap suds with a pack of oats, which meant a very po-faced lay reader became even more po-faced when he found he had a mouthful of detergent rather than porridge.

I reminded Stamford of the incident, and he too started chortling. 'Pompous ass. No more than he deserved. Mind you, funny you should mention that, because that's another reason why I called round today. The Bishop of Pocklington wants you to take Herbert Molescroft under your wing, give him a taste of what it's like to be a vicar. Apparently our saintly Herbert has been bleating on to the Bishop about wanting to be ordained, so the Bishop thought he'd call his bluff and give him a trial run. And you're the lucky man who's been chosen to show him the ropes.'

'But I can't stand him,' I objected, 'he's such a pseud with his black pullover and white sweater and pretentious sing-song voice. He already thinks he could do the job better than ten of the likes of you and me. What can I teach him?'

'The Bishop thought it would be an interesting encounter, David, which I think it will be, although perhaps not in quite the way the good bishop expects. If nothing else, it'll get Herbert out of the Vicar of Warter's hair for a few months. See it as an act of mercy to a fellow clergyman who's had to put up with a real Herbert for over five long years. You deserve a gold medal for service like that, or at least a little respite to give you a chance to recover and recharge your batteries. Go on, give him a try. I suspect that secretly you'll enjoy sparring with him; you've always been an argument-ative bugger!'

I held up my hands in mock surrender. 'With such flattery how can I refuse? When does he start?'

'No time like the present time. Give him a ring and get him in harness by next Sunday. If you act quickly, you might just stave off the poor old Vicar of Warter's nervous breakdown.'

'Speaking of which,' he continued, ominously, 'I hope this piece of news won't give you a nervous breakdown, but the Archdeacon wants to interview you and Rebecca now you've got engaged. He's got firm views about the standards a clergy wife should aspire to, so get your Rebecca to slap on the reddest lipstick and the tightest and shortest mini-skirt, and you can go along and re-educate him. And may God have mercy on the pair of you!'

I groaned for the second time in minutes. The headmasterly Archdeacon treated me like a wayward schoolboy, always finding fault, always emphasizing my inadequacies by stressing how wonderful he was when he was a vicar. He was so full of himself that he had written a string of books of the 'Teach Yourself to be a Perfect Clergyman' variety, including a fair few chapters on the required attributes of a Mrs Vicar. 'A clergy wife should be seemly, dress modestly, avoid make-up, shun gossip and vulgar talk, make her husband's career her career and grace the parish with a vision of holy woman-hood...' If I ever swallowed poison, I know where I would turn to for an emetic.

'Now, David, don't be downhearted. The interview won't last for ever and you only have to go through it once. See it as the bride price for your beloved. Your biblical counterpart had to cut off two hundred Philistine foreskins to earn Saul's daughter's hand in marriage. Even an interview with Stony Sid the Archdeacon can't be as bad as having to do that.'

I felt it was a close call, but said nothing as Stamford departed, leaving me clutching Rebecca's hairspray and my two carrier bags of bleeding pork. Who was it who said 'Beware of Greeks bearing gifts'?

Thursday 28 April

I was tucking into a mountain of a break-fast, a piece of succulent Stamford Chestnut gammon poised on my fork, when the phone rang. Why was it that the thing would be quiet for hours, but as soon as you placed a hot meal before you, then off it would go? I picked up the receiver and answered, 'Beckwith 143,' with all the patience I could muster. Following Stamford's visit, I had thumbed through the Archdeacon's book, *Good Practice for the Pastoral Parson*, and I recalled the rather twee advice: 'The sensitive parish priest should greet each and every interruption with the same joy with which he would like his Saviour to greet him.' Not that my Saviour ever had the choice between greeting me and a piece of gammon, but even so, I could grudgingly see the Archdeacon's point. After all, this phone call could be a matter of life and death.

''Allo, is that you, Vicar?'

I assured the caller that I was indeed me.

'Ay, well, it's 'Erbert Wykeham 'ere. Apparently t' church hall has sprung a terrible leak, with water running down t' kitchen wall like a waterfall. Could you cycle up and have a look at it? I'll meet you there.' And with that the phone went dead. Herbert Wykeham, farmer and church-warden at Beckwith, was a man of few words.

Not quite a matter of life and death. Indeed most of my phone calls went along these lines. Primed by years of study of the Gospel, with pastoral practice fine-tuned, I'd eagerly (or eagerishly!) pick up the receiver only to be bothered by the most mundane of topics. It always amazed me why my opinion had to be sought at all on such trivialities. 'I was wondering, Vicar, how many toilet rolls we ought to buy for the church hall lavatory?'

'A dozen? Two dozen? What's the demand? Is Grandma Weighton doing the catering for the next WI meeting?' I felt like asking. Grandma Weighton, mother-in-law of the famous Ivy of Olympic tea-towel fame, spent most of her day stirring a stew pot by their old Yorkshire range. With no electricity at the farm, light was provided by a thickset candle, which dribbled wax into whatever Grandma was peering into. Beef and tallow stew, cherry and wax cake, rye and tallow bread and raisin and wax scones were all delicacies which the local populace consumed at their peril. Riskier than a dose of castor oil. With Grandma doing the catering at the church hall we'd need toilet rolls by the lorryload.

Another one was 'Vicar, do you think we should use PG Tips or Typhoo for our after-service cuppa?' Since most tea served up in church invariably tasted like a blend of Harpic and mouse droppings, I couldn't see what difference the brand would make anyway. I was too polite to tell the enquirer so, and eventually opted for the tea drunk by chimpanzees. Remember, these were days of innocence, before we realized that monkeys in the TV advert were treated infinitely better than the tea growers.

Probably the *crème de la crème* of stupid interruptions came during teatime on one of my days off. 'Vicar, it's Mrs Ludlow here. I know it's your off day, but I thought I'd ring to tell you I've given the church a thorough clean after the school visit this afternoon.'

'That's very kind of you, Mrs Ludlow.' Mrs Ludlow was the cook at Eastwith School, who daily served up superb mouth-watering lunches. She also had a way with words, or rather of not quite getting the right words. Hence her calling my sabbath an off day; other gems included telling the church house group that her dog was ravishing – because it never stopped eating – and persistent questioning about the Black Sea Scrolls.

'I think, though, Vicar, one of the children must have had dog faces on their shoes...'

At first I thought this was some new sandal that was all the rage, until I realized she was trying to use the posh word for dog dirt.

'...because there was some dog faces left on one of the kneelers. I didn't scrape it off because I thought you would like to see it, so I put the kneeler by your cossack in the vestry.'

'Yes, thank you, Mrs Ludlow, that's very good of you. I'll have a look at it when I'm next down for a service.' By which time my cassock would have a lovely ripe aroma. The Cossack no doubt would have taken offence at having to share the vestry with dog faces and would have galloped back to the steppes long before I appeared.

Compared to dog dirt on kneelers and loo rolls and brands of tea, water cascading down a church hall wall presented a positive errand of mercy, so once my breakfast was cleared, I cycled off to Beckwith without further delay. The injection of protein from the masses of meat I had consumed gave me a surge of energy, so that my feet positively spun around the pedals producing a speed that was positively exhilarating. Beckwith was only half a mile away as the crow flies, but nearly two miles by a road which seemed to go three sides around every tiny field.

I completed the tortuous journey in just over five minutes, a definite record, but even at that speed, I was still able to notice things. The hawthorns blushed at me as they straddled the winding road with a blossom the most delicate strawberry-ice shade of red. The hedges spawned a myriad spiders' webs, made taut by droplets of rain from the deluge the night before, which greeted the morning sunlight with a rainbow of colours. Their gossamer thread seemed to stretch unbroken from With to With, as if you could have twitched a twig at Kirkwith and the vibration would have passed from branch to branch, a hedge-telegraph to tell Beckwith you were coming. The winding approach to the village meant that I did a swoop-past of its entire length repeatedly, each time a little nearer, drinking in the higgledy-piggledy roof-lines of this one-street village.

'By gum, thou's been quick,' was Herbert Wykeham's comment as he greeted me at the hall. Apparently I had completed my breakfast and cycle ride in the time it had taken him to stroll the one hundred yards from his farm. 'Mind you, I'm not as sprightly as I was,' he complained. 'Me father and his father afore him and his father afore him, we've all been prone to rheumatics. It's so damp round here, that river, those Ings, the heavy, clammy soil. You don't want to stay here too long, Vicar, otherwise it'll get to you too.' You'll realize by now that Herbert Wykeham was a fellow who scattered Christian joy and cheerfulness as liberally as the Inquisition, so he was well qualified to be a churchwarden, provided you defined the job as guarding the church against intruders rather than encouraging people actually to enter it.

As we entered the hall, I realized it was our misfortune to coincide with the mother and baby clinic. Privacy was not high on the agenda in those days; a doctor was conducting quite intimate examinations by the kitchen door, which was barely screened from the rest of the room. I was a bachelor who was still prone to blush at some of the even slightly lurid bits in the Bible, never mind encountering them in real life. Although dour Herbert was a family man with six children and eighteen grandchildren, he was of that generation which shielded men from any involvement in the birth (other than at the conception) and allowed them to believe that the gestation period of a human being was five years and nine months, since men seldom encountered a pre-school child other than to hit it. So given our respective backgrounds, bulky farmer and lanky me shuffled through the hall, averting our eyes neither to left nor right of us. Eventually, after what seemed an aeon, we stumbled through the far door to the comparative safety of the kitchen with its weeping wall.

I wasn't entirely unscathed, however, in that one conversation had floated out of the ether and fallen on my ears, which unlike eyes can't be averted.

'If I were you, Mrs Elvington, I'd use a nipple shield.'

'But it's me man who's in the Territorial Army, Doctor, with his flak jackets and body armour. I don't go in for all that warfare stuff, weekend in weekend out. I'd rather stay at home with a good book.'

'No, you misunderstand me, dear.' I could hear the doctor and nurse giving a superior chuckle. 'A nipple shield is to use when you're tender because of nursing.'

'But I didn't give birth in hospital. I had her at home.'

'No, not that sort of nursing...'

With relief I closed the kitchen door

before being assailed by any more. Herbert was of that age when you could quite legitimately feign deafness if you didn't want to hear anything improper, so he pretended that nothing was amiss. But the way his eyes avoided looking at me, and the stiff tilt of his head and even ruddier face than normal, indicated that like me, he had heard every word.

To cover our mutual embarrassment, we inspected the damage ferociously. The previous night's downpour had unleashed a waterfall down the wall adjoining kitchen and hall. The plaster was sodden, the power points connected to the cooker were damp and quietly but ominously sizzled. It was a sorry sight, but Herbert was quick to pronounce a simple remedy. 'It'll be t' lead flashin' thats blown off on t' lean-to. All that needs doing is to 'ammer a bit o' new lead into place, and it'll dry out a treat. I'll get Burt Wold to come round this afternoon. He does a lot of our plumbing round t' farm.'

'That sounds absolutely excellent, Herbert.' But then I hesitated. 'Oh, er, hang on a minute. We'd better get the Archdeacon's permission first.'

'What, just for a little bit o'lead?' exclaimed Herbert, incredulously, 'what's that got to do with him?'

'Well, he's suddenly got very fussy, and wants to know about any work that goes on on church property, however small. Woe betide any vicar whose church buildings spawn stonework, extensions, roof repairs, scaffolding, even a bit of new pointing without his divine permission.'

'Flipping 'eck. And I thought Ministry of Ag was pifflin' with all its rules and regulations. It's nothin' compared to t' Church and your blessed Archdeacon. All these checks and balances. I reckon we're lumbered wi' brakes of *Flying Scotsman* and engine of a lawnmower.'

I laughed at his dour analogy. 'Don't worry, I'll cycle home and give him a ring straight away. I've got to contact him about something else, anyway,' I said, suddenly remembering I still had to book me and Rebecca in for our pre-nuptial interview.

'Well, Vicar, I suppose we'd better be getting on then. But let's just check everything one more time before we go.' Herbert clearly didn't relish the prospect of our return journey through the mother and baby clinic, so we hung around for a few more minutes, prodding and tapping plasterwork, peering at power points, checking every possible square inch of that kitchen. I guess the place had never had such a thorough examination. I even found a piece of fruitcake, buried beneath the dust of ages behind the oven. Herbert was quick to diagnose its origin. 'Bluming 'eck! Last time we had cake like that was for t' Queen's coronation fifteen years since. Grandma Weighton made it for t' village street party. There was a mass epidemic of food poisoning after that. To this day I can't watch Queen's Christmas Day speech without my stomach churning. I'd bury that in a deep hole if I were you!'

Strange archaeological discoveries notwithstanding, the time came when we could no longer delay our departure. We edged through the kitchen door with about as much enthusiasm as lion fodder entering the Colosseum.

If anything, the whole session was livelier than when we had encountered it earlier. One outraged toddler had kicked down the screens, putting paid to even the scantiest attempt to provide some privacy. There were squawks of protest at the double indignity of being stripped naked and then dumped on chilly metal scales. Squawks, I think, from the babies rather than their mothers, although I didn't hang around long enough to check. In fact I tried my best to walk through the hall with my eyes tightly shut, but then I bumped into someone near the entrance. 'Oh, I do beg your pardon,' I exclaimed as I opened my eyes, relieved to find the young mother I was addressing was fully clothed. But then panic set in as I realized this was someone I ought to know. But try as I might, I couldn't put a name to her.

Such amnesia attacks were a common problem with me, and part and parcel of the job. Everyone, of course, knows the vicar. He's the one who christened our Tracy, married our George, buried Uncle Bill, upset Grandma. And they expect the vicar to know them in return. But in the hundreds of contacts, month by month, in sundry situations, it is possible, in that first few seconds of re-encounter, for names to slip. Or wrong names to leap to mind.

'Mrs Green,' I blurted out. 'How are you?' Thank goodness, the name had come to me at last.

'It's Mrs Grey, actually,' the woman corrected me, tight-lipped.

'Of course, Mrs Grey, do forgive me. And

how's your little girl coming on?'

'It's a little boy. You should know; you christened him five months ago.'

'Yes, yes, yes, of course I did, I remember now,' I blabbered ineptly. But I found myself addressing thin air. Mrs Grey had obviously decided she had had quite enough of this idiot cleric, and had walked down the hall to see nurse.

Too late, I recalled her all too well. The vivid details of my visit to her home to arrange the baptism burst into my mind. It had been a foggy November night. By the time I had cycled to Beckwith, chilly droplets of water clung to my clothes and face and hair. As I knocked on her door, I looked forward to a warm hearth and a cheering cup of tea to help me defrost.

No such luck. The welcome I got was as cold as the night. I was shown into a chilly front room, no fire was roaring in the grate, no refreshment was offered. Mrs Grey switched on an electric radiator, which sizzled ineffectively. She rocked the baby in her arms. It was crying loudly and she looked all in.

'Now then,' I shouted, above the noise of the baying child. 'What are you going to call this little chap, then?'

'Jonathan,' she answered tersely.

'What a lovely choice!' I responded, with genuine enthusiasm. Like all Davids, I tend to have a soft spot for Jonathans. 'It means "gift of God", you know. He's an Old Testament hero.'

'Really?' Mrs Grey's eyes glazed over, her lack of interest thinly veiled. 'My old man wanted him named Jonathan after Jonathan Haxby, York City's right wing.'

'Well, whatever, it's a good name,' I soldiered on. 'It catches the wonder that new life and children bring, sheer gift.'

'He doesn't seem like a sheer gift when he wakes you up for the third time in one night, with his father gone to the world because he's had a skinful at the Stack.' Aware that I was hardly making the most brilliant rapport, I decided to get to the point without further delay and then beat a hasty retreat.

'Now about Jonathan's christening. It's going to be a real celebration, a thank you that you've come through the birth safely, a thank you for Jonathan, a thank you to God for loving him from the very beginning. He cherishes the little chap as much as you and your old man, er, er, I mean your husband and family cherish him.'

'Well, God can come and change his nappy, now and again, if he's that bothered,' Mrs Grey quipped with a surly laugh. I decided the best policy was to ignore it.

'Now, I want to make the service special, and most of all, fun, in the best sense of the word. I believe that all services should be like that, not a dirge to set you back, but a boost to set you up. You know, you'll be welcome to bring Jonathan and your husband along to church at any time. It would be good to see you.'

'We go out to the supporters' club in York on Saturday night. It's my only night out with him. We're too tired to get up for church on Sunday morning.'

Oh dear! I wasn't making the impact I had hoped for. We had a brief chat about choice of godparents, the qualification for which seemed to be unquestioning devotion to York City. By now downhearted in the extreme, I concluded with a brief description of the service and outlined a few practical details before bidding farewell to Mrs Grey and her screaming child. Her old man had never even put in an appearance, no doubt imbibing his skinful at the Stack. The weeping night air perfectly caught my sadness over the whole sorry episode.

The christening itself was a hole-in-the-corner affair on a drizzly December afternoon. I tried my very best to whip up some enthusiasm, to make it momentous, even to inject some humour and talk about York City's recent form. But to no avail. The whole stolid bunch had remained distinctly unmoved.

Not a happy set of memories to re-emerge five months on, triggered when I didn't even recognize baby Jonathan and his mum as I staggered out of the hall. I tried to put the whole abject failure to the back of my mind as I cycled home, my feet no longer whirling around the pedals, my heart no longer singing.

Then I was struck by an idea. Herbert Molescroft! He wanted to see what being a vicar was really like. Then I would take him on a baptism visit or two. Encountering a few of the Mrs Greys of this world would soon wear out his holy veneer.

I was so chuffed with my plan that I even rang the Archdeacon free from the heavy dread that usually afflicted me whenever I had to contact him.

'Yes, yes,' he interrupted me, as I gave my name and tried to exchange a few pleasantries. 'What do you want?'

I explained how I needed his permission for the new lead flashing. 'What!' he barked. 'What do you think you are doing interrupting me on a Thursday? Thursdays are supposed to be my writing days. I'll never get the next book finished at this rate. Ring the diocesan office and ask them to send you an Archdeacon's licence, and then damn well get on with it.'

The Archdeacon's sage advice in his *Good Practice for the Pastoral Parson* about greeting an interruption with the same joy as you would hope Jesus would hail you seemed to have been woefully overlooked by its author. But the Archdeacon wasn't through with me yet.

'And another thing, Wilbourne. What do you think you're doing, getting engaged without my permission? You bother me about a piffling thing like a bit of lead flashing, yet fail to consult with me about one of the most important steps in a priest's career. You're only on the first rung on the ladder of being a vicar, and a very shaky rung it is too. You can hardly manage your own life and your new parish, and you have the stupidity to think you have the time and wisdom to take on a woman. There's no undoing it now, I suppose, now that you've pledged yourself and broadcast your intentions to the whole parish and diocese. But you'd both better come along and see me, so that we can make some attempt to salvage this sorry situation. Make it next Tuesday at two p.m.'

Stunned though I was by his outburst, I managed to blurt out, 'I'm sorry, Archdeacon, that's not possible. Rebecca teaches German at the Mount in York. She can't get away during the day.'

'What, you don't mean to tell me she works?' he exploded. 'She'll have to give all that up for a start. Being a vicar's wife is a full-time job. My Beatrice has never worked and I shudder to think what sort of priest I would have turned out without her in harness beside me.'

I shuddered too. Eventually, after much huffing and puffing, he agreed to see Rebecca and me at 7.30 p.m. next Wednesday. After all I'd said, I was sorry we couldn't have arranged an appointment during the day, since high noon would have appropriately captured the spirit of what seemed to be in store.

MAY 1966

Wednesday 4 May

'Now you tuck into these sandwiches, Vicar. Our Rebecca's told us what you've got in store tonight, so you'd better build yourself up. That man sounds like an absolute dragon.' I was having tea at the Weightons' farm prior to our setting off for the Archdeacon's home high on the Wolds. Ivy Weighton waved a massive oval dish before me, chipped around the edges, on which were piled up towers of sandwiches, cut like doorsteps with thick chunks of beef spilling out of them. 'Go on, Vicar, don't be shy, take a couple. Grandma boiled up the brisket specially this morning; she gave it a good stew to make it tender.'

I caught the twinkle in Rebecca's eye as I gingerly picked up the smallest of the sandwiches from the chipped oval dish and put them on to my chipped bread plate.

One of the things Rebecca and I had in common was that we were, in her mother's

45

words, 'too finicky about food hygiene'. I tried to steal a look at the contents of my sandwich to check it didn't contain too much wax; at first sight it looked as though the beef was contained in a tallow parcel, until Ivy caught me inspecting the thing and rushed in with an explanation. 'Grandma spread the bread with thick beef dripping rather than butter. She thought it would line your stomach and settle you if you were a bit queasy about tonight's visit.'

'Oh, Grandma, that's very kind of you. I'm sure they'll slide down a treat,' I lied, as I gulped over the first bite, suppressing a strong desire to regurgitate the meal almost before I even began. I noticed that Rebecca was chewing her portion with a thoughtful look, as if she was trying to recognize a taste she had come across somewhere before, but couldn't quite place it.

Fred Weighton rose from the table and disappeared into the parlour. After a few minutes he returned bearing a chipped glass half-full of what I presumed was whisky. 'Now you just get this down you, Vicar, it'll steady your nerves and put a bit o' fire in your belly.'

I gratefully accepted and took a generous swig – I have to admit not to steady my nerves, but to kill off the strange organisms which would no doubt be swirling around in Grandma's concoction. As I gasped for breath, Mr Weighton turned to his daughter: 'Do you want a drop, pet? You're looking a bit pale.'

'No thanks, Dad, I'm driving. I don't want to be the first casualty of these new breathalysers the police are threatening everyone with.' I also guessed Rebecca would need the kills-all-known-germs drink less than me; after twenty-four years of consuming Grandma's cooking, I assumed she would have developed some immunity.

The sandwiches were followed by an invigorating slice of Grandma's chestnut and wax cake. 'It should have really been walnut, but we'd run out, so Grandma used a few chestnuts we'd got over from Bonfire Night. Once she'd scraped the mould off, they were as good as new,' Ivy reassured me. I washed this down with another generous measure of whisky and hoped for the best.

I looked at my watch. 'Rebecca, we'd better be off. I'm ever so sorry I can't stay to help with the washing up, Ivy.'

'Now then, young man, we'll have none o' that,' Fred Weighton barked, his face deadly serious. 'Leave t' women to do t' women's work, if you don't mind, otherwise we'll have a revolution on our hands.' His two burly sons nodded their heads in stern agreement, as if there was an anarchist in their midst who'd threatened the very roots of their existence. On my frequent visits to the Weightons' farm I had never seen the menfolk lift a finger to prepare a meal or clear one up.

'How do I stop your mum calling me "Vicar"?' I asked Rebecca, as we chugged down the bumpy farm track in her VW Beetle, standard issue for German teachers.

'I don't know, she's always been very proper where clergy are concerned, almost treating them like another species. It's blowing her mind a bit. I suppose having a son-in-law takes some getting used to, let alone one who's also a vicar. I think she comes from a generation who've seen clergy as father figures, father knows best, that sort of thing. All of a sudden she's faced with the prospect of having a father who's also a son. I know Jesus said "the Father and the Son are one", but she never expected his cryptic sayings to suddenly be acted out in her family. Give her time. She'll call you David eventually. She might even call you other things, if you keep on making faces over

Grandma's sandwiches!'

We made easy conversation as we left the Withs far behind, crossed the Derwent at Stamford Bridge and climbed sharply up to the Wolds at Garrowby Hill. At the peak stands a massive cross, on which the crucified Jesus serenely surveys the Vale of York. Sprawled out before him are the silver pencil line of the Humber to the south and the round and darkly maternal Pennines and Dales to the west.

Since we were making good time, we pulled over to the side of the road and gazed at the whole expanse of land before us. York Minster, a tiny silhouette in the evening sun, with York's tinier dwellings gathered around her, like chicks around their mother hen. To the south we could see the cooling towers of the new power station at Drax, handily on site for its fuel from the Yorkshire coalfield, with enough rich seams to keep it going for a century and beyond. In the foreground we could see the patchwork quilt of fields, our fields, with the green shoots of the coming harvest peeping through. Casting our gaze over the whole scene, embracing hundreds of miles in a single glance, brought a sense of great calm.

Fortified for the ordeal ahead, we sped off

49

to the tiny village of Fimber, where the Archdeacon had his massive rectory. We were on top of the Wolds and felt as if we were on top of the world, with the blue North Sea peeping over the horizon to cheer us on our way. The road rolled gently up and down, through dry valleys galore, all cultivated, ploughed fields of dark brown speckled with pieces of chalk and flint.

Only a century before, the place had been wild moor, but it had been tamed by its legendary owner, Sir Tatton Sykes. In my mind's eye, I fondly imagined the lord of the manor hacking away with his scythe at the briars and the brambles and the broom and the brush for mile after painful mile. In reality the project must have been a major industry, employing thousands of hands, callused to bring order out of chaos. And a beautiful order it was too.

Now doubly fortified by such a thrilling journey, we drove up the Archdeacon's drive and parked by the front door of his massive Georgian rectory, paned windows galore, set perfectly symmetrically, their woodwork black rather than the usual white, peering at us judgementally like a thousand dark sunken eyes. Complemented by the dark sunken eyes of the Archdeacon, who swung the front door open with violent force and sternly ordered us to come in.

Feeling like two naughty schoolchildren ushered into the headmaster's study, we were commanded to sit down on the hardest of chairs while the Archdeacon settled himself into a comfortable leather chair behind his desk. 'So you're engaged?' was his opening gambit.

'Yesh, Archdeacon, we are,' I drawled, the double dose of double whisky taking its effect. 'Could I offishally introduce you to my fianshé, Rebecca Weighton?' I only hoped that Rebecca would take over and do most of the talking; drunk in charge of a fiancée was probably an excommunicable offence.

'My dear, I'm very pleased to meet you,' leered the Archdeacon. 'But do you realize just what you have taken on?'

'I hope not,' Rebecca replied, going on to the offensive.

'What do you mean?' the Archdeacon barked, put out by the note of challenge in Rebecca's reply.

'Well,' she explained, 'love in my book is a risk, an unknown, something you commit yourself to be faithful to, come what may. It strikes me that the fun of marriage is the exploring, linked as fellow travellers in a land full of surprises. If I'd got David cut and dried, where would the fun be, where would the love be? To be human is to be a mystery; I doubt if any spouse ever realizes what they are taking on. If they do, then I think they've missed out somewhere.'

'Yes, well, quite,' stammered the Archdeacon. One of the reasons why I loved Rebecca was that she was a deep thinker, who expressed her thoughts as if they had been long weighed in the balance and prepared for a Finals essay. Clearly the Archdeacon wasn't used to encountering this type of woman. 'But what I meant,' he said, trying to recover his poise, 'is whether you're prepared to take on the hard slog of ministry? The Mothers' Union, the flower ladies, the summer teas, the endless callers, your home being available to the parish, that sort of thing.'

'I don't do flowers. I'm too young for the Mothers' Union. As far as I'm aware, there isn't some ontological change that happens to a vicar's wife which equips her to do teas and run stalls better than any other woman, or man if it comes to that. I'm a committed Christian, and I can see that being married to David will give me a platform for some areas of ministry I'm interested in. Other areas I'll leave to others. Why should I hog the show?'

'Well, because a vicar's wife does those things, that's why. She just does them. She's always done them, and if you want your husband to be a success, you have to do them.'

'I think I want David to be faithful rather than a success.'

'Oh quite, quite, no room for ambition in the Church.' The Archdeacon duly trotted out words which he'd spent a career ignoring.

'And never mind all that stuff about the hard slog of ministry,' Rebecca went on. 'Every job has its stresses. Perhaps you'd better ask David if he's prepared to take on the evenings of marking and lesson planning, the hassle of examination time, the draining effect that disruptive pupils unleash.'

The Archdeacon was beginning to look as if he regretted ever asking to see this woman who spoke to him as no clergyman had ever dared. The evening was turning into a tonic, at least for me. 'But surely, you'll give up your teaching when you get married?' he asked.

'Why?' Rebecca replied, fixing him with the gaze of her steel-blue eyes.

'Well, because you'll be too busy around the vicarage with all those duties I've mentioned.'

'I've got other duties. Since childhood I've wanted to teach, I've trained as a teacher, love being a teacher. Haven't I got a duty to use that God-given skill? Or was it just a stopgap until I could fill my days with jam-making and flower-arranging?'

'Well, you could run the Sunday School if you're so set on teaching.'

'What, telling the stories of Jesus to half a dozen kids each week, who've been shoved out of church because the adults don't want them to disturb their slumbers? That's supposed to engage me, is it?'

'I really do find your attitude leaves a lot to be desired,' complained the Archdeacon.

'Well, I'm sorry if I offend you, but if you can't take women speaking their mind, you shouldn't summon them to your rectory. I've got more than enough to do of an evening without hearing you lecture me on wifely duties.'

The Archdeacon was stunned into silence, not knowing what to say, how to end an interview in which he had been so wrong-footed. Rebecca had had the audacity to address him in a way clergy throughout the diocese had only ever dared to imagine in their wildest dreams. I had enjoyed every minute of it.

Suddenly the Archdeacon broke the impasse, but spoke as if he was in a daze. 'Ah yes, wifely duties, wifely duties. I was going to get around to that. Every clergyman is supposed to prepare a couple for the physical side of marriage, explain things to them, give them a bit of guidance. Who's going to counsel you if not me? I thought I'd just spell out to you a few facts...' Rather than fearing him, I was beginning to feel sorry for the old boy, trying to stutter his way through the facts of life.

Rebecca came to his rescue. 'Don't worry about that, Archdeacon.' I wondered what on earth she was going to say next. 'I have to teach seven hundred adolescent girls not just German, but also personal and social development. I have to have more than a passing acquaintance with your facts of life, otherwise the girls would make mincemeat of me with their questions.'

'Oh quite, quite,' the Archdeacon said with considerable relief, grateful that Rebecca's being a teacher had at least one advantage in his eyes. 'In that case, there's nothing more for me to say than to wish you every happiness. Have you set the day?'

'No, not yet,' I replied, recovering my powers of speech. 'But we'll probably go for sometime in August, towards the end of the summer holidays.'

'Good, that'll give you the chance to have a decent honeymoon.' The Archdeacon was becoming quite pastoral as the interview drew to its close. 'Speaking of honeymoons, though, let me give you one tip...'

I cringed. I really had thought we'd headed him off from giving us the advice of an experienced man of the world.

'...for goodness sake don't go too far on your first night...'

Both Rebecca and I blushed.

'...you'll be far too tired after a very stressful day. Beatrice and I went too far...'

Both Rebecca and I blushed an even deeper shade of red at the personal revelations which were about to follow.

'...we drove all the way to Southampton. That was too far, far too far. We'd have been far better breaking our journey at Nottingham or Leicester. Take my advice. Don't cover too many miles, otherwise you'll return from your holiday more tired than when you began.'

Rebecca and I thanked him for this gem, our gratitude made more effusive by sheer relief that his revelations hadn't been at all the sort we feared. We made our farewells and chugged off into the night. At Garrowby Hill we paused again, and gazed on the dark Vale twinkling with a million lights. 'You were wonderful,' I said to Rebecca. 'You stood up to him in a way that I would never have dared. How did you do it?'

Rebecca thought for a moment. 'First of all he might think he's your superior, but he isn't mine, so I wasn't frightened of him in the least. Secondly, I can't stand bullies. Bullying children, bullying parents, bullying colleagues all make my blood boil, and I go for them with all I've got. Thirdly, that Archdeacon's like all bullies: once you stand up to him, he'll mellow; give in to him and all you do is present him with more oxygen to fuel the flames of his tyranny.'

'You seem to have a wise old head on your young shoulders. Where have all these sage views about bullying come from?'

'From Hans I suppose. All from Hans.' And she started to cry. Half, I guess, from delayed shock at having stood up to an ecclesiastical dragon so very successfully.

And half from grief. Hans had been a German prisoner-of-war who had been put to work at the Weightons' farm and then stayed on and become a member of the family. He was the one who had encouraged Rebecca to study German, teaching her the language as a child. Just before Easter, he failed to turn up for work one day. Ivy had found him lying dead on the kitchen floor.

'When he first came to us, he'd been bullied, you know, dreadfully bullied. Bullied in the German army because he was from Transylvania and so not the purest of the Aryan pure. And then bullied here by the local louts who hadn't been called up, and so found him a convenient target for their frustrated aggression. In his time he'd known bullying and bullies galore, and had worked out strategies to cope, strategies he taught me, a little girl teased by her big brothers. They could be real brutes, but he was so kind, so understanding. "Don't you let vem get to you, girl!" he used to say. I didn't and I don't. And it's all because of him.'

She dried her eyes and we set off on the sharp descent of Garrowby Hill, positively shooting past the crawling vehicles that laboured up the hill in the opposite direction. In their headlights I could see her eyes were still red, very red. 'I hope your mum won't think it's the Archdeacon who drove you to tears,' I quipped.

Her sadness broke into a smile. 'No, we'd better tell her it's an early onset of hayfever, all this blossom we've been driving through. I don't think she'd be able to cope if she knew I'd been weeping for Hans. I know she misses him dreadfully, more so than me. I often catch her out of the corner of my eye, laying his place at the table on automatic pilot, and then realizing her blunder, and sobbing, absolutely sobbing, as her loss dawns on her.'

We conducted the rest of the journey in silence, a natural and privileged silence shared between two people at ease with each other, even in grief. A quiet to be cherished, making even a visit to a firebrand of an Archdeacon eminently worthwhile.

Monday 9 May

'Well, you see, Vic-ar, it's all ecc-les-i-as-tic-al,' Bill Everingham pronounced, shaking his head. I was beginning to wonder whether this was his catchphrase, an elixir for every church ill. Just as a GP wrung his hands and said, 'There's nothing I can do, it's a virus, I'm afraid,' Bill's 'all ecc-les-i-as-tic-al' seemed a convenient religious equivalent.

I was sitting in the Everinghams' cosy kitchen, the Yorkshire range blazing away despite the balmy spring weather, their dinner cooking in the black-leaded oven by the fire's side, with the appetizing smell of a roast side of beef thronging the air. 'Ee, Vicar, take your jacket off, it's proper sweltering in here, that fire and that oven have only two settings, either they're a furnace or they're owt,' Hannah Evering-ham explained. She hung my jacket on a huge cast-iron hook which was screwed into their back door. When the door had been opened too heartily or blown open, the hook had repeatedly gouged out a gaping hole in the adjacent plasterwork, which jarred with the well-turned-out appearance of every room in their farmhouse. They were as immaculate as the Weightons were ramshackle.

'Now you'll stop and have a bit o' dinner, won't you? How long will this business take?'

'I just need to pick your brains, really. I'm

sure we can do something for Edna and Flo to make life a little easier for them. But I only know the bare details, that Flo was born blind and has been looked after by her sister since their parents died, that Edna's just retired and is having trouble with her own sight.'

'Well, it's a long story, Vicar, where do you want us to start?' Hannah asked.

'Ay, and it's all ecc-les-i-as-tic-al,' repeated Bill.

'Oh, just tell me what you think are the key bits.' I purposely addressed Hannah rather than Bill. Long stories and his habit of speaking in monosyllables would mean that we'd see the dawn before the tale came to its end.

'OK,' Hannah replied. 'As long as you don't mind if I peel the spuds and prepare the vegetables while I'm talking.' She set herself up at the white pot sink, peeling what looked more like mud than potatoes, great clumps of earth falling off as she scraped each one. 'Flo's the most miserable woman you would ever have the misfortune of coming across. True, she was born blind and we've got to make an allowance for that. Edna, as her older sister, had fair doted on her, so that when their mum and dad died,

Flo grew to rely on her completely. They moved into that little almshouse in t' back lane and have lived there nigh on fifty years.'

'That's where it's all ecc-les-i-as-tic-al,' chipped in Bill. 'Those two almshouses are owned by t' Church.'

'Ay, they are,' Hannah continued. 'And a poor state they're in as well. Anyway, Edna set up house there and made it as comfy as possible. She worked in York, so had to rise early, lay the fires, prepare Flo's breakfast and lunch and then rush out to catch the seven-thirty bus to town. She came back on the early evening bus with a bit of something for tea, and then housework, washing and ironing, and listening to Flo's incessant complaints, completed her long, hard day.'

'What did Edna do in York?' I asked. Hannah had now moved on from earth-encrusted potatoes to equally mucky carrots, the whitewashed wall behind the pot sink speckled with tiny drops of mud, sprayed there by each scrape.

'The most unglamorous job in the city,' Hannah replied, tutting as she gouged out a bit of carrot where a root fly had eaten it away, 'She was the attendant in the underground ladies' lavatory in Parliament Street!'

'That must be t' worst job in cre-at-ion,' Bill butted in again. 'I love to be out and ab-out. I could-n't stand be-in' shut in all day, esp-ec-ial-ly in that dark sh-sh-fet-id place.'

'Yes, well, don't worry, Bill, I don't think you being a ladies' lavatory attendant was ever even a remote possibility!' Hannah joked. 'And nobody could have made a better job of it than Edna. She ran a special service for t' women from t' Withs, Vicar.'

My mind boggled for a moment, as to what special service Edna could have offered over and above the usual. Pre-warmed toilet seats? Or maybe a special supply of exclusive floral toilet paper: 'Have a few sheets of this, love. We don't give quality of this sort to any old riff-raff.' Or maybe she gave readings of Doris Harsley's infamous poetry to move Withs residents when they were enthroned, such as her most recent ditty:

Can you guess where I live?
I live in Kirkwith,
where the church tower is Tudor
and the graffiti on it is ruder
than anything I've ever seen that is lewder!

My wild speculations were brought to an

end as Hannah continued. 'As you know all too well, Vicar, we only have one bus a day to York at seven-thirty in t' morning and it doesn't come back until teatime. We women like to get to t' market stalls early on, so we can buy our fruit and veg before it gets picked over.'

'Troub-le is, you had to then hump heav-y bags round York all day,' Bill explained. 'Or rath-er, hen-pecked hus-bands had to hump heav-y bags a-round all day. Un-til Ed-na came up with a scheme which was pos-it-ive-ly brill-iant.'

'Oh yes?' I said, wondering what this rambling tale had to do with underground lavatories.

'She used to let us leave our bags with her by the lavatories, so that we could then browse around town for the rest of the day, unencumbered by our baggage. And don't you take any notice of Bill; it was us women who used to have to cart it all around. Menfolk used to always go off to cattle market to look over a few beasts. They'd rather be seen dead than appear before other farmers carrying their missus' shopping and looking as if they were under their wife's thumb.'

'Ee, by t' time all t' wom-en from Withs

had park-ed their shopp-in in Ed-na's lav-at-or-y, it was piled up al-most as high as t' keep at t' side o' Kirk-with Church,' Bill chuckled. 'You know what wom-en are like. They fill five shop-pin' bags to our one!'

'And how would you know, either about shopping or the inside of Edna's lavatory?' Hannah replied. 'Amount you and your men eat, no wonder I have to fill six shop-ping bags.'

While this good-natured banter was going on, I did wonder about the state of the shopping after it had been aired all the day in a smelly underground lavatory. Many of my parishioners tried to tempt my appetite with an enticing, 'Ee, have some of this cheese curd tart, Vicar, it's fresh from town!' I suppose there's fresh and there's fresh.

'And another thing about Edna,' Hannah said, 'her cheerfulness shone through, de-spite her grim surroundings...'

'*While Ed-na watched her bags by day,*' Bill flatly intoned to a tune which bore only a slight resemblance to 'While shepherds watched their flocks by night',

All seat-ed in the loo.
The an-gel of the Lord came down
and said, 'Good God, what a poo!'

Hannah raised her eyebrows as if to apologize for her husband's vulgarity before continuing, 'She always was there with a ready smile, always returning the right bags to the right woman, often lugging a couple of bags back to the bus herself if their absent-minded owners forgot about their early-morning purchases.'

'Flo must be deeply grateful that she's got such a sister,' I commented, as Hannah's lecture on the underground lavatories of York drew to its close.

'Ay, you'd think so, wouldn't you? But not a bit of it, not a bit of it,' Hannah complained. 'She doesn't lift a finger to help, not a finger.' Bill and I watched passively as Hannah opened the oven and took out a tin, smoking blue with hot fat. Into it she poured a generous jug full of batter which she had been beating while she talked. The batter sizzled in loud protest at its forthcoming roasting, but to no avail. Mercilessly, Hannah quickly reopened the oven door and almost threw the tin in before rapidly slamming the door shut. It was an impressive performance, although I felt uneasy as she catalogued Flo's laziness around the home; Bill and I had watched

66

Hannah's labours for the last half-hour without lifting a finger to help ourselves.

'When Edna went out to work, Flo just sat all day, listening to the wireless, morning, noon and night, waiting for her sister to wait on her. Once transistor radios had come in, she deigned to sit outside in t' garden on warm summer days, savouring the scents of the flower beds which Edna patiently tended on her Sundays off. But on colder days, she stayed sitting on her chair indoors, warming herself by the fire that Edna had laid, only breaking off to hobble to the lavatory, or eat the lunch that Edna'd prepared. And what's more, she never stops complaining or listing poor old Edna's shortcomings. Never!'

'Tell 'im a-bout t' boiled egg,' Bill drawled. 'She nev-er stops go-in' on a-bout it!'

'Ay. "Do you know what she did, do you know what she did?"' Hannah shrieked, doing a mean impersonation of Flo in full flood. '"Not only did she forget to shell the egg" – as if this was the most heinous crime since the beginning of creation – "but she hadn't boiled it for long enough. There was yolk all over the place, over my hands, my cardigan, my chair. Did I give her a piece of my mind when she eventually rolled in from gallivanting round the town."'

'This was in 1946, mind,' Bill explained. 'A slight over-sight twen-ty years ago, which Flo has ne-ver for-got-ten or for-given, let-tin' it fest-er in her dark mind year in year out. Poor old Ed-na. I would-n't have both-ered boil-in' t' egg at all. I'd have just smashed it raw ov-er her un-grate-ful face.'

Flo must have been a thoroughly nasty old stick to draw such vehemence from my meekest and mildest of churchwardens. Over a delicious meal we discussed what we could do to help, now that Edna's eyesight was failing too. 'Could we do anything to modernize their house?' I asked.

'Well, it's all ecc-les-i-ast-ic-al,' Bill explained for the fourth time that afternoon. 'Church owns their alms-house and maintains it wi' rent from t' Glebe Field.'

'And how much is that?' I pressed.

'Well, it's a big fi-eld, stretch-ing from 'ere to Beck-with and tak-in' in t' Ings. We get about a hun-dred and fifty-three pounds el-ev-en shill-ings and six-pence a year,' Bill pronounced, giving away his farmer's trait of noting every scruple. 'Not rea-lly e-nough oth-er than to patch t' roof and do a bit o' point-in' from time to time.'

'But couldn't we get a mortgage with the Glebe Field as security and use the rent as repayment?' I asked, drawing on my background in Martins' Bank, where I'd worked prior to ordination. 'I'm sure there must be low-interest loans available for updating almshouses. A steady income of a hundred and fifty pounds a year would easily repay a two-thousand-pound mortgage over twenty years. Just think what two thousand pounds would do to convert a slum into a tidy little cottage.'

'Oh, I don't know,' Bill said, shaking his head. 'I don't like ow-in' owt to an-y-one. That's why we've nev-er done an-y-thin' maj-or with those hous-es. Us trust-ees are caut-ious men.'

'Ay, and men being the operative word,' Hannah burst out, reverting to a broad Yorkshire accent which she, like others, tried to mask in front of me. 'Men don't have to do t' cleaning just with one cold tap and a pot sink. Men don't have to do t' cooking just with a smoky old range. It's us women who scratch and scrape and make do.

'It takes me all my time to look after this old farmhouse, and I'm fully fit. God knows how I'd cope if I couldn't see. You trustees huff and puff at your meetings about a tile

69

here or a bit of plaster there. Surprise yourselves, give Edna a break in her retirement
and do the place up for her. Now who's for
some more roast beef?'

'Come to think of it, Bill, doesn't our
Bertha's niece work in t' housing depart-
ment at Leeds City Council? We could ask
her if council has any money to spare for
renovation works.'

'Yes, that's a good ideal' I enthused. 'It
always helps to have a personal contact. I
read an article in this month's *Yorkshire Life*
about almshouses, and it mentioned there's
a National Almshouse Association based in
London to encourage improvement and
renovation. I'll drop them a line and see
what they can do. Provided Bill and the
other trustees are in agreement.'

'Oh, I'm sure they'll come round, Vicar.
Now who's for more roast beef?' Hannah
repeated. Meekly, Bill held out his plate. As
I'm sure it says in the Book of Proverbs
somewhere, 'She who controls the roast
beef and Yorkshire pudding wins the day.'

Tuesday 10 May

Herbert Molescroft ground the gears of his

black Hillman Imp as we bumped along a potholed road that had clearly seen better days. We were bound for Landings Cottages, a clutch of houses perched by the river at the end of a long lane between Beckwith and Eastwith. In days gone by there'd been a ferry crossing to the West Withs, my parish's mirror-image at the river's opposite bank. Now all that remained was a dilapidated jetty with a few bits of rotting wood jutting out of the muddy bank. Here and there a frayed mooring rope dangled, slack and unemployed, whiling away its time clanging in the breeze against iron poles carbuncled with rust, a high-pitched death knell for an industry that was no more. No more ferrymen, no more ferries, instead the luxury of being jolted eight miles by car via the bridging point at Bubwith to get to another side that was only ten yards away. The whole place had an eerie, abandoned feel: the end of the road.

Herbert ground his gears for the tenth time, and for the tenth time his whole body exuded a stiff, sanctimonious pride that he had done so well to refrain from swearing. The body language shouted, 'I've got every reason to swear at this wretched car, every excuse, no one could blame me. Yet I'm so very, very holy, that I'm not going to.'

'Do you believe in ghosts, Herbert?' I asked, a gambit to distract him from his pious meltdown.

'I most certainly do not,' he snapped. 'Holy Scripture forbids us from having anything to do with them.'

'Holy Scripture forbids us from having anything to do with a lot of things, but that doesn't stop them existing,' I countered.

'Mm. Well, I don't believe in them, and that's that. Why are you asking me about ghosts, anyway? You're supposed to be training me to be a vicar, not a medium,' he sneered.

'It's just that they say the Landings is haunted. The tale goes that on Boxing Day night in 1877 the ferry was packed with folk who were to form the choir for a carol service at Wheldrake. There'd been deep snow on the North York Moors until just before Christmas, with the thaw starting on Christmas Eve, so the river was high with melt water. As the ferryman struggled to row them across, the choir beat time with "Christians Awake", their favourite carol, sung to "Yorkshire", a local tune.

'The post barge from Pocklington was late that evening, making up time as it sped down the river in full flood, and came upon the ferry before any alarm could be given, slicing it in two. The ferryman and his fifteen passengers had no chance, and perished within minutes in the dark icy waters.

'Locals claim that whenever the waters run high, the strains of a choir can be heard, trilling the carols they never sang to that waiting congregation in Wheldrake, the ferryman's raucous, tenor voice singing the most poignant lines of them all: *"Trace we the babe, who hath retrieved our loss from his poor cradle to his bitter cross..."*'

'Pah, what superstitious nonsense! Honestly, these country folk will believe anything.' Herbert gave the handbrake a dismissive crunch as we drew up to the Landings. The evening sun was setting in the west, with the Ings, the Derwent's flood water, a sheet of blazing red. The ramshackle cottages were black silhouettes against this fiery background, creating a two-tone scene which took your breath away. Or at least took my breath away; Herbert seemed oblivious.

A woman with a mewling baby in her arms let us into the end cottage, nearest the river bank. The house had a heavy smell about it, in fact several smells. The pre-vailing aroma was must, tinged with boiling nappies and the sicky reek of toddlerhood. The sole downstairs room was sparsely fur-nished: cheap, wooden, ill-matched chairs, a mock-leather sofa with cushions torn and stuffing spilling out, the odd rug scattered on stone slabs sweating with damp. All bore the mark of the poverty of a farm-labourer constrained to live in a neglected tied cottage.

I had encountered Mrs Riccall before. Her face had a contradiction of features. Her long hair was brushed back carelessly into a ponytail, which at first glance made her look more youthful than her thirty-five years. But then you revised the estimate of her age by two decades as you noticed the flecks of grey. Her complexion was natural, no make-up, with the ruddiness of a young girl, but the worry lines betrayed the anxieties of full womanhood. With four children under five and underfed, you could understand the worry lines. In one sense, her eyes were a contradiction too, shining with a brightness, a glee, a love which belied her pauper existence.

I had often come across her struggling back from Beckwith, her children and shopping weighing down a massive old-fashioned pram so that its carriage scraped on its axles. I'd get off my bike and string a carrier bag or two on my handlebars and chat to her as we walked along, impressed by her resolute cheerfulness and tenderness in the midst of all her deprivation. The children were always laughing because Mum was laughing too, no tension, no crossness, no bitterness, when she could have been forgiven all three.

'Mrs Riccall, can I introduce Herbert Molescroft? He's on a placement with us to see what vicars get up to.'

'Pleased to see you, love,' Mrs Riccall beamed, in stark contrast to Herbert's frosty demeanour. 'So do you want to be a vicar, then?'

'Oh yes, oh yes,' Herbert replied, as if ordination were a foregone conclusion. 'People never cease telling me, "Mr Moles-croft, you've got such a lovely holy voice when you read the lessons. When are you going to take it up full-time?"'

'Well, I see you've already got the uniform,' Mrs Riccall breezed, pointing to his white polo-necked sweater which peeped over a black pullover.

'No, no, I just happen to like wearing this,

a sheer coincidence,' Herbert lied.

'So how did this birth go?' I asked, to move us on from Herbert's holier-than-thou show.

'Oh, it was all right. Very quick though, they only just got me to York in time. The ambulance took two hours to find us down here, and then it must have been more than an hour wending our way before we reached the hospital.'

'And no complications?' Though the mother and baby clinic had embarrassed me, I found these one-to-one situations easier to cope with, and felt it was important to talk through any traumas. Birth could have its brutal side, with bossy medics, who should have known better, lording it over an all-too-vulnerable mum.

'Not really. But I had to wait for four hours for the surgeon to put the stitches in. Two hours had gone by, when I gently asked what was delaying things. Sister told me the doctor had had to go and treat a private patient over in Thirsk and would attend to me when he got back. She spoke in the sort of voice that implied I was the dregs and was lucky to be seen to at all.'

'Oh, I'm so very sorry.' Over the years I had heard too many of these tales, and each time they made me seethe with fury. Women giving birth deserved better than this.

A silence followed, a silence of compassion for this mother, lying for hours unattended, uncomfortable, in pain, a holy silence brought to an abrupt end by Herbert Molescroft. 'Tell me,' he intoned in a superior voice, 'what do you think about the Holy Trinity?'

I had told Herbert to keep quiet and simply observe, so I was miffed, to say the least, at his hijacking things. Mrs Riccall looked nonplussed, and wasn't even given the time to frame an answer as Herbert droned on, answering his own question. 'Because the baby will be baptized in the name of the Father, and the Son, and the Holy Ghost. I always think the best way to understand the Trinity is to picture a good meal, all contained on one, single plate. God the Father is the roast meat, God the Son the vegetables and the gravy, yes, you've guessed it, is God the Holy Ghost...'

But with the ominous word 'Ghost', Herbert stopped his lecture in mid-flow and looked horrified as the strains of raucous singing filled the air: *'Trace we the babe, who hath retrieved our loss from his poor cradle to his bitter cross...'* The latch of the door rattled as the colour drained from Herbert's face.

'Oh, here's my Jim, back from the Stack,' Mrs Riccall explained. 'Forgive his un-seasonal solo, Vicar. It's the only hymn he knows, a carol he positively wailed his way through in Miss South's class for the school Nativity play in 1940; they always tried to find him a non-singing part after that! You're looking a bit pale, Mr Molescroft, are you all right? Now what was that you were saying about the Trinity?'

Herbert was too stunned by his near encounter with the Landings' ghost to continue his doctrinal exposition, so I regained the ground, talking about the timing of the christening, who would be there, what we were saying about God being this little babe's friend, right from the start. We left the cottage with a cheery, 'Well, see you next Sunday at two-thirty; make sure you get there in good time to settle everyone down.'

As his car bumped back over the lane, Herbert recovered his voice. 'I really do feel you should have given them something more substantial. All that dribbling on about the maternity hospital was really quite irrelevant. And what do you mean, saying, "God's the little lad's friend right

78

from the start?" There's got to be a response, a promise to keep a holy and good life, an appreciation of our sinfulness. I bet that lot hardly ever darken the church's door, and yet you made out that God was their dearest chum.'

He said the word 'chum' with such a sneer that I felt like strangling him. But I managed to resist the temptation and coolly replied, 'If you feel like that, Herbert, at the next baptism visit I'll do the listening and you can do the talking.'

'I will,' he declared. 'I nearly got a good discussion going on the Trinity tonight before you interrupted me.' He averted his eyes from me, lest I should challenge his version of events. 'One thing I won't do. I won't end the interview with a "see you next Sunday at two-thirty", as if we were all going to a race meeting.'

I suddenly latched on to a way to muzzle him. 'Now then, Herbert, what were you saying before our visit about not believing in ghosts?' I teased. For the remainder of the journey back to the vicarage, Herbert treated me to a surly silence. If I succeeded in getting him to shut up occasionally rather than always spouting forth, then his time with me would not be in vain.

The next night our venue was another ramshackle cottage by the river, but this time three miles north of the Landings in Eastwith. The predominantly red brick of the buildings gave the place a far more cheery air, a welcome foil to the dank evening mist that crept down the river and spilled into the village.

This time the poverty we encountered was abject, with nothing to redeem it. The cottage was occupied by a couple who had been married just before I took over the parish, with their first child arriving before they had been wed five months.

The girl's parents had disowned her because she had got into trouble, her husband being forced to support her and their newborn child with the pittance he earned working as a coalman. Both of them had clearly been cast into marriage too soon, in that, even allowing for the fact that they had little money, they didn't seem to have the first clue about how to run a home.

The young man's trade was all too evident as we stepped into the cottage, for there was barely any furniture at all, just used coal sacks scattered around, serving a variety of purposes: rugs, seats, even the baby was wrapped in a rough sack instead of a shawl.

It seemed that one piece of sacking had even been used to set food out on, in that a half-eaten fried egg and a few scraps of greasy bacon nestled between its folds. Herbert, full of himself as always, strode in, failing to notice the breakfast remnants adorning the floor. He plumped his foot straight on to the fried egg and skidded across the room, crashing into the wall and landing in a filthy pile of unwashed baby's nappies.

The stench almost made me retch as I helped a very soiled Herbert to his feet. I would have defied him to have gone paler than he did the night before, when he thought the ferryman was coming to haunt him, yet his pallor had turned a very nasty shade of grey. So much so that it prompted the girl, who normally was clearly oblivious to the squalor and drama surrounding her, to take action. 'Oo, I'm so sorry, so very sorry. Sit him down on a chair, er, on a bit of sacking, and I'll get him a cup of sweet tea. He looks as if he needs reviving.'

She lifted up a long piece of sacking that

hung from the ceiling; behind it was a room no bigger than a cupboard, which obviously had to serve as a kitchen. Having filled a battered aluminium kettle from an outside tap, she placed it on a Primus stove which flickered with a flame barely stronger than that of a candle. Time stood still as we waited and waited and waited for the kettle to come to the boil.

It never boiled. Instead the girl decided that even tepid water would be better than waiting any longer, so she disappeared further into the dark cupboard to mash a cup of tea. She came out carrying two rusty baked bean tins, brimful with a milky grey liquid which had tea leaves floating on its surface. Or at least I hoped they were tea leaves. 'I'm ever so sorry, we're a bit short of cups,' she explained.

I was immensely impressed by Herbert. He still looked in a bad way, a very bad way indeed, yet he summoned the courage to sip, albeit gingerly, from that baked bean tin. I felt an absolute heel, because while I was racking my brain trying to think of a way to dispose of the tea without it ever touching my lips, he was gracious enough to drink the stuff.

Nor did he embark on his pompous 'meat

and two veg' lecture on the Trinity Instead he took time to listen to the couple, cooed over the baby and talked to them about how difficult it was to set up a home and to make ends meet, even promising to drop around the next day with a few sticks of furniture he had going spare. And then, as we rose to take our leave, he said the words which fell on my ears like soft rain on an arid desert, 'Well, see you next Sunday at two-thirty; make sure you get there in good time to settle everyone down!'

Friday 13 May

'I see you've brought a friend with you.' The matron of Eastwith's old people's home screwed up her eyes and peered through tiny slits at Herbert Molescroft, as if she were trying to weigh him up. Actually, she was shielding her eyes from the spiral of acrid smoke from the cigarette dangling as usual out of the corner of her heavily made-up mouth.

'Yes, Matron, this is Herbert Molescroft who's on placement with me to see the ins and outs of being a vicar.' I was getting rather weary of trotting out this explanation at every turn.

'Oh, there's nothing to it, Mr Molescroft, you only have to work one day a week!' Matron laughed so raucously at her own joke that she triggered her smoker's cough, spluttering till her face went a deep crimson. Miraculously the cigarette remained in place, although a fall-out of ash cascaded on to the carpet with each rasp.

'Well, since today is a Friday and I'm here working, I think we can safely say I've proved that old joke wrong,' I quipped, while we waited for her to get her breath back.

'You might as well have the TV room as usual,' she wheezed. 'Just give us a few minutes to clear away one or two things and see which ones want it and which ones don't.'

Herbert and I were left standing around in her seedy office. Her desk was littered with a half-eaten cream cake, the cream yellowing and congealed, and half a dozen mugs stained with coffee dregs, as well as the inevitable ashtray full to the brim with fagends. She was an untidy person who ran an untidy home. 'Did you not tell her you were coming, then?' Herbert asked, rather pompously.

His manner reminded me of the long-winded Bishop of Pocklington, who had been severely disappointed at the small congregation which had turned up to hear him when he was a guest preacher at Charm-on-Spalding-Moor's harvest. 'Did you not tell them I was coming?' he had asked Stamford Chestnut haughtily.

'No, my lord, but the word seems to have got around,' Stamford replied, deadpan.

Chuckling inwardly, I refocused on the present. 'I always bring Communion at the same time on the second and fourth Fridays of the month,' I patiently explained. 'Before I leave, I always make sure she writes my next appointment in her diary, and I always ring the day before to check she knows I'm coming. Yet it always turns out like this. I think they'd be less surprised at Jesus and his second coming than they are by me turning up. The only exception was when the Bishop of Pocklington toured the parish with me; the place was so spick and span you could eat your dinner off the dining tables

'Don't you mean off the floor?' interrupted Herbert.

'No, I most certainly don't,' I continued. 'In the normal run of things the dining tables are the last place you would want to eat your dinner on, what with the false teeth, used tissues, even bedpans, that sit shoulder to shoulder with the cutlery and crockery. The hygiene in this place is appalling. If she offers you anything to eat or drink, for God's sake say no, unless you want to end up in the District Hospital tomorrow, having your stomach pumped.'

Our discussion was interrupted as Matron breezed back in. 'They're ready for you now. One or two of them didn't seem so sure, but we wheeled them in anyway. Another old dear thought you were the chiropodist, and started taking her stockings off, but we put her straight that it was Communion you were bringing.'

Immensely encouraged that our congregation was so expertly primed for our ministry, Herbert and I made our way to the TV room. The television set was on as usual, just the test-card and background music, the only show in town for the sad residents who gaped at it as in a trance. 'I'm not having this thing compete with the Supper of our Lord,' Herbert declared, striding over to the set and attempting to turn it off. The old people's dazed look was instantly replaced by faces contorted with dark anger, and the air was filled with cursing, curiously juxtaposed with the Bachelors trilling 'I Believe':

'Oi believe for every drop of rain that falls a flower grows...'

'Ay you, piss off out of here, you're blocking my view!'

'Oi believe that somewhere in the darkest night, a candle glows...'

'Who the hell's he think he is fiddling with our set?'

'Oi believe for everyone who goes astray, someone will come to show the way...'

'Leave it alone, you sod, we were watching that!'

'Oi believe above the storm, the smallest prayer will still be heard...'

'Jesus Christ, you turn it down and I'll smash your face in!'

'Oi believe that someone in the great somewhere, hears every word...'

'God in heaven, people bloody well walking in here, telling us what we can watch, what we can't. Can you credit it, can you bloody credit it!?'

'Oi belieeeeve!'

And so, in the twilight of their lives, the residents of Eastwith's old people's home prepared to make their Communion with their Maker. As the dulcet tones of the Bachelors faded out, I used the brief lull to restore order. 'Herbert, could you help me give out the Communion cards, please?' Herbert shuffled over and took the cards from me, his shoulders bowed, both unnerved by all the verbal abuse that had come his way and frustrated that he hadn't been able to find the set's on/off switch. A long time ago I had concluded that the contraption didn't have one, but blared out for ever and ever without end.

'No, you are not the Archbishop of Canterbury, you're a very rude inmate of an old people's home near York and you are not to do *that* with your Communion card,' shouted Herbert, doing a passable impersonation of Joyce Grenfell.

'Oh, and how are you going to stop me?' an old man glared at him. Undeterred, he stuffed yet another Communion card down his trousers. I gestured to Herbert to leave it at that. I tended to write off three or four such cards a month: seepage is what I believe commerce euphemistically calls pilfering, a fun word to conjure with in these particular circumstances.

'Will this Communion stop me corns throbbing?' demanded an old lady, presumably the one who had thought we were the chiropodists.

'This sacrament has many benefits,' Herbert proclaimed in a preachy voice. 'I always think of that great hymn, "And now O Father mindful of the love", with its verse,

And so we come, O draw us to thy feet,
most gracious Saviour who canst love us still.
And by this food, so awful and so sweet,
deliver us from every touch of ill…

'I don't want to be drawn to his feet,' the old lady complained. 'I want someone to draw the pain from my feet. Now can you do it or can't you?'

Herbert should have seen it coming, choosing a stanza where feet loomed so large. He muttered something about being sure the service would make a tremendous difference, and moved on. Personally, I'd always felt the verse would have made an excellent grace before the sickly meals that retreat houses tended to lay on.

'Now shall we start the service with a hymn?' I shouted cheerfully. 'Any requests?' Most of the residents knew a few traditional hymns by heart, and having a sing helped set the scene for worship. Or so I fondly believed.

'Can we have "It's a Long Way to Tipperary"?'

'No, dear.'

'But it was me husband's favourite. Why can't I have it?'

'Because it's not a hymn.'

'What about "Land of Hope and Glory", then?'

'I don't think so.'

'Tut! What's the point of asking for requests if you won't let us have them?' I was beginning to wonder about the point of the exercise myself, regretting my good idea ever saw the light of day.

'"The Old Rugged Cross", "The Old Rugged Cross", let's have "The Old Rugged Cross", it was me dad's favourite,' the Archbishop of Canterbury and Communion card pilferer par excellence piped up. Though by no means my favourite hymn, it was a hymn, so I decided to go for it and to quit while I was winning, or at least while I was not losing too humiliatingly.

'Right, we'll sing "The Old Rugged Cross",' I announced, still preserving the remnants of my original cheerfulness. 'I'll lead the words, you join in with as much of it as you can remember.'

'On a hill far away.' I intoned. 'Stands an old rugged cross...'

Our undoing came with 'old'. I had never before realized that the hymn's tune bore a passing resemblance to Tom Jones' hit, 'The Green, Green Grass of Home'. I did now, because one old boy, who'd obviously been a bit of a bar crooner in his younger days, struck up the ballad at the word 'old', where it coincided with the lyrics of the hymn:

'The old town looks the same, as I step down from the train...' he warbled, immediately forging the way for an alternative choir. Herbert and I and a few loyal old dears struggled on with the hymn; the rest rebelled and sided with the crooner, resulting in a rather peculiar canon:

'On a hill far away stood an old...'

'...*old town looks the same, as I step down from the train...*'

'...rugged cross...'

'*And there to meet me are my momma and my poppa.*'

'the emblem of suffering and shame.'

'*Down the road I look and there runs Mary...*'

'And I love that old cross, where the dearest and best...'

'*...hair of gold and lips like cherries.*'

'...for a world of lost sinners was slain.'

'*It's good to touch the green, green grass of home.*'

'So I'll cherish the old rugged cross, till my trophies at last I lay down.'

Our voices rose in crescendo as we each strove to win the day. With the most amazing sense of co-ordination, we finished together:

'And exchange it some day for a crown...'

'*...as they lay me 'neath the green, green grass of home.*'

'Oo, what a pity we didn't have "Land of Hope and Glory". Such a pity!'

I felt positively wrung out, and I hadn't even begun the service proper. Fortunately Eastwith's version of the Choir of the Year competition had exhausted everyone else as well, so I was spared the usual interruptions, and we were able to steam through the Prayer Book service at a rate of knots.

The resident Red Indian encircled Herbert and me and our makeshift altar (a coffee table decked in a tea-towel featuring the delights of Blackpool), chanting 'Wha, wha, wha!' incessantly. Though Herbert had the alarmed look of a European settler surrounded by Sioux with murder on their mind, I remained calm, by now well used to this harmless old soul trapped in her Wild West dreams. And the other residents, who normally infuriated me with their loud attempts to shut her up, either slept or reverted to their TV-enhanced trance.

That is, until the time came for them to receive their Communion. This was always a tense moment, with communicants often chewing up the consecrated wafer for a few seconds and then returning it to me, or trying to stash it away in their handbag for consumption later, or posting it down their cleavage instead of putting the thing into their mouth. And the problems I encount-ered with the bread paled into insignificance compared to the difficulties I faced trying to get an obdurate and intractable group, often engaging in open hostility with each other, to drink wine from the same cup.

''Ere, I'm not 'aving that, not until you've wiped her gaudy lipstick off the rim.'

'Excuse me, sir, but could I drink from the chalice before him? I don't want to catch what he's got. Just the smell of him makes me want to puke!'

Time fails me to tell in detail of the wine-taster, who habitually took a swig, swirled it around his mouth, and then spat it back into the chalice. As the months in my new parish had gone by, I had got wise to him and used to snatch the cup away before he could use it as a spittoon. As I got wise to another chap who took Jesus' instruction, 'Drink ye all of this', literally, taking a great gulp and draining the chalice to the dregs, leaving not a single drop of wine for the dozen or so people still waiting to communicate.

Today I gave out the consecrated bread, Herbert administered the chalice. All was fine until Herbert inadvertently stood on a communicant's foot. 'Oh God, me corns, me corns, you've trampled on me corns, you clumsy oaf,' she shrieked in dire pain. Of all the people he had to tread on, it would be the woman desperate for the chiropodist's services. In her distress, she kicked out with her injured foot, which made contact with Herbert's groin and sent him reeling across the room.

Herbert made a valiant attempt to keep his balance and avoid spilling the precious contents of the chalice, but after doing a set of pirouettes which were worthy of Margot Fonteyn, he crashed down beside the altar, managing to set the chalice down on the coffee-table's top as he did so. For a few anxious seconds the chalice wobbled on its base, threatening to topple over, but then righted itself. All the inmates applauded heartily. This was live entertainment which was infinitely better than any test-card with Bachelors accompaniment.

Herbert, however, was horrified. As the chalice had wobbled, wine had spilled over the rim and run down, soaking into the tea-towel, staining the delights of Blackpool deep red.

'The blood of our Lord, the blood of our Lord, I've spilled the blood of our Lord,' Herbert moaned. 'Can he ever forgive me?'

'Oo, me corns, me corns, God help me,' the woman wailed.

I helped Herbert up and sat him in a nearby chair, after which I took the chalice and finished communicating everyone. Having concluded the service, I gathered up the vessels, tea-towel and Herbert and made a hasty retreat to the car. For five whole minutes Herbert simply sat at the wheel, too stunned to drive. 'I've spilled his blood, I've spilled his blood. And that service was so ghastly, such a nightmare. How did I ever dream that I could cope with being a vicar?'

I felt his new-found humility indicated he

would cope very well indeed, and tried to put him out of his misery. At theological college we had been taught that if we ever spilled consecrated wine there was a special order of nuns who could be called on, who would eat up whatever the wine had been spilled on, carpets, robes, or whatever was vaguely edible. If the stained substance proved inedible despite their considerable appetite, then they would lick it clean. Apparently they drove up and down the A1 in a Mini, and could be summoned by radio.

Though the college principal had looked deadly serious when he passed on this advice, I had always had my doubts, and preferred a common-sense approach to any Eucharistic mishap, which is what I put into practice now. 'For goodness sake, Herbert, stop fretting. You managed brilliantly and averted a disaster.'

'But I spilled the blood of the Lord,' he protested.

'Well, we always have a cloth we wipe the chalice with. Wine invariably gets on to that, and I just soak it in cold water, which I then pour out on consecrated ground. It's simply God returning to the earth he made to start with, if you want to think of it like that. That's what I'll do with the Blackpool tea-towel, a slightly unconventional altar cloth, I admit, but that was Matron's fault not ours. What I really think is that if Jesus can jump through two thousand years and get into the sacrament, then he's quite capable of getting out if the going gets tough. Otherwise I don't think I'd ever be able to take Communion to that lot ever again.'

Herbert smiled a relieved smile. 'Yes, I can see that, I can see that. Thank you. I feel I'm going to learn a lot in my time with you.'

'No, you know a lot already. It's what you're prepared to let go of which is the make or break of ministry. And another thing,' I began, looking serious.

'Yes?' he replied, anxiously.

'You told that woman that the service would make a tremendous difference to her corns. Well, I think we can safely say it definitely did that, although not in the way either she or you expected!'

Herbert burst out laughing. I felt, after all, that he was not far from the kingdom of Heaven.

Friday 20 May

It was all very well having Herbert Molescroft as my shadow, and kind of him to chauffeur me around everywhere in his little Imp, but to tell the truth, I was missing my cycling. I craved a cycle ride like a drug addict craved his fix.

Ironic, really, when I'd found cycling so tough to begin with. I had never ridden a bike until I ended up as a clergyman in East Hull, with sprawling council estates and a mesh of streets and roads to get around. 'You'll need to get a cycle, otherwise you'll spend all your time walking from one visit to another,' was my new boss's bald comment. No offer was made to lend me a bike, no suggestion was made about help with finance to buy a new one. I had to scrape by on £8 a week, most of which I spent on my board and lodging, but I managed to do a deal with Halfords: a sparkling new bicycle for £20, with a hire purchase agreement where I had to pay off ten shillings each week. After a year of making weekly pilgrimages back to the shop bearing my ten-bob note offering, the beautiful machine was mine.

Unfortunately it wasn't beautiful for long. As I learned to ride it, it proved to have a mind of its own, taking me places I didn't want to go, homing in on innocent pedestrians over a hundred yards away with the precision of a heat-seeking device. My knees and hands were perpetually scuffed, the bike's gleaming paintwork was soon scratched and scraped. But one undoubted advantage was that the experience of learning to ride the thing was a tremendous ice-breaker, and brought me into contact with a wide cross-section of people who otherwise I wouldn't have encountered.

First there were the pedestrians I thudded into, who waved aside my profuse apologies, 'Ee, don't worry, Vicar, we've all got to learn sometime. I remember teaching our Wilf to ride and running behind him, holding on to the back mudguard. He was too scared for me to let him go, until one day I tripped over a black cat and he soared ahead, oblivious. He'd achieved his balance at last. It's all a long time ago, yet seeing you makes me feel as if it were yesterday. He's grown up and got a bairn himself now. It's funny I bumped into you, because I was wondering about getting him christened...'

And then there were the garden walls I collided with, and the gardens I ended up in, sprawled on all fours, usually having to extricate myself from some malicious rose tree. Generally, as I struggled, hoping that no one had noticed my catapulting act, a housewife would emerge. Generally there would also be her friend with whom she had been having a gossip over a cup of coffee. Generally they would be huge women, decked in aprons with a floral pattern, with their arms folded, bolstering a huge bust. 'Hallo, Vicar, good of you to drop by!' they would generally quip, cackling at the brilliance of their wit. But generally and genuinely they changed their tack to a note of concern, 'Ee, you look all in. Doesn't he look pale, Brenda? Come on in and have a good sweet cuppa. You'll soon feel right as rain.' And generally, as I drank their tea, they would talk about their families, their triumphs and their tragedies, their homes and their fears, what they thought of the Church, how it had let them down, how it had made their day. It was worth scarring my knees and hands for such rich contact.

Once I was visiting by the docks when the right pedal crank fell off. The holding nut had worked itself loose, and try as I might, I couldn't fix it back on with my fingers sufficiently tightly. I'd get the thing to go back, but only manage to pedal ten yards before the nut had unscrewed itself and the crank crashed to the ground once again. I tried pedalling with one pedal, but sufficiently acrobatic to get the knac. kept falling off.

After the crank had detached itself for tenth time, I gave up, and was preparing push the bike home, until I realized I had come to rest by a dockside engineering works. It looked a rough place, its yard littered with discarded wheels and machinery and rusting iron rods. The workforce who were hanging around in the yard looked even rougher, unshaven apprentices with long hair who shouted coarsely and guffawed at each other. This was not a place that a black-suited and cycle-clipped young Oxbridge cleric, with short back and sides, normally ventured into. Not if he was wise.

'But why not?' I thought to myself. 'Why not? Why should I spend an hour walking home when they can probably help me?' And so, wheeling my bicycle, I ventured into the yard.

The lads stopped shouting at each other, and turned their bemused attention on me. 'Excuse me,' I stammered. 'But I wondered if any of you had a small sprocket?' Perhaps not one of the greatest chat-up lines in history, but undoubtedly original.

'Ee, you speak for yourself,' the tallest of

he obvious ringleader, replied. 'We
take kindly to vicars asking us
onal questions like that!' They all burst
o laughter, and I laughed too, and the ice
as broken. I haplessly waved the detached
pedal crank at him. 'Eh up, lads, he's come
armed!'

'No, I come in peace,' I declared, impersonating the latest alien figure starring in
Doctor Who. 'I wondered if you had a tool
you could put this back on with.' Again
there was loud laughter: a hapless cleric
spouting on about sprockets and tools, apparently oblivious to the double entendres,
was entertainment indeed.

But the ringleader took pity on me. 'Yeh,
I'm sure we can find something that can put
it on again. Wheel your bike into t' works
and we'll see what we can do.'

I often think of that incident, and see
myself as a brave pioneer for industrial
chaplaincy. I'm sure if the Church had
commissioned a thousand clergy with a
thousand detached pedal cranks, we'd have
made great inroads into the world of
engineering.

As time went on, I found that cycling
became sheer pleasure rather than danger-
ous chore, and I used my time off to leave

the sprawling council estates behind
glide out into the plains of the S[c]
Riding, made famous by Winifred Holtb[y]
eponymous novel. To get there I had [t]
wend my way through the industria[l]
wasteland of the paint factory and oil
refinery, but then suddenly I was free, and
there was a new-world feel, a surprise world
squeezed in between city and sea. I used to
enjoy the desolation of the coasts, the little
village of Paull, cottages huddled together,
peeping over the wide expanse of the
Humber, with the feel of the seaside rather
than the riverside. And then the coast
became more forlorn and more elusive, as I
cycled through field after field, wondering if
I would ever find it again. I enjoyed
watching the ITV series *The Fugitive*, and I
vowed that if ever I found myself cast in the
role of the runaway, then this was where I
would hide out. Evocative names like Sunk
Island and Stony Creek, a muddy harbour
sheltering a couple of rusty hulks and not a
single person to be seen for mile upon mile.
Real solitude from which I could drink and
be refreshed, time out as a foil to all the
contact with people that could be so cloying
in my day-to-day work. A hero of mine was
Francis Kilvert, Welsh clergyman and

...rian diarist, with my favourite entry 7 ...l 1870:

...had the satisfaction of managing to walk ...rom Hay to Clyro by the fields without meeting a single person, always a great triumph for me and a subject for warm self-congratulation, for I have a peculiar dislike to meeting people, and a peculiar liking for the deserted road.

Most people I shared that extract with thought it a bit rum that a clergyman, of all people, should want to escape from contact with humanity. But sometimes I knew all too well the need to get away from everyone, simply so you could come back again.

Cycling was a retreat for me in every sense of the word, something I thirsted for, and so I had arranged with Herbert Molescroft that he would meet me at Eastwith School rather than pick me up from home, to allow me to treat myself to the three-mile cycle ride there.

And what a day it was for a cycle ride, spring in all its glory, the sky a typical Vale of York sky, deep blue stretching for ever. The greens of the trees were fresh and glistening, with none of the jaded look of later summer. I left Kirkwith's avenue of poplars behind, soaring down the lane to the ford, which, when I had first moved into the village the autumn before, had threatened to engulf me. Now it was just a trickle, hardly having the energy to splash me as I sliced through it.

I was in real country now, no house, no farm to be seen, just sown fields alternating with woodland and brush. The smells had a delicious heaviness about them, a sweet drowsy feel, with wild garlic prevailing, clean and appetizing. But there were other more subtle aromas too, which my urban nose could detect but not name, like a musically untutored ear delighting in a symphony yet not able to identify the instruments. Some things I could recognize, the obvious fragrance of wild mint, the fecund scent of the first cut of vergeside grass, the morbid aroma of leaf mould and humus from the forest floor – yet even the rotting smell of death was pardonable on this most lovely of mornings.

I turned a corner and came across an isolated farmhouse, smartly turned out in Elizabethan brick. For nearly four centuries the farm had belonged to the same family, from generation to generation, from father to son, all seeing these sights, drinking in these smells day after day, lean year in, fat year out.

And the sounds: the rasping call of a pheasant which ripped apart the silence; the haunting call of black Russian geese, flying in formation over my head, far swifter than my pedal power could achieve; and, even when Eastwith was still a good mile away, the shrieks of the children playing in the schoolyard, the sound of youthful promise bouncing along the Derwent's surface and echoing for miles. I thought of the nuns, enclosed at the other side of the river, whose open day condemned our garden party to compete with the World Cup. What thoughts, what prayers, what despair arose from the sound of children dashing against their silence?

Renewed by my journey, I pedalled into Eastwith and parked at the school gates, where Herbert was sitting waiting for me in his car. I would have missed so much if I had travelled with him.

The school's head, Geoff Goodmanham, was striding around the yard, joking with the children, teasing them, listening attentively to their news, at times a laughing face, at times a serious face. In his arms was

Elizabeth, his baby, who had shocked us just after Christmas by arriving too soon. By now Geoff was an experienced father, and yet the way he held her, just a wee bit too tightly, betrayed the stance of a man who had nearly lost his darling.

Geoff bounded towards us, his Harris tweed jacket, far too heavy for this warm spring day, flapping in his slipstream. 'David, just great to see you,' he boomed. 'June's gone to York for the day on the bus, so I'm doing the baby-minding. Perhaps you can give a hand?' As I've mentioned before, the sort of bus service we had in the Withs meant that you could never go to York for less than a day, making every menial shopping expedition a major excursion.

'Yeh, I'll be delighted to,' I replied, picking up Geoff's rather over-enthusiastic speak. 'I used to look after my younger brother in my teenage years, so I can change a mean nappy.'

'Good man. Now who's this you've got with you? A vicar's HMI?'

'No, a vicar's HMI is called an arch-deacon, and I'm pleased to say he's at least fifty miles away. Let me introduce you to Herbert Molescroft, who's following me around to see what a vicar gets up to and

107

whether the job's worth taking on. We went to the old people's home last week, so we're rather nervous of another excursion to Eastwith.'

'My goodness, you poor things. If only I'd known, I'd have brought the whisky over! Well, anyway, welcome to Eastwith's young people's home, Mr Molescroft. Feel free to wander around, ask the children questions, that sort of thing. And be prepared for them to ask you a few.'

'I'm sure I'll manage,' Herbert replied, his eyes narrowing, the corners of his mouth turning up to make him look rather snooty. It was a pity, in that I thought his experience at the old folks' home would have managed to defrost him. Clearly he'd decided to revert to aloof-man.

The other teacher, Miss South, emerged from the building ringing a huge handbell to summon the children inside for their assembly. Herbert and I followed them into the hall and waited while they settled down, sitting cross-legged before us. 'Good morning, boys and girls,' I declared. I always felt this greeting sounded so false.

'Good morning, Vicar,' they shouted back. At least they'd moved on from 'Good morning, Mr Wilborn/MrWelborn/Mr Willesborn/Mr Wilbraham/Mr Wilberforce,' and all the other hundred and one variants of my surname visited upon me by adults who should have known better as well as by children whose lapse could be forgiven.

'Now, I've brought a very important person with me this morning. His name is Mr Molescroft.'

'Good morning, Mr Molescroft/Mr Molescrotch/Mr Molest/Mr Noseblow,' they intoned.

'Now, Mr MOLESCROFT is with me today because he wants to find out what a vicar does, so what can you tell Mr Molescroft about the things I do?'

Twenty-nine hands shot up. 'Yes, Yvonne.'

'You help people die,' a little girl with blonde pigtails informed me.

'Well, er, yes, in a sense...'

'My dad calls the knackerman to help our horses die,' Paul Broadley, the naughtiest boy in the school, chipped in. Paul had been a shepherd in the school Nativity play which had been staged at the church. His attempts to lasso an eagle with his father's long dressing-gown cord had caused the angels to divert from their planned route, with one little girl brushing against a candle and setting her wings on fire. Bill Everingham had rushed on to the stage and bravely beaten out the flames, adding some high drama which had been entirely unscripted.

'No, I'm not like the knackerman,' I hurriedly tried to explain. 'I don't make people die. In fact I'm very sorry when anyone is dying, and I try to help them to be happy and know that God loves them.'

Most of the children looked disappointed, as if they'd been rather taken with the idea of me being a sort of ecclesiastical hitman, putting a few trying and wretched humans out of their misery. To be honest, when some of my charges were particularly trying, I could see the attractions of the role myself.

I noticed one of the girls in the top class was waving her arm in the air, desperate to speak. Sharon Dubbins had starred as a muscular Virgin Mary in the afore-mentioned Nativity play, and her family regularly won the bale-tossing competition at the Howden Show. Brawn rather than brains tended to be the order of the day with the lot of them, so I didn't have very high hopes about what she was dying to say.

'Sharon?'

'When a girl gets in the family way, you tie the knot and make it proper,' she cannily pronounced. I guess she'd been unduly influenced by the recent marriage of her sister, who, even with the Dubbins' renowned muscular frame, had found a six-month pregnancy difficult to disguise on her wedding day.

'Yes, I do marry people who dearly want to spend the rest of their lives together and start a family,' I explained, as diplomatically as I could manage. 'David?' I asked.

'You circumstrate babies,' he declared.

'No, I think you mean christen them,' I corrected, wondering whether he had confused me with a cross between a rabbi and a vet. 'I've never heard of the word circumstrate.'

'I have,' Paul Broadley blurted out yet again. 'We've been circumstrating lambs on farm for t' last fortnight. Me dad holds lambs and knackerman bites off their knack—'

'Paul Broadley, out!' Miss South shouted. 'We've heard quite enough from you this morning. Go into the classroom and sit at your desk, and I will see you as soon as Mr Wilbourne has finished.'

'And what do I do to babies when I christen them?' I continued, as Paul Broadley shuffled out in tears.

'You give their hair a wash with cold water

111

and they shriek and that makes the devil come out, and then they're done,' Lee Moss informed us.

'Partly true, Lee. I do pour water on their heads, really as a sign that God loves them, right from the very start of life. The water is a sign of the life and love God freely gives.'

'Funny sort of way to show you love someone, pouring cold water on their heads. I gave Sharon a ring, didn't I, Sharon?' Lee was physically well developed for his age, and was known to be more than slightly keen on Sharon. Their puppy love had injected a surprising note of passion into the normally chaste environs of the Nativity play, with Lee as Joseph giving Mary more than one amorous embrace. He had also exceeded his brief, with hilarious consequences, by trying his hand at obstetrics, delivering a baby doll Jesus who unfortunately had got wedged in his cot.

Sharon waved her hand, showing off a cheap plastic ring to all and sundry. 'I got it out of a cracker,' Lee explained, oblivious to its tackiness. 'It's got "for ever" engraved on it.'

'Well, a baptism is a way of saying that we belong to God for ever,' I butted in, attempting to reclaim the argument. 'It's a way of celebrating that he'll never leave us, never let us down.' Most of the children started shuffling their feet; a squawking child having its demons exorcised, à la Lee Moss' rite, was obviously more exciting.

Baby Elizabeth was gurgling in Geoff's arms, so I decided to reclaim their attention by staging a mock baptism. I dispatched Miss South to the kitchens for a bowl of water and, placing it on a high desk, asked Geoff to hand Elizabeth to me. 'Name this child,' I intoned, with mock seriousness.

'Elizabeth Mary,' Geoff declared. And then his eyes filled with tears. I realized that our role play had cast him back to that night at the end of December, when I'd stood by June's bed in the maternity hospital and christened their dying child. As we'd gazed on the infant, so tiny, so frail, a little tongue had come out of her mouth and licked the drops of baptismal water which had run down her face. Until then Matron had been sorrowfully looking on, but as soon as she saw that baby's reaction, she decided the little one was a real survivor, and so she pulled out all the stops to save the child. And save her she did.

'Elizabeth Mary, I baptize you in the name of the Father and of the Son and of the Holy

Ghost.' I avoided catching Herbert's eye as I pronounced the word 'Ghost'. It was bad enough causing Geoff to have a flashback; I didn't want to produce another nervous wreck by reminding Herbert of the Landings ghost.

As I said the words, I cupped the water and let it fall clear of Elizabeth's head, not wanting to disturb her good humour. Also, with Herbert watching my every move like a hawk, I didn't want him reporting me to the bishop for the heinous sin of Anabaptism. Though no one had been tried for it since Reformation times, I feared it could still be a burnable-at-the-stake offence; or at least a dressing down from the dreaded Archdeacon.

To give Geoff a chance to recover his composure, I showed the children an ancient church register I had brought with me and at the same time set a mental arithmetic poser: 'Grandad's age is three score years and ten. How old is he?'

Nine-year-old Peter Broadhurst, son of professor George, had the answer in no time. 'Please sir, seventy!' Miss South beamed

'Yes, well done, Peter. I have to admit that when I had that question in an exam when I was your age, I confused a score with a gross and came up with three times a hundred and forty-four plus ten, with a grandad who was the ripe old age of four hundred and forty-two.' All the children tittered at this clerical numskull before them, their ridicule triggering my own flashback.

I had been marked wrong and cruelly mocked by my teacher for failing to twig that grandparents didn't achieve that ripe old age. But there again, his imagination hadn't been saturated like mine with Old Testament patriarchs who strode through centuries as if they were decades. As a clergy child I had moved among them since the cradle, and assumed that all humans routinely lived hundreds of years. And another thing: I reckon I should have got extra marks for completing a sum that was far trickier than the one intended.

I fast-forwarded from my childhood back to 1966, and waved the register in front of the children. 'This book is almost as old as that poor old grandad in my exam – four hundred and twenty-seven years to be exact. When anybody was born, or got married or died, the vicar wrote their details in here. But just think for a moment, about all those years, and all those vicars who would have come and gone, and what they would have

115

seen, what they would have been frightened of, what great events they would have witnessed. Anyone got any suggestions?'

Sharon Dubbins waved her hand eagerly. 'Please, sir, the Stone Age?'

'No, a bit early, I'm afraid, Sharon. Anyone else?'

David Harsley blurted out, 'Robin Hood, Vicar?'

'No, again a bit early. But it's good to see you've lots of ideas,' I said, trying to sound encouraging. Geoff and Miss South were looking at their feet in embarrassment. 'Lee?'

'The Lone Ranger?'

'Well, not really, he was an American, and I think he's just a story,' I replied.

'No he i'nt, I've seen him on the telly, so he must be real,' argued Lee, with unassailable logic.

'Help!' I cried, silently. Every time I took assembly, it always ended up like this: I always felt like the driver of a Formula One racing car, whose steering wheel had just come off at high speed.

Help came in the guise of Peter Broadhurst, who treated us to a *tour de force* of British history. 'Well, first there was Henry the Eighth, then there was the Armada, then there was Charles the First and the Civil War, then there was a lot of boring kings, then there was Stephenson's Rocket and Queen Victoria, and the Zulu War and the Great War and the last war...' Not so much an answer as an encyclopaedia.

'Charles the First had his 'ead chopped off.' It was Sharon Dubbins who was giving us this explanatory gloss. 'There'd be blood everywhere. When me dad kills chickens, he wrings their necks. Sometimes their necks are too thin and their heads come off in his hands and blood spurts and spurts all over the place. Charles the First would be like that, blood everywhere, over everyone...'

'Thank you, dear, that'll be quite enough of that.' Miss South's voice was firm and brooked no argument.

'Well, thank you, Peter, and er, thank you, Sharon too,' I continued. 'Just imagine, all those things going on as this little book was being written up. But there were local things too. Just look at this entry: "Second of September 1566: Harry Rume baptized. Third of September 1566: Mary Rume buried. Fourth of September 1566: Harry Rume buried." What does that tell us?'

'That the Rumes ate something at the christening party that disagreed with them!'

quipped Lee.

'Oh, don't,' said Sharon. 'The little baby's mum died and then the little baby died. That's it, isn't it, Vicar? So many women died giving birth in those days, my mum told me. Our Mabel had a fever after she'd had their Colin, but they cured it with some antibionics. A few years back she'd have died with that, that's what my mum said.' Precocious Sharon might have been, but her knowledge of her sister's recent confinement held the hall spellbound.

'Thank you, Sharon. We've got a lot to be grateful for, that mums and their babies seldom die these days. And other things as well. Listen to this: " Fourth of May 1837: Harry Jenkinson buried, aged seven. Ninth of May 1837: Martha Jenkinson buried, aged nine. Fifteenth of May 1837: Joseph Jenkinson buried, aged three. Eighteenth of May 1837: Rebecca Jenkinson buried, aged one. Twenty-first of May 1837: Stephen Jenkinson buried, aged five. Twenty-sixth of May 1837: Nathaniel Jenkinson buried, aged eight. Thirty-first of May 1837: Elizabeth Jenkinson buried, aged thirty-two." What does that tell you?'

This time there were no clever quips from Lee, shamed by his sweetheart. Instead he answered in a low voice, 'All the children died of some horrible disease, and then their mother died?'

'Yes, Lee, it was a disease called cholera, caught from dirty water. And can you make out the signature of the vicar who took all those funerals?' I strode across to the juniors in the back row and held the register open for them to read.

'George Jenkinson,' the children all cried out together.

'Yes, George Jenkinson. The same surname because he was married to Elizabeth and those were his children. Just imagine the poor man, what he must have been feeling, as day after day he not only had to bear another death, but also take the burial. This book's got a lot of tragedy in it like that, and a lot of joy too, sweethearts married, babies born and surviving to old age. Each little register entry tells such a story, sad stories, happy stories, life going on, year in year out.'

I had them eating out of my hand now, moved by the plight of their ancestors, grateful for the luxuries and health they enjoyed in the present day. I should have left it there. Instead I decided to follow on with my party trick.

'Just look, as we turn the pages of this register, how the writing changes.' I showed them the grudging scrawl of the parish priest in the 1530s, none too fussed at being commanded by Henry VIII to keep appropriate records. Then I flipped through to the neat and exact copperplate of Victorian times. Finally I turned to the present day: 'And just look at how untidy we are today, when we've got all the pens and equipment and health and good fortune that our ancestors never dreamt of a hundred years ago.'

Ever one for visual aids, I had brought along a sharpened quill and a bottle of indelible black ink to demonstrate the pains taken. I dipped the quill into the bottle, which then for some reason decided to assume a will of its own, leaping off the table and landing (fortunately without shattering) at the feet of Miss South's class. The impact splattered spots of black ink over their socks, legs and faces, making them look like victims of the sort of instant mass epidemic that had taken out the Jenkinson dynasty in one month. The rest of the ink glugged out of the bottle and soaked into the oak floor.

Panic-stricken, I looked at Geoff. He was

back to his usual carefree self, smiling indulgently at baby Elizabeth, assuming that this was all planned and just another of my carefully arranged skits. Herbert Molescroft was no use either. He was squatting on the floor by the side of Miss South's class, and so had been in the line of fire, with spots of indelible ink speckling his precious white sweater. Now he was frantically dabbing at these with his handkerchief, oblivious to my need for help.

'Mr Goodmanham, I'll go out and get a cloth,' Miss South boomed, signalling to Geoff that all was not well. Actually a whole succession of cloths was needed before the infants resumed any sort of normality. We mopped up the floor as best we could, but the stain remains to this day. And Dalmatian socks were all the rage in the Withs for months afterwards, despite the scrubbing and the bleaching that mums throughout the parish frantically engaged in, cursing the stupid vicar and his stupid assemblies as they did so. As Geoff told Herbert over break, in all innocence, 'David's only been here a short time, but he's really left his mark on this school.'

Three days later the phone rang as I was eating my breakfast, the sadly diminished remainder of Stamford Chestnut's engagement present, the bacon by now a little high. 'David, it's Geoff here, Geoff Goodmanham. I wonder if you could come down, something terrible's happened.'

There was an anxious edge to his voice which took me back to those days after Christmas, when he'd rung me from the maternity hospital in Howden, fearing that his new-born daughter was dying. 'Of course I can, Geoff, what's the matter?'

'It's Mrs Ludlow,' he explained. 'She's just popped in to school to tell me she wouldn't be coming in for a few days, because her husband had a heart attack last night and died. She was amazingly matter-of-fact about it all, but she seemed to be functioning on automatic pilot, not all there really. I offered her a cup of tea, but she refused and said she had things to do at home. As she walked off in a trance-like state, I felt she needed someone to be with her. I'm ever so sorry, I can't leave the children, but then I thought of you, whether you might have the time?'

'Of course, Geoff, I'll cycle over straight away.'

As I cycled the three miles to Eastwith once again my mind focused on Mrs Ludlow, alone now after all those years of marriage, both grief-stricken and overwhelmed by the hundred and one things that have to be done at the time of death. My cycle ride wasn't all morbid, however, in that I replayed a conversation I had had with Geoff on my visit to the school three days before. Geoff had been changing his daughter's very dirty and smelly nappy in the staffroom during break. The tiny room doubled up as the kitchen, and as excreta oozed everywhere from the soiled nappy, Geoff became uncharacteristically stressed, all too aware of the threat to hygiene. To relieve the tension, I told Geoff about Mrs Ludlow and her dog faces.

'You should hear some of the things she comes out with here at dinner time,' Geoff had commented, laughing as he visibly relaxed. '"Now then, love, do you want another scoopful of salmonella? It's lovely and creamy."

'I just note them down for posterity, but Miss South tries to put her straight. "It's semolina, Mrs Ludlow."

'"That's right, love, salmonella. We had tapioca last week."'

'Any more?' I had asked, passing Geoff the talcum powder.

'Well, we often have lionized potatoes rather than Lyonnaise potatoes, on our jelly we pour condescending milk rather than condensed milk, Welsh rabbits must be a near-extinct species by now, judging by the number which must be culled for our regular Monday menu slot, and on Wednesdays we delight in salivas of liver in gravy, which makes a change from the slivers of offal I used to have as a boy.'

Geoff was in his stride, as he thought of more and more examples.

'Occasionally we have quench Lorraine, which sounds more like border territory that France and Germany perennially fight over. When there's a lot of mashed potato left over from the day before we have bubble and squawk. On Fridays we try to abstain from meat except when we have kestrelee rather than kedgeree. The raffioli can understandably be a bit chewy, but Mrs Ludlow's *pièce de résistance,* or "pass the resistor" as she would say, is undoubtedly her non-alcoholic variant of that great British sweet, the syllabub trifle. Who can

124

resist her plea, "Have another spoonful of sillybugger trifle, it'll only go to waste"?'

'The thing is,' Geoff had concluded, 'I don't know what we'd do without her. She's an absolutely brilliant cook and so motherly with the children. She's riddled with arthritis, you know, not helped by that damp cottage she's lived in all her married life, but she does wonders as she hobbles around this cramped school kitchen.'

He waved his hands expansively, or as expansively as the minuscule room would allow. 'She copes with temperamental ovens and equally ancient utensils, and somehow manages to concoct a meal which is both satisfying and popular. Not a single child goes home for lunch or brings a pack-up, since no alternative could remotely equal Mrs Ludlow's fare. Roast beef, lump-free mashed potatoes, treacle sponge, apple pie, bread and butter pud, whatever the menu, the meal is the five-star highlight of our school day.'

Of course, he had been preaching to the converted. Whenever I took assembly, I always conspired to hang around until lunch-time and benefit from Mrs Ludlow's cuisine, or cousin as she persisted in calling it.

As I neared Eastwith, my thoughts came

back to the present. The school kitchens and the hall would be a very different place today and for the next few days. Tins of lukewarm stew, swede and tapioca would have to wend their way from Salvington School, six miles down the road, sloshing about in the van as it drove three sides around every field. Eastwith would indeed feel the loss of Tom Ludlow deeply.

I leant my bicycle against the ivy-covered wall of Mrs Ludlow's house, a shower of mortar falling as my handlebars caught pointing which should have been replaced long since. Mrs Ludlow opened a stiff front door whose planks were warped, with gaps in between them which let the light shine through, and no doubt the wind and the rain and sundry small creatures to boot. She proudly showed me into the parlour, where there was a fire, newly lit in the grate, spluttering, doing its best to dispel the heavy smell of damp. How many such rooms had I been ushered into in my time as a priest? The parlour, the front room, the cold, posh, never-inhabited place, reserved for the visits from the vicar, and other important people who sadly never came.

In the centre of Mrs Ludlow's parlour was the most important person of them all, at least in her eyes. In a newly made coffin lay Tom Ludlow's body, laid out during the night by his wife, the last act of a woman for her man. I thought of her old, arthritic fingers, closing his eyes, washing him down, dabbing him dry, looking over the cold grey body which, in its time, in her time, had been one flesh with her. And then easing the cold, rigid limbs into his best white shirt, his best, and only, suit (the suit, no doubt, he had married in), trying, trying and trying again to tie his tie, fumbling over the knot that was so infuriatingly unfamiliar. Making this farm-hand, normally decked in an open-necked shirt, tatty worsted trousers, a dirty rope for a belt, making him look his best for death, laid out in her best room.

Mrs Ludlow stood beside me as I silently looked at the body of her husband. It was the smells that loomed: the new wood of the coffin, the smoke of the fire, the camphor of mothballs, the coal tar soap with which she had scrubbed him down, the damp of the room, all masking, but not quite masking, the smell of death. Dead men smelt differently from dead women, distinct smells which often preceded death, often heralded it, which we nice people pretended not to notice.

'He looks very peaceful, Mrs Ludlow,' I said, as I put my arm around her. Her body juddered as she fought to control the sobs.

'Ay, it was a quick end, Vicar, mercifully quick. It was half-nine, just last night,' she explained. I noticed the inflexion she gave the word 'just', as if death had drawn unacceptably close, as if something as ultimate as death should have given notice of its coming, as if it were remarkable that death had visited only yesterday, within a day's span, like an impostor trespassing in a kingdom which should never have been his. 'He were listening to t' farmers' forecast on wireless one minute, then he shuddered, and the next minute he was gone. Dr Seaton was round within the hour and pronounced him dead. "Don't fret, Becky, there's nothing you could have done, absolutely nothing. It's over for him; he's at peace now."

'I couldn't rest, Vicar. Who could? Dr Seaton had left me something to help me sleep, but I didn't want that. So I spent the night cleaning him up, getting him dressed. And then Bert popped round with the coffin early this morning, ready-made, we didn't want anything fancy. He helped me to lay him out in his last resting place.'

I had encountered Bert, the local joiner and undertaker, a fair few times in my first six months. He had told me how he kept a stock of ready-made coffins for men in just two sizes: large for the bulky farmers, medium-small for the wiry farm-labourers. 'No point in measurin' 'em up, Vicar. They're either one size or t' other round 'ere. Women are a different matter, widths and heights all over t' place, so have to be made to measure. I've got me work cut out for me, gettin' t' coffin ready in time for women's funerals. Just you remember that, if you please. We can bury t' men virtually straight off, for women I need three or four days to get job properly done.'

I said a prayer over Tom, the same one I used in season and out of season whoever it was who had died, Cardinal Newman's prayer, a prayer whose sheer loveliness could never be diminished by overuse:

O Lord, support us all the day long of this troublous life until the shadows lengthen, the busy world is hushed, the fever of life is over, and our work is done. Then, Lord, in thy mercy, grant us and those we love, safe lodging, a holy rest and peace at the last. Through Jesus Christ our Lord. Amen.

'Amen,' Mrs Ludlow chorused, as the prayer came to its end. We stood for a further few minutes before she broke the silence. 'Let's go into kitchen, Vicar, and I'll put t' kettle on. I think we both could do with a cuppa to warm us up.'

I followed her out into the kitchen, a damp little lean-to propped up against a damp little house. The crudely made cold tap creaked as she turned it on, with the old lead piping beating a tattoo of protest as it was disturbed from its slumbers. Mrs Ludlow noisily filled the kettle, blackened by use, and clattered it down on its rack over the stove where the flames licked around its base. It was funny that in the parlour it was the smells that had loomed. Now in the kitchen, it was the sounds. Death made every sensation seem sharper.

'We'll have him done in church, if that's all right with you,' Mrs Ludlow pronounced, as the kettle slowly came to the boil. 'And I've booked a plot for him and me in t' new graveyard. I know he didn't come to church much, he used to leave that to me, "Women's work," he used to call it. Even so, he had a soft spot for that old red-brick building in which he were christened and where we got wed. It was his church, where his family's births, marriages and deaths had been marked for centuries. He wanted to go there at the end, I'm sure of that. "It's all continental," he used to say.'

'From one generation to another,' I said gently, deliberately avoiding the word 'continuity' so as not to appear to correct her in her grief. 'I'd often see him, you know, as I cycled by when he was cutting back the hedges, and sometimes I'd stop and chat with him. You're right about him not being churchy, but he had faith nevertheless, a wider faith than a narrow churchiness, and at the same time a hidden faith which didn't shout itself from the rooftops. Faith in the wonder of nature and the seasons, faith in the rich characters around him, who he talked of tenderly. Faith in you,' I added, dropping my voice, realizing that in a real sense I was walking on hallowed ground.

'Do you think so, Vicar?' Mrs Ludlow asked. 'He was never very demonstrable, never made an outward show of affection, specially not in public. He'd been brought up very strict, Victorian, where a man kept his feelings private, to himself, kept himself bottled up.'

'The way he talked gave away how deeply fond he was of you,' I replied. 'And you should have seen his face light up as he described the tea you'd served him the night before.'

'Oh, he liked his meals, true enough,' Mrs Ludlow agreed. 'He'd come home at five on the dot every day, "Let's get stuck in right away, lass," he'd say. He'd want his meal there and then. Woe betide me if I was a bit behind and the potatoes still had a few minutes to boil. You can understand it, can't you? After working in them fields all day, with all that fresh air, any man would be positively ravishing.'

I was glad that even in the valley of the shadow of death, Mrs Ludlow had not lost her way with words. Or maybe she was trying to signal that her husband was a 'demonstrable' man after all. 'I'm pleased you liked him, Vicar,' Mrs Ludlow said, noticing the slight smile come to my lips and mistaking it for fondness. 'It'll make the service meaningful, you knowing him and liking him. It's true what Mr Goodmanham says of you' I braced myself to hear her latest revelation. '...."He reads people like a book, that vicar. He's a highly percentage man."' Praise indeed.

'Have you got any idea about hymns?' I asked, keen to move the conversation on.

Mrs Ludlow looked thoughtful as she poured out two steaming hot mugs of thick brown tea, routinely shovelling a couple of dessertspoons piled high with sugar into each cup. 'I don't know,' she said, shaking her head. 'I don't know what would be approximate. How many do you have?'

'Normally two,' I replied.

'I suppose we'd have to have "Abide with Me". He loved his Cup final, Tom did. 'That match last month between Sheffield Wednesday and Everton absolutely thrilled him. "Ee, would you credit it!" he exclaimed after t' game had finished. "Wednesday had it in t' bag, two-nil up at half-time, and then Everton came back and thrashed 'em with them three late goals. Wednesday were just too comp, comp, comp..."'

'Complacent,' I said, coming to her rescue.

'Yes, that's it, Vicar, "too comp, comp, compl, er, too smug", that's what my Tom said.'

'And what about the other hymn?' I asked, slurping my tea, too sweet and too strong.

'Well, he always liked "The Old Rugged Cross" when they sang it on *Songs of Praise*.'

'Sadly, I don't think that's in the hymn book, Mrs Ludlow,' I said, secretly grateful. I still squirmed as I thought back to Herbert Molescroft's visit to the old people's home and the way the hymn had been shouted down in favour of 'The Green, Green Grass of Home'. I didn't want to run the risk of that happening again at so solemn occasion as a funeral.

'In that case, we'll have "The King of love my shepherd is",' Mrs Ludlow decided.

'Tom would like that line, "Thou spreadst a table in my sight", what with his love of food,' I commented.

'Yes, I can just imagine him, being ravishing in heaven like he used to be on earth,' Mrs Ludlow added.

'Mm,' I said, nodding, with the inane smile for which we vicars are famous.

We talked for a long while after, about big things and little things, about the funny ways of grief, about treating yourself tenderly in the months ahead. 'Now don't hesitate to contact me for absolutely any reason whatsoever between now and the funeral,' I said to Mrs Ludlow as I took hold of my bicycle, a shower of mortar once again cascading from the ill-kept wall.

'Don't worry, I will, Vicar, I will. I've

found your visit very comforting, very comforting indeed. That picture of my Tom being ravishing in heaven is just lovely. That'll keep me going.'

It kept me going too, even enabling me to chuckle as I cycled through a hailstorm on my way back to Kirkwith. The hard pedal home gave me a tremendous appetite, even for the congealed bacon I'd had to abandon because of my breakfast call-out. I had every sympathy for Tom; what it is to be ravishing!

Tuesday 24 May

I was tucking into a more meagre breakfast of Weetabix and toast the next day, when once again the phone interrupted my meal. The sense of *déjà vu* grew stronger by the second as I heard the caller say, 'David, it's Geoff here, Geoff Goodmanham. I wonder if you could come down, something terrible's happened.'

'Yes, Geoff,' I replied, hesitantly. I was feeling a bit like Patrick McGoohan in the TV series *The Prisoner*. Every morning he woke up and found himself back in the very situation he thought he'd escaped from the day before. I rubbed my eyes to check I wasn't dreaming. 'What's wrong?' I asked.

'It's Mrs Ludlow again. She's come over to school because she had nowhere else to go. Her home was broken into whilst she was asleep. She's not the only one, I'm afraid. Quite a few of the children have been coming in this morning with tales of their home being burgled last night. But it seems to have hit Mrs Ludlow the hardest of them all, what with her husband's death and everything.'

'Right, Geoff, tell her I'll be with her in twenty minutes. I'm so very, very sorry for her.'

As yet again I cycled towards Eastwith, I grieved for Mrs Ludlow and indeed all the others who had had their homes violated. It was such a trusting village. I must have visited nearly all the hundred homes in the place, and yet hardly ever had I found a front door or back door locked, even when the house was empty. It was such a marked contrast to my parish in East Hull, where everyone bolted their houses with the fastidiousness of warders locking up their evil charges at the nearby Hull Prison.

Ron, proprietor of the infamous Ron Ran Run bus service, was also my churchwarden at Eastwith, and had patiently explained things when I expressed my surprise at everyone having an open-door policy. 'Everybody knows everybody else, here, Vicar. In fact, most of us are related one way or another. We trust each other like members of a family. Besides, most of the door locks are broken or painted up, most of the keys to them are either lost or too bulky to carry in your jacket or handbag. As Mae West would say, "Is that an Eastwith doorkey you've got in your pocket, or are you just very pleased to see me?"' He halted and put his hand over his mouth, suddenly realizing his transport-café repartee was a wee bit out of context. 'Oh, I'm sorry, Vicar, I forgot I was talking to you. No offence, I hope.'

'No, Ron, none at all,' I had laughed. 'So nobody ever has any trouble with things being taken?'

'Well, we do have the occasional bout of petty pilfering. But generally we can find out who the culprit is and then the village sorts it out for itself. Usually a wayward teenager's backside gets a good tanning by his dad and, surprise, surprise, the pilfering stops straight off. And we'd rather have that state of affairs than wasting our time always locking and bolting doors. We all like to be

137

in and out of each other's houses, and would be surprised, nonplussed, no, dammit, we'd be offended if we suddenly found ourselves locked out.'

'They've paid a very high price for avoiding offence,' I thought, as I parked my bike for the second time in twenty-four hours against Mrs Ludlow's crumbling house. Once again I found myself sitting in her dark and dank kitchen drinking another mug of her strong and sweet tea, listening to her story. Or rather attempting to draw her story out of her, since she didn't do much else but cry.

'Was very much taken?' I asked.

'No, not really,' she replied, dabbing at her nose with a handkerchief as she fought to stem the tears.

'You probably feel your privacy has been invaded,' I said, after a long, painful silence. I was aware that I was fumbling for words, and when I did manage to say anything, it sounded so inadequate and contrived.

'No, not really,' she said again. 'It's always been an open house, people coming and going. You never have that much privacy in a small village, anyway.' Her sobs continued. What was causing her to be so upset? Was it the grief coming out, nothing really to do with the burglary?

'Yes, but I really feel for you with this coming so soon after Tom's death, I really do,' I stuttered, trying my best to comfort her. 'Did the burglar get as far as the front room?' I asked, wondering if she was upset because Tom's final resting place had been disturbed.

To my surprise, Mrs Ludlow stopped crying and started laughing. 'Ay, he did. And he got the shock of his life, apparently, seeing Tom lying there.'

'How do you know that?' I asked.

'T' policeman said that t' burglar was going through t' village sympathetically like...' I mentally transposed 'sympathetically' to 'systematically'. '...and that all the signs were that he'd made a hurried exit after entering our parlour. Mine was the last house to be burgled – it must have been seeing Tom that scared him off, and stopped him doing any more homes. Ee, my Tom would have laughed at that. Mind you, I suppose in death he saved t' rest of t' village, so there'll be a fair few who'll be grateful to him!'

And then she began crying again.

'What is it, Becky?' I gently asked, reaching out and taking her hand in mine.

She sniffed, and dabbed at her eyes once again. 'Oh, it's so silly, really, Vicar. I'm doing all this crying over nothing at all.'

'Don't worry, the tears do flow when someone you love dies. There doesn't have to be a reason.'

Again there was a poignant silence. 'It is to do with what was taken, I suppose,' she explained. 'It's funny, as I looked over the rooms to see what was missing, I didn't feel upset at all. The clock had gone, the brass one, the one that had been given to Tom after twenty-five years on t' farm,' she said, as if there was an array of clocks to choose from in their poor little home. 'Well, it never kept very good time from the first day, and I always know what time it is anyway from t' church clock strikin', so I won't miss that.

'And I know it sounds funny, Vicar, but I won't miss my engagement ring. It seemed to cost a small fortune at the time, Tom had to save and save and save for it on his meagre farmworker's wages, but he was always embarrassed by it. "It's too cheap for you, a thin band of gold, a tiny diamond, you deserve better, much better," he used to say. I treasure those words of his far more than any ring.'

We shared yet another silence, a silence

140

which was becoming more holy than awkward. Again there were tears. 'See how much he must have loved him' came to mind, the bystanders' comment as Jesus wept over his dead friend, Lazarus. 'See how much she must have loved him,' I thought.

'It was the rattle, Vicar, the little silver rattle. I can't bear that being gone,' she blurted out. 'He bought it me when I fell pregnant. I was only six weeks gone, barely started, but he was over the moon, so proud, so very proud. Off he went to York, on t' bus, all sheepish like. He came back with this little parcel, all clumsily wrapped up, and handed it to me. "This is for him; or her," he said, his eyes moist with tears. I'd never seen him like that before. You see, he wasn't demonstrable, as I think I said yesterday.'

'I never realized you had a child,' I said.

'Well, I didn't. When I was seven months gone I slipped on t' licheny step outside t' back door, and went a real wallop, twisted myself terribly, felt something crack.' She rubbed her side, vaguely indicating the area of injury. 'They took me to York in t' farm truck. Oh, Vicar, I felt every bump, every pothole, excruciating pain, stabbing at my insides. I prayed and I prayed and I prayed, "Let my baby live, let my baby live."'

Once more a silence, definitely holy this time. 'She died, of course. I'd broken my hip, my pelvis, mucked up my insides. She stood no chance. Perfect she was as well, a real beauty. They let me see her before they took her away. "God must want her to be his angel in heaven," the hospital chaplain had said. He meant well, I suppose. But I wanted her here, I wanted our baby here, here on earth, never mind God in heaven. Sorry, Vicar, I sound terrible, talking like that, I'm so sorry.'

'I'm the one who's sorry,' I said. 'Sorry for you and for all you went through. Was that, er, was that when all the arthritis set in?'

'Yes, the bones never healed probably, made worse by this damp house, I suppose. But it's a funny thing, you know. The pains of arthuritis are sharp, very sharp, and yet I don't curse them like a lot of sufferers do. It sounds really odd, Vicar, but I almost welcome them, they mark, they draw the sadness for the daughter I almost had, for all the other children we never had. After that accident on that wretched step – how I hate this house! – there was no chance of having another child.'

She often got the wrong words, and yet she had managed better than most to put

142

into words something very deep; they were words I felt privileged to hear. Her lack of children seemed particularly poignant when I saw, as I often did, the motherly way she dealt with Eastwith School's children even at the most stressful of times. Listening to her comments over just one mealtime charted the breadth of her concern. She was generous to a tee: 'Yes, of course you can have another carrot, dear.' Tolerant too: 'Don't worry, love, spilling a jug of gravy isn't the end of the world. You mop your friend down with this cloth, whilst I go and boil up some more.' And to top it all, she was so deeply sympathetic: 'Oh come on now, don't cry. Your first day at school will soon be over and then you'll be home to Mum. Go on, have a lick of the treacle spoon.' Without a doubt, she was the best mother the children never had.

By the time I left her, it was nearly midday. The village was all hustle and bustle. Bert the joiner was out and about, hurriedly fitting a lock here, a lock there, competing for trade with the locksmiths from Selby, Howden and Pocklington, whose vans clogged up Eastwith's narrow street. I walked my bicycle and chatted by each gate as people indignantly recounted their own losses and told me, in no uncertain terms, what they would like to do to the so-and-so burglar.

It was well after lunchtime when I cycled away from the village, having talked to every victim. Though their loss weighed heavily on me, the loss of innocence and trust weighed more heavily, as I witnessed people turning their houses into fortresses and open doors into barricades.

As I rode along, the scents and the scenes I took in acted as a gentle balm to soothe my sorrow. I was particularly cheered by the sun's rays dancing about, making the leaves, moist after bursting from their buds, glimmer like silver. One hedgerow shone so much that I stopped my bicycle to take a closer look. There in the middle, camouflaged by the silver leaves, was a tiny silver rattle, presumably discarded by the thief as worthless as he took fright and took flight.

Cradling it in my hands like the most precious treasure, I put the rattle carefully into my jacket pocket, turned my bicycle around and headed back to Eastwith, with a piece of good news to cheer Becky Ludlow's dark day.

Friday 27 May

Sleep eluded me as I reflected on the previous day, the day of Tom Ludlow's funeral, with a kaleidoscope of memories flashing before my tired eyes. The little red-brick church full to capacity, mourners spilling out into the churchyard, dividing with the greatest of dignity to let me through, to let Tom's coffin through, to let his widow through, staying divided as if to let the children-who-never-were through. Becky Ludlow weeping as she saw how many had turned out in honour of her man. Becky Ludlow singing lustily with the congregation, her Yorkshire twang lengthening some words, shortening others: '...'eaven's mooorning breaks and earth's vain shadows flee; in liiiife, in deaaaath, O Lord, abiiiide wi' me.' Becky Ludlow bearing up so well that she brought tears to my eyes, I who was supposed to be brave, I who was supposed not to break down, I who was supposed to carry the congregation in their grief. Becky Ludlow looking down into the double grave hewn into the rock and commenting spontaneously to me, 'Ee, that's deep, isn't it!' Simultaneously staring into her man's last resting place and her own future.

145

And lighter moments? The procession from the church to the cemetery, people walking six abreast along the road for a quarter of a mile forming a motley fashion show: burly farmers compressed into ill-fitting formal dress, like Sumos in suits, women with shapeless black hats and thick black coats like rugs wrapped around them, making them sweat, beads of perspiration trickling down their foreheads on this balmy spring day. A red Post Office van careering around the corner and braking fiercely as its driver saw the human wall ahead of him, grinding his gears and having to back up, our advance unstoppable. The driver revving the van's engine to prevent the further indignity of stalling before such an audience, creating a pall of blue smoke which wafted over Tom's coffin like incense.

The grave was squeezed in by the lattice fence which bordered the new and select housing estate. A plot next to a graveyard is hardly the most choice of sites for superior dwellings; the fence was deliberately high so the inhabitants could pretend the cemetery wasn't on their skyline. As the mourners and I tramped silently through the grave-yard and gathered by the grave, I suddenly realized that something was going on at the other side of the fence, only about a yard away from me. It was too high actually to see anything, but I could hear a dog yapping and scratching as if to burrow under the lattice-work. The terrier was obviously all too well aware of us, the mute crowd who had dared to threaten its boundary, and was tunnelling to see us off.

His mistress, on the other hand, was clearly oblivious to our existence, in that she began to cajole the dog. 'Come here, Susie, there's a good girl,' she called, initially with considerable restraint. But the dog's scratching and excited yapping continued, so she threw restraint to the winds as she vented her feelings more volubly, clearly still unaware of the considerable audience on our side of the barrier: 'Will you leave off that fence, you bloody stupid bitch!'

The coffin was duly lowered into the grave. Bert the joiner gestured silently to the pallbearers, a rope was taken hold of here, a resting block was removed there, the whole business conducted as if on tiptoe. Gentleness was the order of the day, from the soft sound of the ropes slithering through the handles to the merest of thuds as the coffin touched base. All was done quietly, matching the reverent hush of the sizeable crowd of mourners: 'Sh! We've got this far, we've nearly got him home. Don't let us wake the dead now.'

A stillness in stark contrast to the sheer cacophony at the other side of the fence. As a feeble attempt to voice-over the language that was getting bluer by the second, I launched into the familiar words of the burial service, 'Man that is born of a woman, hath but a short time to live, and is full of misery. He cometh up, and is cut down, like a flower...'

'You little sod! You've dug up all my tulip bulbs!'

I boldly continued, '...he fleeth as it were a shadow, and never continueth in one stay.'

'For the last time, will you come away from that flower bed?!'

'In the midst of life we are in death'

'What was that you said, love?' my unseen neighbour shouted over the fence, suddenly aware that she was not alone.

I soldiered on. 'Yet, O Lord God most holy, O Lord most mighty, O holy and most merciful Saviour, deliver us not into the bitter pains of eternal death.'

'Bloody hell!' she shrieked as the penny finally dropped. I heard a scuffle as she swept the dog up and carried it away. A door slammed, and only then did the loud yapping subside.

With the dignity of the occasion restored, I concluded the burial service, '...earth to earth, ashes to ashes, dust to dust.' Each mourner followed Becky Ludlow's lead and threw a handful of dirt on to the coffin. Then everyone hung around by the graveside, uncertain of what to do next, not wanting to be the first to leave, no one knowing what to say, hesitant over how to make the transition from death to small talk. The impasse was broken by Mrs Ludlow. 'Well, we'd better get on to t' receptacle. Ivy will be waiting for us.'

The mourners processed in dribs and drabs back to the heart of the village and to Becky Ludlow's 'receptacle', the funeral tea in the school hall. I usually avoided wakes. People invariably said to me, 'Lovely service, Vicar,' or 'Lovely sermon, Vicar,' which tended to be a conversation stopper rather than a conversation starter. I also felt like the spectre at the feast, too proper for the party, a stark reminder of death and tragedy when people wanted to loosen up, laugh a little, let their hair down. But today I made the exception. As we all hovered in the cemetery, Mrs Ludlow took my arm:

'You're coming to the hall, aren't you, Vicar? You being there will be such a constipation.' I hope she meant 'consolation'; and with an invite like that, how could I refuse?

As soon as the school day had come to its end, Ivy Weighton had rushed in and had hurriedly laid out tables and put out plates, each containing standard fare: a slice of ham, tired and curling at the edges, a wizened pickled onion, a parched tomato, two slices of white bread smeared with butter, whose switchback crusts competed with the ham for undulation, all topped off with a piece of cake which I suspected was the spawn of Grandma Weighton's infamous walnut and tallow variety.

'You've done very well to have managed all this in so short a time,' I overheard Geoff Goodmanham compliment Ivy.

'Yes, it was a bit of a rush. Fred was using t' Land Rover right up to three o' clock, spreading muck on t' fields. As soon as he came home for his mid-afternoon snack, I took my chance, rushed out into yard and started loading stuff into t' wagon. I'd plated everything up already, so I just spread t' plates around on t' floor. T' plate backs got a bit o' dirt on them, what with floor being mucky after t' spreadin', but I soon wiped them clean. I brought t' tea-towel along, you see.'

'Oh, very good, Ivy,' Geoff said, putting his empty plate down and surreptitiously wiping his hands on his Harris tweed.

'Are you not eating anything, Vicar?' said Ivy, thrusting a plate at me.

'Oh, I'm very tempted,' I replied, lying through my teeth. 'But to be honest, funerals make me a bit nervous and I find I can't eat anything for a couple of hours afterwards.'

'Now don't you worry, Vicar,' she said, patting my arm consolingly. 'I'll put a plate aside for you and take it back in t' Land Rover. You can have it for your supper when you come round later to see Rebecca!'

And so I did. She'd saved a plate for Rebecca too, so we both gingerly picked our way through ham now twice as curled up as it had been at the wake, seasoned with a pickled onion that, even in the kindly evening light, looked more like a pickled raisin. Rebecca's brothers and father had ambled off on their nightly pilgrimage to the Stack at Beckwith, leaving their customary places at the table free for us to occupy, which was just as well, since there were no other seats available. Grandma sat on her customary stool by the fire stirring a stewpot which, like God, went on for ever and ever, world without end, Amen. The two sheepdogs were in their customary place, sprawled out on the sofa, snarling and growling in their sleep and defying anyone to disturb them. The customary pile of *Farmer's Weekly* perched precariously on the only stool. They looked even more precarious as Mrs Weighton flicked them with a duster, making a show of doing a bit of housework. On screwing my eyes up to peer at the duster more closely, I realized it was none other than the multi-purpose tea-towel.

Rebecca was marking as she ate. Or more accurately, she was marking as she tried to avoid eating, feeding the less choice items on her plate to the sheepdog pup waiting eagerly beneath the table. Each morsel she gave him caused him not so much to wag his tail as his whole rear end, which thumped rhythmically against the table leg. I was delighted that my future mother-in-law's fare had at last found an appreciative audience of one, and started feeding him the curlier bits of ham from my plate. At this his ecstasy doubled into seismic proportions, shaking the whole table, making me fear that the disturbance would catch Ivy's eagle eye.

Which it did, although she came to the wrong conclusion. 'Now you two, stop playing footsie and get on with your meal,' she chided, good-humouredly. And then all of a sudden her mood changed, a change as dramatic as when a dark cloud blots out the sun and brings a chill to the warmest summer day. Her smile was replaced with a frown as she fixed the two of us with the weirdest sort of stare, a stare which looked beyond us, far beyond us, rather than at us. Even though it was the kind of momentous look that time seems to stands still for, it was a look I couldn't quite place. Not one of horror, although there were aspects of horror there. Not one of grief, although there were elements of grief there. Not one of yearning, although there were features of yearning there. And then the frozen moment passed as time kicked in. Her lip started quivering, she burst into tears and ran out of the room, thumping up the stairs. Rebecca leapt up, knocking her chair backwards and startling the puppy, who shot over to the sofa yelping, seeking the protection of his sleeping mother. As Rebecca ran up the stairs, I made as if to follow, but she turned me back. 'If you don't mind, David, I'll see to her. She often has these dos these days.'

I returned to the table, so dazed that I absentmindedly consumed the parched tomato which I had spent all the evening trying to avoid. Grandma seemed unaffected by the drama, staying seated by the fire, stirring her stew with one hand, holding a candle in the other. 'You didn't get to the funeral, then?' I asked.

'Neh,' was her monosyllabic reply.

'But you did know Tom Ludlow?'

'Yeh,' she grunted, giving the stew a vigorous stir, scraping the charcoal from the bottom of the pot.

'I always enjoyed my conversations with him,' I added, realizing that I was prattling on like an idiot.

'Yeh,' Grandma said, refusing to enjoy any conversation whatsoever with me. My prattling dried up and I watched agape as hot wax ran off her candle and straight into the stew. 'A bit o' fat gives t' stew a bit o' body,' Grandma cackled, suddenly moved to eloquence.

There was really no response I could make to such a homely dictum, so I buried my head in the books Rebecca had been marking. The children had written an essay in German on any subject of their choosing, their narrow repertoire of experience impoverished further by a limited German vocabulary. *'Mein Haus'* seemed a popular theme, containing startling information on the number of rooms, doors and windows, colour of paint, presence of roof *etc*. *'Meine Stadt'* came next in order of popularity, with flat descriptions that made even an enchanted place like York sound graceless. The most promising by far was an abstract piece on joy. 'Praise to Joy, the god-descended daughter of Elysium!' the essay began with a flourish, which certainly had the edge on 'I live in a street', or 'My house has a roof and a ground floor'. 'Ray of mirth and rapture blended, goddess to thy shrine we come. By thy magic is united...' I suddenly twigged: the girl had cribbed the whole piece from the blurb on the record sleeve for Beethoven's Choral Symphony, which sets *Ode to Joy* to music.

I never had the chance to ask Rebecca whether she would mark the girl down for plagiarism or mark her up for presenting an oasis in an otherwise cultural desert of *mein Hauses* and *meine Stadts*. For at that moment Rebecca came back downstairs looking terribly drawn, her face pale, her eyes red with crying. 'Mum'll be OK now. I've persuaded her to try to get some sleep—'

'But what was the matter with her?' I asked.

'Well, it's Hans really. You've talked to her, I've talked to her. You know what people are like when grief hits them. She's simply missing him,' she explained.

'But it seems to run so very deep,' I said. 'She looked as if she'd seen a ghost just now.'

'Well, yes, yes, you're right, there's more to it than a normal bereavement,' she admitted. 'Instead of seeing the two of us at the table, she saw her and Hans twenty years back. As I said, there's more to it than a normal bereavement.'

'If you can call any bereavement normal,' I added gently, trying to encourage her to talk about her feelings, her mother's feelings.

But I was thwarted because at that moment the kitchen door crashed open as Rebecca's father and two brothers returned from their jaunt to the pub. 'Ee, put t' kettle on, our Rebecca. I could do with a cup o' tea,' Mr Weighton ordered. 'Walk from t' Stack is a long and thirsty one.'

'Ay, and make us a coffee while you're at it,' her brother chipped in. 'And don't be at it in t' kitchen, otherwise we'll be waiting till midnight,' he added, raucously, gales of beery breath filling the room.

Rebecca blushed, but wasn't cowed. 'I'd have thought you three would have had enough to drink at the Stack,' she retaliated.

'Now don't start being school ma'amish with us, just get us a hot drink. You know we'll never get to sleep if we don't have a hot drink.' The banter was good-natured up to a point, but there was an edge to it. I remembered what Rebecca had said about being bullied by her brothers, and how Hans had given her tips to cope.

'If you want a drink, you can get it for yourselves, I'm not your slave,' she shouted. And then, turning to me, she added, 'If you don't mind, David, I think I'll have an early night. I'll take the books up with me and see if I can mark a few before I nod off, but I really do feel all in.'

'Why, what have you been up to, Sis?' her brother jeered.

'Just shut up!' Rebecca shouted furiously, in the sort of teacherly voice which would have put the fear of God into God. Her brothers and father shuffled into the kitchen to get their own drinks, like sheepdogs who had felt the rough side of their master's, or rather their mistress's, tongue. Immensely proud of her, I gave her a hug.

'They're not bad, really. It's just the drink gets to their head a bit, and then they start throwing their weight around. Or at least trying to.' She still looked pale, and couldn't stop herself yawning. 'I know it seems dreadfully inhospitable, but I really do think I'll turn in.'

'Don't worry, I understand,' I said. 'G.K. Chesterton described sleep as the eighth sacrament, so let's hope it delivers the calm and restoration you and your mum deserve.' And before I became any more preachy, I kissed her on the forehead and left.

As I cycled away from the farm, Rebecca stood in the doorway, silhouetted against the candlelight, giving me a sleepy wave. Her brother's continued banter emanated from the house behind her, echoing through the night air. 'Has he gone? Tut, just when I've made him a cup of coffee. I hope he didn't take offence at me ribbing the pair of you. These clergy can be a bit touchy.'

'Oh, for goodness sake, why don't you drink your coffee and sober up?' I heard Rebecca answer, her voice fading the further I cycled from the farm. 'You three are absolutely pathetic, make me really ashamed ... what will David think of us?'

'Where's your mother? She'd have made me a cup of tea, wouldn't have got on her 'igh 'orse like you,' Mr Weighton bellowed.

'She's gone to bed, Dad, she got a bit upset.'

'She's always getting upset these days, why...' I strained my cars to hear the remainder of the comment, but by this time I was too far away and the door had been shut. Metaphorically as well as literally, I felt shut out from a family clearly not at ease with itself. Not the first family I had come across which was dysfunctional, admittedly. But disturbing when that family was to become your family before the summer was out.

A long day with a lot of memories, a lot of concerns to keep me awake. How was Becky Ludlow faring, alone in her widow's bed in that dank and damp house which had made her barren? How were the Weightons faring in their candlelit farm, with so many shadows looming that night? Although, as I recalled my supper with ham twice as curled up as it had been at the wake, I guessed it wasn't just memories and concerns that were making sleep elusive.

I eventually drifted off, with Beethoven's *Ode to Joy* being sung by a bloated Becky Ludlow, shrouded in black. 'Praise to joy, the god-desiccated daughter of an Electrician. Roy of mirth and rupture blinded, goddess to thy shrub we come...' She disappeared in a mist as God's eighth sacrament came and soothed my troubled mind.

JUNE 1966

Wednesday 1 June

I was sitting in my study, facing an immaculately dressed Herbert Molescroft. He was sporting his usual black jacket, black trousers, black jumper beneath which lurked a white sweater, clerical to a tee, or clerical to a 'do have another cup of tea, Vicar!' I felt underdressed in my distinctly unclerical jeans and T-shirt.

We were having a session trying to make some sense out of the ministry situations he had encountered with me. I started the ball rolling by asking Herbert to pull no punches and identify those places where he felt I hadn't delivered the goods.

'Well, your visit to the school, for a start,' Herbert said, sliding into the critic's role just a mite too easily. 'The children seemed woefully ignorant about Christianity, and you didn't help, dribbling on about this and about that, gabbling on about the registers, about what a vicar does, making no particular point. And then that farce where you sprayed all that ink around. What do you think you achieved by that? I just can't see why you waste your time going there.'

'Mm,' I replied, reeling from Herbert's all-out assault. 'I don't mind looking foolish in front of them; I guess it does them good to see that adults, especially adults in positions of authority, aren't infallible. I'm not sure how much information I can actually load them with at their age, other than planting seeds of faith which grow later. I just like being with them, I suppose. I've always had a soft spot for children, enjoying their sense of fun, but also tender to the worries that loom so large for them.'

'Pah! They need more than your wishy-washy approach at their time of life. Discipline, that's what they deserve, and some strong Christian teaching, the Ten Commandments and the Catechism and learning Bible verses off by heart. That'll set them up!' pronounced Herbert, in full flood.

'I'm not sure what precisely that will set them up for. I agree that we've got to do all we can to help them prepare for adulthood. I look at those children and see the tragedies lurking in the wings, tragedies that none of them will be immune to. I want to advertise that when those tragedies inevitably come, then I'm a friend they can easily approach. More than that, I want them to see that the faith I hold dear is a key to coping. And not just a key to coping but more than that, a key to flourishing, in spite of all that life throws at you.'

'Well, I still think you've got to be more structured in your approach,' Herbert lectured, as if he were already a bishop rather than a budding priest. 'You allowed the children's comments to set your agenda.'

'That's probably because I wanted to address where the children were rather than where they weren't,' I retaliated, although my irony was lost on him.

'Yes, I'm sure,' he said, looking down his nose. 'Even so, I would very much like to have a crack at talking to the children myself.' He didn't add 'to show you how it's done', although the implication was there, sure enough.

'Fine,' I said. 'I'll give Geoff Goodmanham a ring when we've finished this session and we can set a date. Any other areas you feel you'd like to talk about?'

The knives were clearly out, because

Herbert immediately latched on to another criticism. 'I didn't think much of that sermon you preached at Tom Ludlow's burial.' Herbert had discreetly observed the whole funeral. Though perhaps discreet wasn't quite the right word, in that his immaculately well-tailored garb made him stand out like a sore thumb compared to the other men there, most of whom were squeezed into wedding suits which had been worn when their waists and chests were six inches narrower.

'Oh, quite a lot of people at the reception told me how much they liked it,' I replied, not adding that people always said that at a wake, whatever you'd preached. 'What was it that worried you?'

'He never went near church, did he?' Herbert asked, seeking clarification before he launched his broadside.

'Not really, no.'

'Well, in your sermon you talked as if God would be absolutely thrilled to see him. You made no mention of judgement or punishment or the hell that unbelievers like Tom Ludlow are bound for. You had a great evangelistic opportunity, you could have really spelt out the Gospel, laid it on the line, called people to repentance before it was too late. But you blew it.' As Herbert delivered this tirade, he repeatedly thumped his fist down on my desk as he made each point, working himself up into a religious frenzy.

I said nothing, simply giving him the space to calm himself down. After a couple of minutes, I opened a prayer book and showed Herbert one of my favourite prayers, simple, short, but lovely: 'Father, we commit to thy merciful care those who have confessed the faith, and those whose faith is hidden, known to thee alone.'

'I reckon Tom firmly belonged to the latter category,' I explained, after a further period of silence. 'What I was trying to do in my sermon was draw people's attention to that hidden faith and how it had been expressed in a distinct life, mentioning his major tragedies and major joys, moments and events which had moved him. I'm not in a position to judge people, declare who's gone to heaven and who's gone to hell, that's for God to decide. But at a time when grief is so very sharp, I want to proclaim a God who is utterly loving and utterly merciful. A God who weeps with those who mourn rather than a God who compounds their misery.'

By now Herbert had a distinctly shriven,

thoroughly-ashamed-of-himself look, so I decided to temper my message with a post-script. 'And speaking of mercy, you know, you come across as a very merciful man.'

'How do you make that out?' he asked.

'Well, for instance I found it very moving that you had the nerve to drink tea out of that rusty baked bean can at that poor couple's home in Eastwith. I was all for pouring the contents of my cup, or rather can, over the pile of dirty nappies in the corner! And your offer of furniture was so very kind. You saw a genuine need and offered genuine help.'

'But that visit was a total fiasco,' Herbert protested. 'I was all set to give them the talk I had prepared on Church doctrine and belief about baptism through the ages, but I felt so queer when I fell over like that, that I never got around to it.

'I felt such a fool, writhing about in all that filth, messing up my clothes, a poor ambassador for the Church. I was reading the Archdeacon's book, *Good Practice for the Pastoral Parson*, which gives some useful advice about visiting. "A well-dressed priest advertises a well-ordered Church; a shabby priest only advertises a shabby Church." Getting my clothes into such a mess really let the side down.'

'I don't know,' I countered. 'When I ride around on my old rusty bike, cycle clips round my ankles, my turn-ups smeared with oil, I feel akin to Jesus who rode into Jerusalem on a tatty old donkey. Posh priests only advertise a posh God, a God too posh for the likes of us.'

'Oh no, I don't agree at all,' Herbert replied, all huffy. 'The Church has got such a ramshackle reputation; we ought to make her look slick and professional. You really ought to think about getting a car, you know. You look so unprofessional wobbling up to people's homes on your bike like that. It's beneath a priest's dignity.'

'OK, Herbert, you didn't preach your little sermon in that home, but you proclaimed something far more important,' I said, ignoring his slur about my beloved cycling. 'By what you did rather than what you said, you preached acceptance and concern. And yes, your pratfall made you feel stupid, who wouldn't feel stupid falling over like that? But it made the girl see you in need and respond to you, so the ministry that night was two-way rather than one-way. She was able to minister to you, the minister, albeit with a rusty baked bean tin,' I grinned.

167

'But don't you see what a failure it all was? I never said a word about Christ to them,' he said, with genuine regret.

'No you didn't, but something touched them. They've been coming to Eastwith Church ever since, sitting huddled at the back, the baby crying during my sermon, putting up with the hostile stares of the congregation, cross at having their slumbers disturbed. In my book they deserve a medal for coming at all. You have to ask yourself, what did they see in you that night that drove them to come?'

'Hm,' Herbert said, looking thoughtful. 'I still feel the visit was an absolute botch-up. But let's leave that. Has there been any other time where you felt I came across well?' Herbert rubbed his finger around the inside of his white collar, anxious for me to name an 'Oh Mr Molescroft, you really ought to be ordained' situation where he came across as a real vicar.

'Mm,' I said. 'There was another occasion.' Herbert sat up straight, primed, alert for a compliment. 'But I think it's more about promise at this stage.'

Herbert's shoulders drooped with a disappointed air. 'What was this other occasion, then?' he asked, barely able to disguise the fact that his interest was waning.

'It was at the old people's home,' I answered.

'The old people's home, the old people's home? But that was another utter fiasco!' he spluttered.

'Well, it's always a fiasco there, and I always come away feeling useless. But I sense that the danger points in my ministry are not so much when I'm feeling useless, but when I feel what a jolly good fellow I am, and how well its all gone, and what a lucky chap God is to have me on his side, and how I deserve grand recognition for being so fantastic. At times such as that I fear people see too much of clever old me, and not enough of God. St Paul said, "When I am weak, then I am strong." I guess what he meant was, "When I am weak, then God is strong."'

'I think it's blasphemy, messing about with Scripture like that. It's not for us to rewrite St Paul,' Herbert said, rather priggishly.

'No, and it's not for us to rewrite God,' I added mischievously.

'What do you mean?' Herbert asked.

'Well, we can make God out to be so perfect, so aloof, so above it all that he strikes ordinary folk as having little to do with them. When you were falling over yourself in that old people's home, you really had a lot in common with those poor old folk who are always falling over. We could have conducted a perfect service, preached eloquently, but actually missed their condition by a light year. In a sense when you stooped to reach them, you were just like God.'

'Now you are talking blasphemy,' Herbert sneered.

'No, I'm not.' I insisted. 'I'm talking orthodoxy. Both the Bethlehem stable and the cross of Calvary are signs of just how low God is prepared to stoop to reach us. A good priest in my book is someone who, on God's behalf, has absolutely no pride.'

There was yet another period of silence, with Herbert frowning as he took it all in. 'Speaking of having no pride, I wondered if you would like to come with me tomorrow on my home Communion rounds?' I asked, mischievously.

'What do you mean, no pride? Surely you must be proud and privileged to take the sacrament to people in the twilight of their lives?'

'Well yes, that's the theory. But just remember what it was like in practice at the old people's home. I feel that going around a few of my sick communicants will help both of us. Your theory can inspire my practice with a bit of vision, and at the same time my practice can root your theory in a bit of reality. What about it?'

'That's fine with me, that's just what the bishop sent me here for,' Herbert replied, in the sort of voice which implied that I needed the vision much more than he needed the reality.

Thursday 2 June

Our first port of call was normal enough: a retired farm-worker and his wife who shuffled about their little home on sticks, both crippled with rheumatism. The man's build was lean with a wiry, taut frame. I guess once that frame had been taut with energy; now it was taut with pain. In contrast to her husband, the woman was plump and bell-shaped, her weight making her arthritic legs balloon out obscenely. *'And we most humbly beseech thee of thy goodness O Lord to comfort and succour all them, who in this transitory life are in trouble, sorrow, need, sickness or any other adversity...'*

I introduced Herbert to them; he immediately enthroned his immaculately dressed self on their tiny settee, and bestowed a regal and pious look over everyone. *'We beseech thee also to save and defend all Christian kings, princes and governors...'*

So much for my lecture about a priest having no pride! Herbert read the Gospel for us with an imperious air. *'Give grace, O heavenly Father, to all bishops and curates, that they may both by their life and doctrine set forth thy true and lively word...'*

As I read the Prayer Book service, I glanced around the room. Brass candlesticks, brass vases, a brass clock, a brass harness, brass knick-knacks, all polished to perfection, their finish a mirror. The mantelpiece was cluttered with photos of children and grandchildren and great-grandchildren, frowning children, anxious children, smiling children. A son with hair plastered down by brilliantine, with collar bleached white and tie knot smart, with eyes full of terror: clearly the first day at school. The same son, now with hair more unkempt, collar loose, scowling at the camera with the eyes of an adolescent: the first day at work. And then him again, hair cropped and barely visible beneath his soldier's beret, eyes full of terror once more: the last photograph before he was killed in action.

'And we also bless thy holy name for all thy servants departed this life in thy faith and fear...'

My gaze moved from the mantelpiece to a flimsy table in the corner, on which was perched a tiny television set. Beneath the set lay the latest copy of the *TV Times*, with a glossy picture of Elsie Tanner from *Coronation Street* leering at us on the cover. *'Ye that do truly and earnestly repent you of your sins...'*

The man and his wife raised their hands to receive their Communion, hands gnarled with arthritis and shaking with age, hands that had tilled the soil and washed the nappies day after day after day. *'And to all thy people give thy heavenly grace, and especially to this congregation here present...'*

'You must be very important, going round checking up on our vicar,' the man said to the enthroned Herbert when the service had come to its end. Herbert let the comment pass, and flushed with pride. 'Oh by the way, Vicar, we don't want it next month. Me and the missus will be going to t' Yorkshire Show. Our son's fetching us – it's always a grand day out at Harrogate.'

173

'So what did you make of that?' I asked Herbert as we drove away from their home.

'I think you should have told them that if they were fit enough to go to the Yorkshire Show, then they were fit enough to come to church,' Herbert pronounced, his brow furrowing with concentration as he steered around a stray cow which had wandered on to the road. 'You should only take the sacrament to those who are truly housebound, not those who want you to go just for their convenience.'

'I think I go to that couple for my convenience, not theirs,' I replied, deliberately goading Herbert.

'What on earth do you mean?' he said, rising to the bait.

'Going there and being surrounded by their things and memories and trappings of a full life actually brings the sacrament alive for me. You feel that God's reality is touching their reality, a very rich and full reality. Communion in church can feel so false, so superficial, there's so little real contact – so many are playing just pretend games.'

'Hm,' said Herbert, making it quite clear what he thought of that. I was saved from further comment as he swerved to avoid another cow that was frolicking around on the road. This time the cow was being chased by a very red-faced Herbert Wykeham, Beckwith's churchwarden, the very same churchwarden who had braved the mother and baby clinic with me. Herbert Molescroft stopped the car and wound down the window to have a word. 'What's the matter with her? Obviously she doesn't fancy being milked this morning!' he joked, speaking as one expert on farming to another.

Herbert Wykeham gave him a look full of disdain, puffing loudly as he struggled to get his breath back. 'Ay, well, she wouldn't fancy being milked, seein' SHE'S a bullock!' His gaze shifted from Herbert to me. 'Oh good mornin', Vicar. Sorry, I didn't realize it was you. I didn't expect to see you in a car. You couldn't spare a couple of minutes and help me to catch this bug, er, this bullock, could you? Some clot left gate to t' yonder field open and him and his friend have made a run for it.'

'No problem, Herbert,' I replied, opening the passenger door and leaping out. 'I fancy a bit of exercise. Are you coming too, Herbert?'

'Well, course I'm coming. It's my bullock

after all. I wouldn't expect you to catch 'im on your own,' Herbert Wykeham replied, with a puzzled look.

'Oh, I'm sorry,' I said, suddenly realizing that I was faced by a confusion of Herberts. 'Let me introduce you. Herbert, this is Herbert Molescroft who's on placement with me. Herbert, this is Herbert Wykeham, churchwarden of Beckwith and cow-catcher par excellence.'

Herbert Wykeham wiped his right hand on his corduroy trousers and shook hands with his namesake, who had reluctantly inched his hand out of the wound-down window, like royalty deigning to touch a peasant. 'Ee, glad to meet you,' Herbert Wykeham said cheerily. 'It's 'Erbert by the way. I don't like to put on airs and graces. But I'm always delighted when I come across another 'Erbert.'

'Oh, I'm definitely a *H*erbert,' Herbert Molescroft replied, frostily. 'If you don't mind, David,' he added, as he turned to face me, 'I'll stay here while you round up the cattle. I've got some rather fine shoes on and I don't want to get them soiled.'

'Fair enough,' I said. 'Come on, Herbert, or rather 'Erbert. Let's catch him before he gets to Howden!' We soon cornered the beast by a nearby gate and shooed him back to his field, picking up the other wandering bullock en route.

'Ee, that chap you've got with you is a snooty bug, er, snooty so-and-so, in't he?' commented 'Erbert, who almost managed to watch his language in my presence. I was trying to wipe the soles of my shoes on the grass verge, having inadvertently run through a couple of cow-claps during the chase. 'What's he on placement for?'

'Oh, he's wondering about being a vicar,' I replied.

'Ff, ff, flippin' 'eck!' 'Erbert exclaimed. 'He'll 'ave to come off his 'igh 'orse. He talks to you as if he's the bl, bl, blumin' Archdeacon!'

'Yes, well, perhaps he should be shadowing the Archdeacon rather than me. There's an idea! Anyway, good to have got those bullocks back into the right field, 'Erbert. I'd better get on. We've got a few home Communions to get through.'

'Ay, well, thanks ever so much, Vicar. If you ever want a job as a farm 'and, just give me a call! But don't bother bringing your snooty friend!'

I walked back to the car where Herbert was drumming his fingers on the steering wheel impatiently. 'Honestly, this is just what I meant yesterday when I said clergy should be more professional,' he complained, crashing the gears as we moved off. 'Just look at your shoes, look at your clothes, look at your hair. You look as if you've been dragged through a hedge backwards.'

'Well, not quite. It's just that one of the bullocks tried to crush me against a hawthorn tree when we were penning him in. I'll brush myself down before our next port of call, don't you fret. Anyway, people round here like to see their vicar looking a bit fresh, rather than turned out like some official from the dreaded Min. of Ag.'

Herbert treated me to yet another of his contemptuous silences as we pulled up beside a little cottage on the outskirts of Beckwith. Mrs Shipton, my communicant, answered the door with an overall draped over her, her hair wet and in rollers. 'Oh, hello, Vicar,' she said nonchalantly. 'Ee, do you know, I totally forgot you were coming today. I've got the hairdresser here at the moment. Would you mind giving it me under the dryer?'

'Well, would you prefer it if we came back later?' I asked. Herbert tutted and looked at his watch.

'No, I'm afraid me sister and her husband are coming over and taking me out for lunch. That's why I'm having me hair done,' she said. 'T' hairdresser won't mind you giving it to me now. He's a good Catholic lad, he's always going on about saints and things. His dad's Italian, you know,' she concluded, dropping her voice to a whisper.

'Erm, er...' I dithered for a moment. 'Well, if you're sure, and you'd really like your Communion now, then I wouldn't want to disappoint you.'

'I might as well. What with having me hair done and having Communion, I'll be right set up for a grand time with me sister,' she breezed, cheerily showing us into a front room which had been transformed into a hairdressing salon.

I followed her in, not entirely happy, with Herbert following me, not happy at all.

The hairdresser was a swarthy-featured young man, of a slight build, with a feminine grace to his movements as he glided around the room. Like Herbert, he was dressed entirely in black, but with a tailored black shirt which was open-necked and black trousers that were skin-tight. Like Herbert he had an aloof air, and regarded the both of us sniffily, making us feel as if we were mongrels who had just walked into Crufts. I got the distinct feeling that this 'good Catholic lad' didn't rate Protestant ministers that highly.

'Right,' I said, deciding that things needed taking in hand pretty quickly to show that it was me and not the hairdresser who was in charge. 'I think we'll begin the service, if you don't mind.' I handed Mrs Shipton a prayer book, found her place for her and prepared to start. The hairdresser responded by turning on the drier, which filled the room with a loud whine, droning like a small jet.

'Lift up your hearts!' I bellowed at Mrs Shipton. She responded with a blank look. The hairdresser ignored us both, standing behind the drier, alternating examining his fingernails with fussing over the wisps of Mrs Shipton's hair which peeped out from beneath the drier. Herbert was enthroned on the sofa again, and had that air about him which positively shouted, 'I may be sitting here, but I've nothing to do with all this whatsoever.

'Lift up your hearts!' I shouted again, at the very top of my voice.

'Oo no, I don't think we'll be eating tarts.

Me sister's husband is going to take us out to Terry's in York. It's very posh there. They serve tarts in cafés, not in restaurants like that.'

'No, not tarts, hearts!' I shouted.

'Well, I'm quite partial to a bit of ox heart – it can be very tender. But again, Vicar, they're not going to serve that there. Ox heart won't be high-class enough.'

'Oh, never mind,' I said. 'Lift up your hearts,' I repeated, more softly this time.

'We lift them up unto the Lord,' I said, replying to myself in a rather novel form of ecclesiastical double-speak.

'Let us give thanks unto the Lord our God,' I continued.

'It is meet and right so to do,' I informed myself. Herbert fixed me with a deeply pitying look as I hurtled on through the rest of the service. I pressed the consecrated bread into Mrs Shipton's hot hands which reeked of perm solution, gabbled through the Lord's Prayer and gave a hurried blessing. I whipped my robes off in record time and bellowed farewell at Mrs Shipton. 'And have a good lunch!' I shouted.

'Yes, and you enjoy your tarts and hearts,' she shouted back. The hairdresser dismissed us with a disdainful sneer as he began to take Mrs Shipton's curlers out with the victorious relish of one who has seen off his opponents good and proper.

'I think we can safely conclude that Communion and having your hair done are incompatible, and leave it at that,' I said, as we drove to our next appointment, just two hundred yards down the road. I was fairly confident that this would be a holy contrast to the fiasco we had just endured. Miss Felixkirk, a retired civil servant, had decked out her kitchen as if it were a sanctuary. A large picture of Holman Hunt's *Light of the World* hung over the fireplace, and on the mantelpiece there were two candles burning, with a crucifix in between them. In the centre of the room Miss Felixkirk had covered her small kitchen table with a delicate starched white cloth trimmed with lace, on which I laid out the chalice and paten and placed my prayer book. It was a setting which Herbert Molescroft fitted into perfectly; Miss Felixkirk purred with obvious delight as he intoned the Gospel reading, oblivious to the severe attack of church-voice-itis which Herbert seemed to be suffering from: 'And it came to parss, that ars he wars cam nigh untooo Jerichow,' he intoned. I found it so excruciating that my toes curled up involuntarily and I literally rocked on my heels. Miss Felixkirk sighed and smiled at me sweetly, clearly assuming that I was swaying with ecstasy at hearing the song of an angel.

My experience of home Communions is that wherever you go, there will always be a hitch. It came at the point of the administration, the most sacred part of the service, as I placed the bread in Miss Felixkirk's eagerly held out hands and said,

'The body of our Lord Jesus Christ which was given for thee...' But at that moment I was interrupted by a loud knock on the back door, and the Rington's Tea man breezed in, his wicker basket on his arm, totally uncowed by my presence. At the very least, I would have expected him to have reeled from the shock of finding a surpliced figure standing in the middle of his customer's kitchen, especially when accompanied by a man dressed like Adam Adamant sitting at the table. But not a bit of it. Treating me and Herbert as if we were invisible, he addressed Miss Felixkirk, 'Just 'alf a pound o' loose tea this week, love?'

Amazingly the good Miss Felixkirk was as unfazed as he was. 'Yes, that will be fine. Just let me get my purse.' She sprang up with an agility which belied her infirmity, and would have put many healthy church-goers to shame, rushed out of the kitchen and returned after a few seconds with the 1s9d which she counted into the tea man's hand.

He left with a cheery 'See you next week then!' I waited a moment to regain my composure before continuing, '...preserve thy body and soul into everlasting life. Amen.' It was a totally surreal experience, almost as if I'd switched TV channels from *The Epilogue* to *Till Death Us Do Part* and back again. I suddenly found myself yearning for the false and superficial setting of a church building which I had so pompously lectured Herbert about. False and superficial a church may be, but at least there you are safe from tea men and hairdressers interrupting you.

Friday 3 June

And nurses bullying you. It was the next day, and Herbert was proving a glutton for punishment by shadowing me for a second set of home Communions. 'She's just in the bath at the moment,' a district nurse informed us in stentorian tones as we knocked on our first communicant's back door. 'You can give it her in there if you want!'

'No, it's all right, tell her I'll come along at the same time next month,' I stammered, beating a hasty retreat.

We did not escape so easily on the next call. Martin was a retired antique dealer who lived alone in a little cottage, white-washed on the outside, spick and span on the inside. Each room was furnished with fine furniture; delicate porcelain festooned every shelf. When well, he had cleaned the place himself, setting the highest and most exacting standards. This was a standing joke among the locals at the Stack. He was the butt of the laughter of men like Fred Weighton and his sons, who never lifted a finger to help clean their own homes, and who scorned Martin 'in his little pinny doing women's work'.

Now too ill to do the work himself, a woman had to do his work for him, but only under the strictest supervision, his eagle eye watching her every move: 'If you could just polish that tap a little more, my dear...'

He was a very proper person, his speech and behaviour as exact as his tidy little home. Whenever I visited he was consistently polite to the point of being reverential. 'Father, how good of you to come. I'm so touched that you can find time for me when you must be so very, very busy.'

This morning Martin's door was opened by a nursing sister who let us into the kitchen. Or rather ordered us into the kitchen would be nearer the truth. 'He's on the commode,' she barked out, as matter-of-fact as if she were wishing us 'Good morning'. 'He's been constipated for weeks, so I've given him an enema.'

Poor Martin! Waves of sorrow rippled through me as I thought of him. He was the last person in the Withs who would have the nerve to mention such delicate issues, let alone experience them. The least I could do would be to leave him in decent solitude with his tormentor. 'Well, if that's the case, Sister, we'll take our leave. Give Martin my regards and tell him I'll come along at another time.'

But the wide-hipped nurse blocked our escape route. 'Don't be such a prude, Vicar,' she boomed. 'He's quite decent and he'll be on the commode for hours before anything happens. His insides are as solid as concrete. Just you carry on as normal.' I had no doubt whatsoever that this was an order, not just an encouragement.

Reluctant to cross an enema-happy sister built like a battleship, Herbert and I meekly obeyed and wandered through to the front room. There we found Martin duly en-throned, red-faced with embarrassment. Or at least I assumed that that was the cause. We caught each other's eye, both hapless victims of a tyrannical nurse's regime. 'Oh Father, I'm so very, very sorry,' Martin apologized profusely.

'There's nothing whatsoever to be ashamed of,' I reassured him, getting robed to cover my own embarrassment.

Both to avoid further explanation and to get things over as quickly as possible, I began the service without delay. Herbert decided to deviate from the Gospel he had been reading at all our services the day before. Instead he chose a protracted lesson from the beginning of the Acts of the Apostles, about God's Holy Spirit energiz-ing the disciples when they were gathered together in Jerusalem, which had been read at our Whitsun services the Sunday before.

The second verse provided fate with an irresistible temptation: 'And suddenly there came a sound from heaven, as of a rushing mighty wind, and it filled all the house where they were sitting.' At that precise moment, Martin's enema did its stuff and his relief came, complete with massive sound effects.

Like the good English gentlemen we were, we all pretended nothing had happened and I carried on, bringing the service to as rapid a conclusion as possible. We made our farewells to Martin and left the formidable sister to clear up the mess.

As we drove away, Herbert and I stared zombie-like through the windscreen, in a total daze: two days of episode after episode of disaster had taken their toll. 'Do you know, Herbert,' I drawled, making a valiant attempt to edge out of utter stupor. 'There's one glimmer of light that I draw from our visit to Martin.'

'Oh yes,' Herbert replied, in a voice that sounded like a drug-induced monotone. 'And what would that be?'

'Well, I'm heartened that I've discovered at least one thing in the whole of creation that did not have to wait on that wretched sister's permission before it could happen.'

Our final Communion that morning was at Flo and Edna's in their decrepit almshouse. No sooner had we settled ourselves in their dark kitchen than Flo started on with a litany of her sister's faults. 'Do you know what she did, do you know what she did? Not only did she forget to shell the egg...' Flo shrieked in a perfect impersonation of Hannah Everingham doing a perfect impersonation of her. Of course, I already knew what Edna had allegedly done, so I ignored her outburst and busied myself with putting my robes on. Herbert tilted his head on one side at a degree which he clearly thought oozed compassion and fixed Flo with an intensely pastoral and interested gaze. Of course, all this posing was wasted on her, but Herbert seemed to have forgotten that I had told him Flo was blind. '...yolk all over the place, all over my cardie, all over the chair. Did I give her a piece of my mind when she rolled in! It's a long time ago, now, the fourteenth of April 1946, but it's a day I'll never forget!'

'It's a day no one in the Withs will ever forget,' I thought to myself. Throughout this tirade, Edna sat with her eyes closed, preparing for her Communion, a slight smile on her lips, the look on her face positively beatific, no sign of sourness or of resentment or of wanting to retaliate.

For understandable reasons, our experience at poor old Martin's home had put Herbert off reading about the mighty rushing wind. Even so, it clearly wasn't his day for choosing lessons, since he reverted to the Gospel he'd used the day before, about Jesus healing the blind man. This jarred just a tad with the plight of the two women sitting before us, one blind from birth, the other edging towards blindness, and I felt my heart racing as Herbert, seemingly oblivious, approached the punchline. 'Jesars arsked him,' he read, the churchy voice only adding to my discomfort, '"Whart do you warnt me to do for yew?" He said, "Lord, lert me receive migh sight." And Jesars saird to him, "Receive your sight. Your faith has made yew well."'

'Well, he hasn't healed me, has he? He hasn't healed me!' I heard the malevolent Flo whisper under her breath.

'Ee, how lovely!' Edna chipped in spontaneously, drowning out her sister's moans. 'What a lovely, lovely story.' No jealousy, no bitterness, just a determination to focus on sheer joy. Tears filled my sighted eyes.

Once the Communion had come to its end, we talked about a visit the couple had endured the previous day. 'Ee, he made a real nuisance of himself,' Flo complained.

'Poking in every cupboard, wanting to go into every nook and cranny. He even lifted a floorboard in the bedroom, and then didn't have the decency or the sense to put it back flush. When I was going to bed I went flying over it and could have broken my neck for all he cared. Proper mucked up my routine he did.'

It was news to me that Flo's activities managed to achieve the status of ever having need of a routine, but I kept my counsel and instead turned to her sister.

'And what did you make of him, Edna?'

'Oh, he was a perfect gentleman, Vicar. He kept apologizing for causing any trouble or inconvenience, not that he caused us any bother whatsoever. And he was so thorough, and so very kind. "You ladies deserve an indoor bathroom at your time of life," he said, really concerned, he was, as if it were his own mother he was worrying about. "And a damp course will soon put paid to all this mould that's growing on your walls."'

The visitor had been an architect financed by the National Association of Almshouses, which I had contacted after my chat about things ecc-les-i-ast-ic-al with Bill and Hannah Everingham. They had been very helpful and had offered a grant to help pay for a survey. Bill and I and the other trustees had acted swiftly, incredibly swiftly by the Withs' standards, resulting in yesterday's visit.

After he had been fawned over by Edna and chewed over by Flo, the architect had popped in to see me, to share his initial impressions. 'The best thing we could do is to gut the place and go for a total internal rebuild,' he'd announced clear-sightedly. 'Anything less would just be patching and mending, with the damp biding its time to cause you more problems year after year. This area is so low-lying that you either lick the damp or it will lick you. So for a start we need a damp course.'

'Yes, I can see that that's an essential,' I agreed. 'But what can we do to improve the look of the property? And what can we do to make it less of a chore for Edna, and any other old people who are tenants in years to come?'

'You could take out the massive chimney breast and heat the place with storage radiators, which would save poor old Edna laying a fire and clearing it up every day. That would give us a lot more space on both levels, with room for a small bathroom upstairs. As you know, at present they've just got one cold tap in the kitchen which has to serve all their needs. It's incredible that they have to live like that in this day and age. We could refit the kitchen as well as moving the lavatory from the outside lean-to and installing it in the bathroom.'

'That sounds absolutely super,' I enthused. 'What gets to me, though, is that the place seems so dark. Is there any way we could make it lighter?'

'Well, yes. The bedrooms are very dark with just one tiny window at the south gable end. I thought of putting dormer windows in, which would make them five or six times lighter.'

'And what about downstairs?' I asked. 'I've always thought that the little house is so well set, overlooking the church and the Ings, yet downstairs they don't have a single window looking out that way. What about installing one in the living room on that south wall?'

'Mm, yes, I can see that that's possible,' the architect replied, consulting his notes and sketches and scribbling a few alterations with his pencil. 'It'd be in a load-bearing wall so we'd have to do a proper job, which means that it would add to the total cost. I reckon on a hundred pounds extra as an approximate figure.'

'Making a total cost of?' I asked, steeling myself.

'Three thousand one hundred, or thereabouts, if we're to do up both cottages. We'd work on the empty one first and then move Flo and Edna into that whilst we repeated the same job on their home. You really do need to have a crack at both properties whilst we're at it, otherwise we'll never lick the damp.'

I thought of the terrible damp: the green growth on the skirting boards and window frames, the black fungus disfiguring the whitewashed walls, the white mould creeping like grey cotton wool across the exposed beams. I really wished the architect wouldn't keep repeating that phrase 'licking the damp', since it turned my stomach, a stomach which balked at Grandma Weighton's waxy stews and Ivy Weighton's multi-purpose teatowel and was queasy at the best of times.

Or maybe my stomach was churning because of a price that was way beyond the trustees' budget, a fantastic figure that was over three times my annual salary and £1,000 more than the capital we could raise, even if Leeds City Council were able to give us the cheapest of mortgages.

194

'Oh, I forgot about another idea I had,' the architect added chirpily while my mind reeled from the figures. 'Those outside sheds at the back of the property, they don't seem to be used for anything and at present they're an obvious rat-run. We could convert them into a nice little bungalow whilst we're on site doing the work on the cottages. That would keep the costs down to about two and a half thousand, making just five thousand six hundred in all.'

He made it sound like a bargain I could hardly afford to miss, rather than a figure which was totally out of our league. 'Er, is there any way you could renovate the cottages for a bit less?' I asked, hesitantly, sounding like a timid customer trying to get an antique dealer to knock a pound or two off a piece of porcelain.

'Not really,' he replied. 'My guestimate is based on good but basic materials and hiring a builder who won't try to fleece us. I do a fair bit of work on almshouses and so I'm used to getting the best of work out of the tightest of budgets. The only way we could reduce the cost would be to limit the project. Is a bathroom negotiable, or a kitchen, or making the place light? Whatever we decide, I don't think we can do without the damp course. As I said, that damp will lick us unless we lick it.'

I felt myself turn green as my imagination ran riot. Lyons Maid had recently stormed the market with their 3D lollies, and I pictured one, lichen, mould and fungus-flavoured and coloured, the architect eagerly devouring it, me gingerly sniffing at it and retching. 'I'll tell you what, I'll get some proper costing done and let you have some detailed plans and figures. In the meantime, you can talk through things with the other trustees.'

'All the talk in the world won't produce a thousand pounds,' I thought, as I waved him off, his little MG sports car leaving a pencil-line trail of blue exhaust. As it hung there, suspended in the middle of my drive, it captured my mood precisely.

I felt we were suspended between action and inaction, wanting so very much to do something for Flo and Edna, but thwarted from doing anything at all, paralysed by a shortage of funds.

Tuesday 7 June

'Good morning, Mr Molescroft/Mr Molescrotch/Mr Molest/Mr Noseblow,' twenty-nine children chanted.

'Now then, boys and girls,' Herbert Molescroft intoned in his most unctuous voice, wisely deciding to ignore the variants of his name. 'When I'm not accompanying Mr Wilbourne on his rounds, I am a lay reader. Does anybody know what sort of creature a lay reader is?'

Twenty-nine hands shot up eagerly, twenty-nine earnest voices shouted 'Sir, sir!' and twenty-nine fervent faces pleaded to be the first to be picked. I also suspected very strongly that not one of the twenty-nine children at Eastwith School had the remotest clue what a lay reader was.

Not exactly a brilliant start to what Herbert had assured me would be the *crème de la crème* of assemblies, the assembly to put mine to shame and show me how the job should really be done.

'Is he someone who lays down to read books?' Sharon Dubbins, Virgin Mary and bale-thrower par excellence, asked.

'Lies, dear,' Miss South corrected.

'Is he someone who lays down to read lies?' a confused Sharon repeated.

'No, you're barking up the wrong tree entirely,' Herbert snapped with a rather cruel edge to his voice, which brought tears to Sharon's eyes. 'What do you think a lay reader is, boy?' He pointed at Lee Moss.

Lee Moss stuck his chin out pugnaciously. He wasn't going to let some upstart insult his sweetheart and get away without a fight. 'A lay reader is a failed vicar,' he said, spitting out the words maliciously.

'No, no, that's certainly not right,' Herbert blustered. 'In fact, I always see it the other way around, that a vicar is a failed lay reader!' He laughed heartily and then stopped abruptly, changing the laugh into a cough as he realized that no one else shared the joke. 'You, yes, you, the little boy in the front with the sticking-out ears.' I put my head in my hands as I wondered how many more children Herbert would manage to alienate.

'Is he someone from the Min. of Ag. who counts chickens' eggs?' a very red-faced David Harsley haltingly asked. Little David was grandson of she-who-never-takes-a-breath Doris, but fortunately hadn't inherited her trait. He had his own little oddity, however, in that he could never tell his left from his right and was invariably wearing his shoes on the wrong feet. That together with his jug ears meant he was prone to be teased and easily blushed.

'I don't quite get you. Can you explain a bit more?' Herbert barked.

'Well, a lay reader, it's obvious, in' it?'

'Isn't it, dear,' the ever-patient Miss South corrected again. The poor woman had probably spent a lifetime getting nowhere trying to iron out her charges' Yorkshire slang.

'Well, a lay reader, isn't it obvious, in' it?' David laboured. 'He's someone who records how well hens *lay* and *reads* the result to his boss. He reads the lays, a lay reader. Get it??'

Ingenious, undoubtedly. But wrong. 'No, that's not right at all,' Herbert stressed. 'Put your hands down, the lot of you, because you obviously haven't got a clue. A lay reader is not a failed vicar,' he said, looking pointedly at Lee, 'but is someone who helps in church to do specific things. A hundred years ago, very few people could read, so the first lay readers were educated lay people who read the lessons from the Bible out loud. Now they spend a great deal of time studying and preaching fine sermons and teaching untutored people more about their faith.'

'But I thought the vicar did that,' a still-piqued Lee Moss piped up, pointing at me.

'Well, yes he does, but he has to do other things as well, and people like me do those things I've just mentioned so he can spend more time on those other menial things.'

'So you can do some of the things that the vicar does, but can't do others?' Lee asked incredulously, sounding like the prosecuting counsel grilling a defendant who was rapidly losing his grip. Herbert would live to regret treating Sharon and Lee so dismissively.

'My grandad's got a tractor that can do some things but can't do others,' Paul Broadley chirped up. 'He says it's buggered!'

'Paul!' Miss South shouted. 'How dare you use such language! And in front of the vicar too. Come and see me at playtime. And at lunchtime and at playtime this afternoon.' Paul's lip started quivering, another victim of Herbert's *crème de la crème* of assemblies.

'Anyway, all you lot need to know is that a lay reader is someone who does lay readerly duties,' Herbert announced patronizingly, dwelling on each word.

He reminded me of a debate that had gone on in the House of Commons about the role of archdeacons. The Prime Minister had consulted several of his learned advisors for a definition of what an archdeacon actually did, but found their responses inadequate. He eventually sent the question to the bishops sitting in the House of Lords and received the answer, 'An archdeacon is an ecclesiastical officer who does arch-deaconly duties.' Apparently this magisterial non-statement entirely satisfied both the Prime Minister and the whole Commons.

Be that as it may. Herbert's dismissive statement far from satisfied me, so I decided to take over the assembly to prevent any further casualties and stop him wrecking the good relationship I'd forged with the school. 'Thank you, Mr Molescroft,' I said, rising from my seat and joining him at the front. 'I found it very interesting what you said about the first lay readers getting their name because they read to others. It sounds terribly easy, doesn't it, just reading?' Twenty-nine heads nodded in ready agreement, the younger ones hesitantly, the older ones more certain of themselves and their ability. 'But I'm not sure that it is that easy,' I continued. 'Let's take a line from a Gospel story that Mr Molescroft has been reading to people who can't get to church any more, so we take the church to them instead. It's a tale you all know well, about a blind man asking Jesus to heal him. But listen to the punchline, when Jesus tells the blind man the best of news: "And Jesus said to him, 'Receive your sight, your faith has saved you.'"

'Now think of the different ways you could read that simple sentence. What about this way: "And-Jesus-said-to-him, 'Receive-your-sight, your-faith-has-saved-you.'"' I read the verse deadpan, in a monotone, like someone who had only recently learned to read. 'Yes, Lee?'

'It sounds like a Dalek, there's no feeling to it,' Lee answered, surprising us with his sensitivity.

'Yes, that's right. Well spotted. What about this way? "And Jesars said to him, 'Receive your sight, your faith has saved yew.'" This time I read in a deliberately churchy voice. 'Yes, Sharon?'

'It makes it sound too posh,' she replied. 'As if Jesus was too good for the likes of us.' Geoff Goodmanham raised his eyebrows as again we were surprised by an unexpected astuteness.

'And what about this one? "And Jesus said to him, 'Receive your sight, your faith has saved you.'"' This time I barked the verse out crisply. 'Yes?' I said, pointing to Peter Broadhurst.

'You make Jesus seem like a general, ordering poor people about as if he didn't really care for them,' Peter answered.

'And do you think he was really like that?' I pressed.

'No, he'd have a softer voice. He was a really, really kind man.' There was something in his voice that made all the adults, including Herbert, catch our breath. The child talked with conviction, as if Jesus was a personal acquaintance. I looked at him and wondered. I wondered about the deep grief into which he had been cast when his mother had tragically died, whether Christ had come to him as a friend to calm him and see him through the dark times.

'What about this then? "And Jesus said to him, 'Receive your sight, your faith has saved you.'"' I tried to imagine the blind man before me, the compassion that Jesus would have had for him, willing him to be healed.

'Yes, that's right,' said Peter, stunning us all because the spine-tingling certainty was still present. 'You're not far off him there.'

I said nothing for a moment and neither

did the children, before continuing in a quiet voice, 'So you see how important reading the right way is, especially when you're reading from a Gospel. You've somehow got to bring Jesus alive for those who are listening to you, which is a massive and important job. You've got to put in lots of study, lots of practice, lots of thinking, lots of praying. The last thing you want to do is to put people off him. So you see how crucial Mr Molescroft's job is. Let's end with a little prayer.'

Twenty-nine pairs of hands squeezed tightly together, twenty-nine pairs of eyes squeezed tightly shut, some not so tightly as they peeped out at their neighbour. 'God, our Father, thank you for stories. Thank you for people who read to us and make them come alive. Thank you for your story and its message that you are a friend to us all. Amen.'

'Amen!' twenty-nine treble voices chimed.

'I failed, didn't I? Totally failed?' Herbert said, as we drove away.

' No,' I said, trying to be reassuring. 'It looks easy, talking to children, but it isn't. You have to find the right words, words that won't patronize them, but words that won't be above them either. And you've got to keep calm, whatever you do, don't put them down, because what sort of message is that? Before I do an assembly, I try to ask myself, "What of Christ will these children see in me as I do this?" It's quite a searing test.'

'But I felt so useless,' he said, tears not far away. 'It went so wrong, I was getting so angry with the children.'

'I've told you before, feeling useless is the first step towards true ministry, not pretend ministry, not looks-good ministry, but the sort of ministry that really counts, really makes a difference. Remember that and you'll get there.'

'Do you really think so?' a very humbled Herbert Molescroft replied.

'Oh yes,' I answered, putting on my best serious look. 'And it certainly beats counting how many eggs hens lay,' I added, and both Herbert and I burst into laughter as the little Hillman Imp swerved from side to side in the narrow country lane.

Thursday 16 June

'My Han-nah 'as 'eard from her Ber-tha. Her legs 'ave-n't been too good of late, swoll-en up like ball-oons they 'ave,' Bill

Everingham announced in his usual ponderous way.

'Oh that happened to my dad,' Doris Harsley breathlessly informed us. 'He had to have water tablets which cured one problem but gave him another.' She lowered her voice to a conspiratorial whisper as she imparted the last piece of information, flagging up that there was a certain delicacy involved.

'Yes, Grandma had those water tablets too,' Ivy Weighton confided. 'To this day we don't know whether the tablets made the swelling on her legs reduce, or whether it was all the exercise, constantly nipping to and from t' lavatory in t' yard. She was up and down at all hours, throughout the night.'

'Why didn't you give her a po?' Sam Harsley asked, before being kicked by his wife.

'Really Sam watch your language when the vicar's present,' she chided.

'Oh, we did give her a gesunder,' Ivy Weighton continued. 'But it was full by midnight, so then she had to trip to t' privy for rest of t' night.'

'Anyway that wasn't me dad's problem,' Doris Harsley explained, snatching back the limelight for this Withs' version of *Ask the Doctor*.

A hasty action she soon regretted. 'Well, what was the problem, Doris?' Ivy Weighton asked.

Doris turned bright red. 'Erm erm well,' she began hesitantly, before taking the plunge, 'Once he started taking them tablets he and mum never had much of a love-life after that.' And then she added in another conspiratorial whisper, 'If you know what I mean.'

I felt my own face redden, and from the blushes of those around me it was clear that everyone present knew precisely what she meant. But it was left to her husband Sam to relieve the tension. 'Ay, but with his legs like barrage balloons he didn't have much of a love-life before he started taking them tablets, either.'

'Sam really!' Doris scolded, giving him another sharp kick beneath the table.

As laughter rippled around the room, I took my chance to bring the church council back to the subject in hand. 'Anyway, Bill, you had something to tell us about a loan for the almshouses.'

'Oh ay,' he replied, taking my cue. 'Our Ber-tha with t' swoll-en legs, her niece reckons Leeds Cit-y Coun-cil would give us a mort-gage to do t' houses up. They've fin-anced lots o' big est-ates in t' cit-y sub-urbs, so this'd be small fry for 'em. We'd need to put a prop-er app-lic-at-ion in, mind,' he added, as if we thought Leeds City Council were in the habit of throwing money around at the merest whim of our Bertha's niece.

'But how much money will they give us?' Doris Harsley asked.

'Well, I gave our Ber-tha's niece de-tails a-bout t' in-come from t' Glebe Field. It's ve-ry com-plic-at-ed be-cause it's all ecc-les-i-ast-ic-al, you know.' Bill's ponderous 'ecclesiastical' gave George Broadhurst a fit of the giggles, which he attempted to disguise by blowing his nose noisily and hiding behind his handkerchief.

'Yes we know all that,' Doris Harsley interrupted impatiently. 'But how much will we get?'

'I was just get-ting to that,' Bill continued, unruffled. 'On t' pres-ent rent of one hun-dred and fif-ty-three pounds elev-en shill-ings and six-pence we could get a mort-gage of two thous-and pounds.' As he said the words 'two thousand', Bill's speech slowed down even more than normal to a pace which was positively reverential.

'Phew!' Sam Harsley whistled. 'That's a tidy sum.'

'But not enough, I'm afraid,' I said. 'I had a letter in this morning's post from the architect confirming that the conversion would cost three thousand pounds for the two cottages, and a further two thousand five hundred for building a bungalow where the sheds are. I think we can safely forget the bungalow.'

'I think we can safely forget the whole venture,' Sam Harsley declared gloomily.

'To think we'd be in debt for all that money, and still need half as much again.'

'Oh, I don't know,' Geoff Goodmanham said breezily, immediately injecting a note of optimism into what had become a very pessimistic meeting. 'Those properties are an absolute disgrace. Just think of the good we could do if we did them up. Flo and Edna would live out the rest of their days in comfort, rather than squalor. And the other cottage, well, there's lots of people who could benefit from it. I was wondering how much longer Becky Ludlow can survive in that hovel she has to live in at Eastwith. It would be absolutely wonderful if we could settle her into something cosy.'

'And how would she get to your school to

cook?' Doris Harsley asked. I have heard church councils nicknamed murder boards, because of their habit of always trying to murder a good idea.

'That would be no problem. June would fetch her and drive her back,' Geoff explained, indicating he had been giving the whole issue substantial thought long before this meeting. Thinking about the agenda before a church council was certainly a novel idea, at least in these parts.

'Never mind about lifts,' Sam Harsley interrupted, thumping the table. 'We're a thousand pounds short. Where the hell do we get our hands on money like that?'

Doris gave him another kick. 'Watch your language in front of the vicar,' she hissed.

'Why don't we start a fund with the money raised at the garden party?' George Broadhurst piped up. 'How much do we usually make?'

'No more than a hundred pounds,' Ivy Weighton answered. 'And that includes the money we make on "Guess the Weight of the Cake." That always proves very popular and a really tough competition, because no one has won it for the past ten years. Grandma bakes the cake special,' she beamed.

'Ay, and everyone makes sure their guess isn't within a ton of t' actual weight,' Sam Harsley whispered to me, cackling.

'That means we still need another nine hundred pounds,' Geoff explained, for those who were a bit dim with figures. He taught their children and grandchildren, so he knew precisely how slow With-dwellers were as far as sums were concerned.

'And where the hell, where on earth are we going to get that from?' Sam Harsley mused. 'Where on earth?'

'We need an ang-el to drop it in-to our laps, that's what we need, Sam,' Bill Everingham said, sympathetically.

'Can't we get the architect to leave out one or two of the jobs for now and bring the price down a bit?' Ivy Weighton asked. I was sensitive to the fact that she herself lived in a substandard dwelling, no electricity, no damp course, just a Yorkshire range for heating and cooking.

'Yes, I wondered about that too, Ivy, but it's all part of a package,' I explained carefully. 'For instance, we could make a saving not having a damp course, but then we'd be throwing good money after bad in that all the restoration work would soon be spoiled by damp. And we could just have the damp course, but it would be nice to see a material improvement for the old folks, like a new bathroom and lighten the place up with a few windows.'

'Well, I think we ought to launch a fund to raise the remaining thousand,' Geoff Goodmanham declared. 'It's a project that will benefit the whole parish and one we can really pull the stops out for. I propose that we start tonight and plan to really boost the garden party's profits.'

'I'll second that,' said George Broadhurst. 'What's more, I'll give a hundred pounds to kick it off. Helping to finance updating the almshouses will be a fitting memorial for Jennifer. Also I have had the immense good fortune to find love for a second time, and this would be a way of simply saying thank you.'

'Thank you very much, George, that's very generous indeed,' I said. He had been in the Withs for less than a year, and yet his generosity put to shame those who had been born and bred here, but were reluctant to give a halfpenny 'to t' Church with all its Commissioners' millions'.

My cynicism was put to shame as Ivy Weighton piped up, 'I'll give fifty pounds towards the fund, Vicar. Hans had put a bit of money aside and left it to us in his will. It seems a good idea to use it for t' benefit of villages he loved so much.' I noticed the tears in her eyes as she said her little speech. Once again I thought of her own deprivation, so found her generosity particularly touching.

'That's really, really kind of you, Ivy. It'll be a good memorial for him, as you say,' I replied.

'Ay, and perhaps we'll rename the almshouses "Bugger-off House" after him,' Sam Harsley quipped.

Ivy's tears turned to laughter as she remembered Hans' malapropisms. 'Ee, when he told that bishop to bugger off, he couldn't understand why everyone else split their sides. "I only said *auf Wiedersehen* in English, didn't I?" he asked, genuinely puzzled. I didn't have the heart to tell him that wasn't quite what he said.'

'Well, it looks like the fund has had a grand start, with us nearly a fifth of the way to our total already. Any other takers?' I asked. I noticed that the rest of the council suddenly started studying my ceiling with an intensity which the Georgian plasterwork, though fine, had never previously warranted.

'We're very lucky indeed to have baby Elizabeth,' Geoff Goodmanham said softly, breaking the painful silence. 'As long as I live, I'll never forget the night she was born and how we nearly lost her. I'll never forget you cycling over all that way, David, and baptizing her and bringing us hope. June and I will gladly give fifty pounds as a thank you for our good fortune, our immense good fortune. I'm only sorry it can't be more.'

'Thank you, Geoff, what you've said is more than enough,' I replied, the tears in my own eyes matching his. 'Well, there's our fifth of our target. I don't want to put pressure on anyone, I know how tight things are, but if anyone else would like to give a donation, however small, you know where to find me.'

We ended the meeting by discussing the forthcoming garden party. My long experience of such deliberations was that they always focused on three issues:

a. what to present to the opener;
b. whether stalls could sell their produce before the official time of opening;
c. where to put the cake stall.

The answers were invariably the same in parishes the length and breadth of the nation:

a. something as cheap as you could get away with, so as to maximize profits;
b. yes;
c. under the trees so that any cream cakes would be in shade and not go sour.

Standard though the questions and their answers were, year in and year out they were raised and pondered on throughout the land, as if no one had ever encountered their like before.

'What do you think we ought to give to the opener?' asked Doris Harsley, kicking off the proceedings.

'Well, she's the wife of our MP and a local landowner, so it needs to look good. What about a bouquet?' suggested Ivy Weighton.

'Well, yes,' Sam Harsley agreed. 'But it mustn't be too pricey, otherwise we'll be spending all our profits. What about your lad, Ivy? He grows a fair few blooms under glass in that lean-to at end o' your farm. I could manage a flower or two from our garden, so if we put 'em together, it 'ould be a grand bunch, and hardly cost us owt.'

215

'Yes, I'm sure that would be no trouble,' Ivy Weighton replied. 'We could get Grandma to sort them out whilst we're busy with t' cake stall.' I only hoped Grandma Weighton's flower-arranging skills were a touch better than her culinary ones, otherwise Mrs MP could look forward to a novel presentation of wilting chrysanthemums speckled with hot wax.

'Speaking o' cake stall where do you think we ought to put it?' Doris Harsley enquired, as eagerly as if it were the first cake stall in creation.

'We need a nice shady spot away from t' sun,' Ivy pronounced ponderously. 'Grandma's going to make a cream and walnut cake this year. We don't want cream turnin' if it's a hot day. We'll set up under t' vicar's horse chestnuts, just like we did last year.'

'We're a bit out of it there though,' Doris Harsley complained. 'What about going underneath his sycamores at top o' t' drive?'

'Oo no, we don't want to do that. Don't you remember, Doris, we put t' stall there in 1954 and t' sycamores spat their horrible green gum all over cakes. We had to pretend it were icing. We just couldn't bring ourselves to throw the cakes away, you see,

216

Vicar,' she explained, turning her head towards me. 'They were so precious what with rationing only just coming to an end. Sugar was like gold.'

'It was that,' Doris Harsley agreed. The rest of us looked from woman to woman as the conversation went on, like mute spectators at a tennis match. 'Mind you rationing wasn't all bad,' she went on, breathless and unpunctuated as ever. 'Carrot cake for instance was delicious so sweet and so moist.'

'Ay, Grandma used to make a fine carrot cake,' Ivy Weighton agreed, her eyes going misty as she savoured the memories.

'Apart from 1950 when she left the carrot tops in though,' Doris Harsley added. 'That caused a few surprises I can tell you.'

'Anyway,' I said, attempting to draw this ramble to a close, 'let's put the cake stall under the horse chestnuts. It'll be nice and cool there. Any other queries?'

'Yes,' said Sam Harsley, puffing out his cheeks and bristling his jet-black moustache, and looking very important indeed. 'I'd like to ask your opinion on a very sensitive subject, Vicar.'

'Fire away,' I said, rubbing my eyes. I felt tired and wondered how I could survive another forty years of councils like these. Still, it was good that Sam was trying to bring the meeting around to a serious issue at last.

'Well, do you believe...' he began. I braced myself expectantly for what lay ahead. Was he going to ask whether I believed in the Trinity, or in infant baptism, or in trial marriages, or in revising the Prayer Book? At last I was going to be able to air the knowledge I'd gained after all those years of theological study.

'Do you believe,' he repeated, 'that goods should be sold before the MP's wife has officially opened the fete, or not?' As he batted this poser at me, he smiled triumphantly at everyone else, with the sort of smile I guess the Pharisees had on their face when they asked Jesus whether it was permissible to pay taxes to Caesar or not.

'We're there to make money, money for a very good cause, so if someone wants to buy something, sell it to them, whether it's before, after or even during Mrs MP's spouting forth,' I answered, crisply.

'But then people who get there early get the pick,' Doris Harsley protested.

'Then that's a good reason for not being late. I'd rather sell out too soon than hold back and be left with a lot of stale cakes and unwon tombola prizes,' I replied, standing my ground. 'Any more questions?'

We had covered the threefold traditional garden party agenda, so there was nothing else to be said. I closed the meeting by saying the Grace and then chattered by the door as people sauntered of. I overheard a dark muttering or two as people disappeared down my drive into the night. 'Now Mr So-and-so, when he was vicar, wouldn't allow a thing to be sold until the opener had finished, would he, Doris?'

'No he was straight down the line over that.'

'Well at least you knew where you were with him. He was firm but fair about it all. If we don't watch it, this next time will be a free-for-all.' They spoke in a deadly serious tone, as if their very lives were at stake.

The muttering was drowned out as Rebecca's VW turned off the road and chugged up the drive, narrowly missing mowing down my critics. 'I thought I'd come and pick Mum up,' she explained, as she leapt out of the car and gave me a kiss.

'I think she and Bill Everingham are still inside,' I said. 'Come on in. We've had a fun-packed evening talking about where to put cake stalls and what to present to openers...'

'I bet!' she replied. 'I've been having a fun-packed evening too, marking a third-form piece on asking a policeman for directions from York railway station to the Minster.'

'No Odes to Joy this time, then?' I asked as we walked through the porch.

'No,' she laughed, her blue eyes sparkling. 'But there was one clever-clogs who wrote *"Ich wurde sagen* 'How do I get to York Minster?'*,* since few York policeman can speak German."'

'Hallo, our Rebecca,' Ivy Weighton cried out, as we met in my hall. 'What are you doing here?'

'Ee, Ivy,' Bill Everingham exclaimed, 'she's come vis-it-ing her fi-an-cé. En-gaged coup-les should see each oth-er from time to time, thou knows! When I was court-ing my Hann-ah, I just could-n't keep a-way.'

'Sorry, I quite forgot,' Ivy said, laughing at herself. 'I find it difficult to switch over from David being the vicar to David being my son-in law.' Then she covered her mouth with her hand in embarrassment. 'Oh, I'm sorry, I hope you don't mind me calling you David. It just slipped out.'

'Not at all,' I replied, smiling at her fondly. 'Actually, Mum, I came to see you,'

Rebecca explained. 'I thought you looked a bit peaky at teatime and could do with a lift home.'

'Oh, that's kind of you, love,' she replied. 'But actually, t' meeting's cheered me up no end. We're going to have a fund to do up t' almshouses and I chipped in with Hans's' money. He'd be so pleased to see it used in that way.'

'That's good, mum, very good,' Rebecca replied.

'And Bill here has asked me back for a bit o' supper with him and Hannah. We thought we'd have a look over t' architect's plans that t' vicar's, er, that David's lent him. It's ever so sweet of you to have popped down, but if you don't mind...'

'Not in the least,' said Rebecca. 'I'm so pleased to see you enjoying yourself.'

'Ay, and it'll give you two love-birds a chance to be to-geth-er,' Bill joked, as Rebecca blushed.

'Yes, come on, Rebecca, I'll put the kettle on. You deserve a break from all that marking. What time do you want picking up, Mrs Weight, er, Ivy,' I asked.

'Give us an hour,' Ivy replied, before she walked off with Bill, arm in arm, friends from childhood days like children still.

221

I hate being cooped up indoors, and I especially hate being cooped up in a meeting, the air becoming staler and more fetid as the meeting drags on. Though she was devoted to teaching and enjoyed the buzz of the classroom, Rebecca had a similar yearning for the open spaces she had enjoyed since birth, so that night we drank our tea on the lawn. The day had been a mild one, creating a store of warm memories which anaesthetized us against the night chill, the grass already brittle beneath our feet, primed for an unseasonal frost. The horse chestnuts and sycamores, welcome shade from the sun for innumerable garden parties, were now dark silhouettes shielding us from a crisp night sky whose stars could have been pinpoints of ice crystallizing in the heavens. On the western horizon, towards the Derwent, was a thin band of light where it was still day, multicoloured light, gold and red swirling with mauve and purple. We drank our tea and silently and gratefully drank from the scene, feeling doubly refreshed.

'I find it quite touching that your mum should give Hans's money for the almshouses,' I said.

'Yes, it's typical of her to be concerned

about the comfort of others rather than her own,' Rebecca replied, putting her arm around my waist. 'But it really does seem to have cheered her, doing something tangible for him. She looked happier tonight than I've seen her for months.'

'I just hope we get the other eight hundred and can actually do the job,' I said. 'I know all too well that donations around here are measured in scruples. It's a rare day indeed when we get a ten-bob note on the collection plate.'

'Oh, don't worry,' Rebecca replied soothingly. 'I'm sure you'll get there. Don't forget you've still got the garden party and Guess the Weight of Grandma's Cake to help the money roll in. Poor old soul, she's never realized that it's a Withs' tradition to make sure your entry definitely isn't the winning one!

'And even if you don't get the money,' she added, 'I know of another good use Mum can put Hans's' bequest to.'

'And what would that be?' I asked.

'Five hundred new tea-towels for our wedding present!' she laughed.

At that moment a jet screeched overhead and there was a great boom as it broke through the sound barrier. 'I do wish

Church Fenton would stop those night flights,' Rebecca said as she jumped with fright. 'They play havoc on the farm, disturbing the animals. It's near impossible to settle the young cattle down once one of those jets has shattered their rest.'

However, this time the jet passed surprisingly quickly and we were able to enjoy the silence once again. As we looked over the village, the roof-lines black and higgledy-piggledy, a flash of white dropped down suddenly from the sky. 'What on earth was that?' I cried out.

'Oh, it was probably just a trick of the light,' Rebecca said, with the reassurance of a teacher used to soothing her teenage charges' irrational fears.

'For a moment, I thought it was Bill's angel,' I joked. Rebecca gave me a puzzled look, and so I added, 'Ee, Vicar, we need an an-gel to drop mon-ey into our laps if we're ever go-ing to do 'owt a-bout those alms-houses!'

'Never a truer word is spoken in jest,' Rebecca replied. 'You certainly need a miracle to raise that sort of money around here.'

Quite early the next morning, I popped around to Flo and Edna's to tell them about our launch of the Almshouse Fund. I felt it was important to give them clear details before they heard the news via the Withs' grapevine, a system of communication which was certainly speedier than a jet plane if nowhere near as reliable. I knocked on the flimsy back door, whose peeling paint and rotting wood typified the state of the house, and, not waiting to be bidden, walked straight through the kitchen into the living room. 'Good morning, Edna, good morning, Flo, sorry to disturb you but...'

I stopped mid-sentence, brought up short by the sight of a man sitting by the fire, with the two sisters twittering around him in attendance. At first I thought he was a tramp, overalls torn and tatty, chin stubbly and unshaven, hair blond but bedraggled, hands dirty. But then he stood up stiffly, towering an inch or two above me, and greeted me, and I changed my opinion. 'Why, good morning, Reverend,' he said, with a Texan drawl to his voice. 'These two ladies have spent most of the night telling me so much about you.'

'Good heavens,' I exclaimed. 'I didn't know there was that much to tell.'

'Oh, they somehow managed to fill the time,' he drawled, giving me a broad but self-deprecating grin at his typical American understatement. I instantly liked him and felt surprisingly at ease in his company.

'Yes, but we told him nothing but good about you, Vicar, nothing but good,' Edna twittered.

'That's most certainly true,' the Texan drawled. 'In fact, I was hoping to come across you because I've never met a saint before.' Again there was that broad but self-deprecating grin. 'Anyway, let me introduce myself since I already know your name and a hell – sorry, Reverend – a heck of a lot about you. Jimmy Benson at your service, sir.'

'Very pleased to meet you,' I said, trying to hide the pain from his strong grip that felt as if it was squeezing the blood out of my hand. 'I must say, Flo and Edna, I never realized that you had American con-nections.'

'Oh no, we don't have, or rather we didn't have until Jimmy dropped by,' Edna replied.

'I should say "dropped by" is the operative word, ladies!' Jimmy added, raising his eyebrows and treating us to that disarming grin again. 'Should I tell him or will you?'

'Oh, we'll tell him, Jimmy, we'll tell him,' exclaimed an unusually garrulous Flo. 'It's the most exciting thing that has happened to us in ages. Probably in our whole lives!' I braced myself to be overwhelmed. Mind you, given Flo's extremely staid existence in a Kirkwith which was sleepy at the wildest of times, I wasn't building my hopes up too high.

'It all started last night, about ten o'clock. Edna had just made us our nightly Bourn-vita when we heard this scratching and scraping at our back door. We thought it was Hannah Everingham's cat, who includes us in her rounds. Edna gives her a saucer of milk now and again, although how we can afford to give milk away like that, I shudder to think,' Flo complained, as her mean streak reasserted itself.

'Anyway,' continued Edna, taking over before Flo lapsed into her usual litany of discontent, 'it wasn't Tiddles at all, it was Jimmy, lying prostrate by our back door, scratching to get our attention!'

'I might add, Reverend,' Jimmy interrupted, 'that I'm a Southern Baptist and life-long teetotaller, so I wasn't rolling around on

227

these good ladies' doorstep because I was blind drunk. I'm a pilot with the American squadron based at Church Fenton, one of these wretched night flyers that keep disturbing the peace of you good country folk.' Again there was the wide smile accompanied with a choice of words which skilfully allayed any hostility over an emotive subject.

'Well, he certainly disturbed our peace last night,' Flo complained. 'Nearly frightened us to death, he did.'

'Now come on, Flo, don't take on so,' Edna chided. 'The scratching on the door didn't frighten us, since we thought it was Hannah's cat. True enough, it was a bit of a surprise to find a man lying on our step...' I smiled at Edna's understatement, 'a bit of a surprise' suggesting that she was really quite accustomed to finding American gentlemen sprawling outside her back door. '...but then you looked up, Jimmy, and fixed us with such a dazzling smile, and said "Ladies I'm so terribly sorry to bother you at this time of the night," in such a sweet, polite way that we instantly felt charmed and certainly not terrified.'

'But what were you doing in Kirkwith at that time of night?' I asked Jimmy, genuinely puzzled.

'I was flying over it!' Jimmy explained. 'One minute I was looking out at all these pinpoints of light from your villages, and having warm feelings about rustic life in good old England, the next minute there was a great boom and I realized I'd totally lost power. I must have hit a flock of geese or something – birds are a lethal danger and can utterly wreck your turbine jets. I had no choice but to press the ejector button and then automatic procedures took over, culminating in my 'chute landing me in these good ladies' back garden.'

'Goodness, so that was the boom and the flash of white that my fiancée and I spotted dropping out of the sky! But you seemed to fall so fast. How did you manage to escape being injured?' I asked, incredulously.

'Understandably I was a fair bit shaken and very wobbly, so all I could do to begin with was to crawl. The lines from my 'chute had somehow twisted around my legs, and try as I might, I couldn't untangle them, which made moving even more difficult.'

'Yes, but we soon got you free of those, didn't we Jimmy?' Edna piped up. 'You see, Vicar, I used to have to untangle my father's fishing lines when I was a girl. Unravelling Jimmy's legs was far easier than child's play, to coin a phrase!'

'Yes indeed, ladies, and once you'd unravelled me I thankfully found that total paralysis hadn't set in after all. A cup of your – what do you call it?' Jimmy asked Flo.

'Bournvita,' Flo replied.

'A cup of your Bournvita soon restored my spirits. Edna kindly popped over to her neighbours and rang Church Fenton...'

'Oh, they were in a right old panic, Vicar,' Edna explained, gleefully continuing the tale. 'You see, Jimmy had totally disappeared off their radar. Once I'd assured them that his 'chute had opened and that he was totally OK, they calmed down a lot. I told them our precise location, and they promised to send a jeep for Jimmy this morning, if we could manage to put him up for the night. They couldn't come straight away, you see, since they were using all their resources to search for the wreck.' Words like 'radar' and 'chute', 'jeep' and 'wreck' just tripped off Edna's excited tongue, as if they'd been commonplace in her vocabulary for a lifetime.

'I was very, very anxious about where the jet had eventually come down,' Jimmy said. 'So I was extremely relieved when I heard on this morning's news on your Home

230

Service that it had safely come to rest in empty marshland about five miles south of here. Before I bailed out, I'd managed to change course so the jet wasn't obviously heading towards any pinpoints of light, but even then, I wasn't certain it would clear centres of population. You Brits tend to go to bed early, so I was afraid some villages might have already switched all their lights off.'

'Oh, he's a real hero, isn't he, Vicar? He risked his life, you know, staying in that plane to save the villages. And he was so worried, so very worried about where that plane would land. We had to calm him with a second cup of Bournvita,' Edna told me, at the same time giving me a wink which was obvious, and very deliberate. The only problem was, I hadn't got the slightest clue what she was getting at.

'Well, that stuff sure is a wonderful drink, ladies. I'll make sure we get some of that Bon, Born, Bourn, whatever it is in our stores at the mess. It sent me off good and proper. I had the best night's sleep on this little sofa of yours since coming to England.'

'And how long have you been in England?' I asked.

'Five months, sir. Ma daddy pulled a few

strings to get me into the airforce and serve with NATO so that I'd be spared the carnage in 'Nam,' Jimmy replied, openly, in a matter-of-fact way. 'It's a total horror story in the Far East, believe you me, Reverend. I'm so very grateful that I'm over here and not over there. Even with jets packing up all around me.'

'Now you two have a little chat whilst Flo and I go and make a cup of tea,' Edna cooed.

'Excuse me, ma'am, but I don't go for tea in a big way. Is there any chance you could fix me another cup of that Bor, Bourn, Borvita stuff?' Jimmy asked with immense courtesy, accompanied by that wide smile again.

'Oh, I think we could manage that, couldn't we, Flo?' Edna replied.

As the two of them disappeared into the kitchen, Jimmy wiped the smile off his face and put on a very serious look indeed. 'Say, this, this house, does it in some way belong to the Church?' he asked.

'Well, it does and it doesn't,' I replied. 'It's an almshouse owned by an ancient trust which was taken over by my church council in the 1920s. It's maintained by the rent from nearby farmland, which your plane no doubt skimmed over last night.'

'But your church does have some responsibility?' he pressed.

'Oh yes, and last night...'

'Well, you ought to be thoroughly ashamed of yourselves, allowing two disabled old ladies to live in this squalor,' he interrupted. The easy smile was definitely gone and there was fire in his eyes. 'Just look at the damp! And only one cold tap stuck in that miserable kitchen to serve the whole house. When I first arrived, I was bursting to visit the john, so as a well-brought-up American, I asked for the bathroom. I really thought I must have banged my head, got concussed and was suffering from delirium, because instead of showing me upstairs, Edna led me outside to some sort of shed. It smelt horrible and was absolutely freezing, and as I went in, I could hear some sort of creatures scurrying off. I'm sorry, Reverend, if I seem abrupt, but really, for the love of Christ, what do you think you're doing allowing anyone to live in such misery?'

'You're absolutely right,' I agreed. 'It's a crying shame that the house should ever have been allowed to get into this state. But help is at hand. We've got plans for renovating the place, and we've already raised a

233

good deal of the cost. The snag is that we've still got to find another eight hundred pounds, and until we've got that we can't really start work.'

'How much is that in dollars?' Jimmy asked

'Well, at an exchange rate of about two dollars forty, it's the equivalent of around two thousand dollars,' I replied.

'Gee, you may be slow about doing up houses, but you're not slow when it comes to doing sums,' Jimmy commented, his wide smile returning.

'Oh, it comes naturally, I used to work in a bank,' I explained.

Once again Jimmy's smile darkened. 'But two thousand dollars would be small fry in the States. I don't see what the problem is.'

'I'm afraid it's a lot of money around here, more than a year's wages for most folks. It'll take some getting there, I'm sorry to say, certainly more than a year or two ...'

'And meanwhile poor old Edna and Flo continue in this squalor,' Jimmy grimaced.

There was nothing more I could say, so we sat in silence for several moments, staring into the fire which spluttered and sparked in a valiant attempt to air that dank room. 'I'll just go and see if the girls need a hand,' I said, walking through to the kitchen.

I caught Edna spooning a generous measure of whisky into Jimmy's drink. 'I think he's rather taken with our version of Bournvita,' she whispered, smiling and giving me that wink again. 'I didn't realize he was a teetotaller until he mentioned it just then. And I daren't stop adding a bit of the hard stuff now, otherwise he'll notice the difference and twig what was going on.'

'Oh, by the way,' I whispered, catching Edna's habit, 'what I really came to tell you is that the church council have started a fund to get this place renovated, completely done up in fact. It might take a bit of time, but please be patient, because I'm sure we'll get there in the end.'

'Oh, I know all about that, Vicar,' Edna assured me. 'It was Bill Everingham's phone we rang Church Fenton from last night. Hannah told me how you'd got two thousand two hundred pounds in the bag but needed another eight hundred. I hear Grandma Weighton's baking a tasty cake for the garden party to launch us on our way!'

I silently ate my words, which though humbling is certainly preferable to eating the good matriarch's cake. Because though I had been right about the Withs' grapevine being faster than a jet plane, on this occasion that grapevine was undoubtedly more reliable.

Sunday 19 June

''Oly, 'oly, 'oly,' the congregation sang, their voices discordant, dropping their aitches, as was the custom in these parts. Doris Harsley was at the harmonium, valiantly trying to keep it and us in tune. Sam was at her side, pumping the bellows up and down.

As the hymn progressed, the organ started emitting a strange wailing sound. It tripped my memory back to childhood, a Sunday School visit to the zoo when we'd all roared with laughter at the weird honking of a lovesick camel. Except that I don't think our harmonium was lovesick, but was rather in its death-throes, singing its swan song.

The wailing rose in a crescendo as Doris desperately tried to quench it, pushing in this stop, pulling out that stop, like an engineer on the *Flying Scotsman* trying to bring his locomotive to an emergency halt because the bridge was out ahead. If Doris was like the engineer, Sam was like the fireman, but pumping instead of stoking, working harder and harder for ever-diminishing returns. Sweat poured off his brow as the wail grew louder and louder, and the strains of the hymn tune grew proportionately softer and softer and became just a distant hint in the midst of the organ's dying clamour.

''Oly, 'oly, 'oly,' some of the congregation valiantly continued singing. Others directed bemused stares and raised eyebrows in the direction of Doris, as if to say, 'Is that sound coming from you or your harmonium?'

'All thy works shall praise thy name in earth and sky and sea,' the discordant voices prophetically trilled as the organ evolved from impersonating a mere lovesick camel and advanced to shrieking a whale's haunting cry. Sam now heaved like a runner completing the Marathon in Rome 1960's sweltering climes. Doris moved stops like a mill-worker teasing a spinning jenny on a treble production day. And then there was an enormous bang as the harmonium finally gave up the ghost. The encore came from the burst bellows, which in their dying moments emitted an enormous raspberry, a mighty sound of rushing wind which was worthy of poor old Martin and his enema.

'I did-n't know Dor-is was cap-ab-le of

play-in' a des-cant,' I heard Bill Everingham naively whisper to Hannah in the merciful silence that followed.

'Ay, but the way you sing, every line's a descant. I wish you'd stick to t' proper tune for once!' Hannah blurted out, causing the congregation to lapse into a fresh state of giggles.

I decided I'd better take command quickly, before the service degenerated into a farce. 'Thank you very much, Doris – and Sam too,' I added, as Sam's perspiring and blotchy face edged up over the harmonium's side, like an exhausted climber scrambling over a cliff-top, 'for that very impressive performance. I think we can safely say that it is a production which is unique in the long history of church music, and I for one dearly hope that it remains so! We always do things in style in the Withs: today we've launched the new organ appeal in the most novel of ways!'

I was a bit nervous and realized I was rambling a bit, putting things awkwardly, if not pompously. Today was the baptism of Simon Broadhurst, the son of George and his late wife, Jennifer. Baby Simon had been recovered from the wreck of the car crash which had killed his mother. The child didn't have a single scratch, and wasn't even crying when the firemen had eased him out of the mangled metal. The crying had come later; for him and for the rest of the family. Dealing with the massive grief meant that Simon's baptism had to be postponed until now, almost a year since his birth.

The tragic memories swirling around at the service made me tense enough, but on top of that there was a posse of George's colleagues from York University, high-flying academics to their bushy eyebrows and half-moon spectacles, and I was anxious to give them a good impression of the Church. The new university was a bit snooty about Christianity and all its works, so I was keen to redress the balance and show them what a serious matter religion was. Beginning the service with a performance from a dyspeptic harmonium and a congregation rolling around in fits of laughter wasn't quite the virtuoso performance that I had had in mind.

I stuttered and stammered through the rest of the service without a major hitch. The godparents, consisting of my Rebecca, George's fiancée Pam and a couple of Classics lecturers, with one foot in the twentieth century and the other in Ancient

Rome, stood surety for the child and answered their promises boldly. The whole christening party moved to the font for the high point of the drama, with the rest of the congregation swivelling 180 degrees in their pews and looking fondly on.

I turned to Pam, who was holding Simon, or rather was doing her best to hold on to a hefty youngster who was bursting with life and wriggling like a worm with St Vitus' Dance trying to escape. 'Name this child,' I said.

'Simon David McGregor,' she replied, softly but unhesitatingly, her steel-blue eyes fixing me with an assured gaze. She passed the writhing bundle to me. Tucking his flouncing waist as best I could under my left arm, I held his head in my left hand and gently, or reasonably gently, tipped it over the font.

'Simon David McGregor,' I began, breathing heavily with the exertion of holding on to this bundle of nuclear energy singlehandedly. 'I baptize you in–' And then I came to an abrupt halt as I peered into a font where there was one crucial ingredient missing. The thing was as dry as a desert, with not even a single tiny drop of water clinging to its lead bowl.

I did a double-take, because I had poured a full jug of water into the thing at the start of the ceremony only minutes before, yet now the whole lot had simply vanished. 'I'm afraid the water's done a disappearing trick,' I announced, trying to sound as calm and as suave as the magician David Nixon, but feeling I was coming across as clumsy as Tommy Cooper.

'Ay, lead linin' tends to leak a bit,' Sam Harsley shouted from his perch by the organ. 'Give me jug and I'll go and get some more from home. I'll only be a couple of minutes.' As well as pumping the organ, Sam was Kirkwith Church's verger, so was well used to helping in such ways. Even so, the exertion of staving off the harmonium's death had clearly taken its toll, since he was wheezing heavily as he bustled importantly out of church, clanking the heavy door behind him. We'd be lucky if he made it back in five minutes, never mind two.

I held Simon in both hands and rocked him up and down to try and keep him happy, simultaneously walking around the Norman font like some ancient witch-doctor encircling his place of work. As I looked at the font's base I realized where all the water had leaked to: there was a substantial pool, which was still seeping out of the stone. 'Look, Daddy,' Sally Broadhurst shouted, as her eyes followed the direction of my gaze, 'The font's done a wee-wee.'

'Wee wee wee wee wee...' Simon began chanting, showing a considerable grasp of language for one so young. I was beginning to feel like a beleaguered continuity announcer on TVs new BBC 2 channel, trying to hold the fort while normal service was resumed as soon as possible.

In my mind I flicked through the services I had taken in my short time in Kirkwith. I remembered the tower falling down on the Archdeacon when I was made vicar. I recalled the angel spontaneously igniting at Christmas, with the baby Jesus staying firmly wedged in his cradle while his father did a spot of tree-felling. A shiver went down my spine as I recollected how shy old me had stammered over the word 'circumcision' not once but an embarrassing fifteen times at a New Year's Day service to celebrate Jesus' naming. Then a heavily pregnant winter's bride flashed through my memory, fainting with shock after her father-in-law 'accidentally' forgot to bring his wife. In my imagination I saw bats playing with ladies' hats on Easter Day... It suddenly dawned on me that no service at Kirkwith was ever normal.

I prattled on to try and keep the congregation amused as we all eagerly awaited Sam's return. 'Just as we can't do without water for a christening, we can't do without water for life,' I began, the congregation's eyes glazing over as they got bored with me stating the obvious. I thought of the canon from York Minster who had gone shopping with his wife in the Saturday market and had come across the fish stall, the dead fish gawping up at him with lightless eyes. 'That reminds me,' he said, raising his hand to his worried brow, 'I'm preaching at the Minster in the morning!'

'We're made mostly of water,' I continued, soldiering on despite the gaping fish. 'We can't survive very long without a drink of water, and yet our friend water is simultaneously our foe, in that it can drown us, sweep us away, sink us, kill us.

'This font this morning should be full to the brim, and if it was, it would look deep and very threatening to this little chap...'

Unfortunately at that moment Simon screwed up his face and looked like a mini-gangster, who would be menaced by absolutely no one, not exactly the best visual aid for my little spiel. But still I persevered. 'But this service is to celebrate that what looks like a threat is actually a friend, what looks like a curse is actually a blessing. This service challenges us to think of God like water, essential to life, yet sometimes seen as terrible and threatening to life. Mostly it's us and our prejudices which make God a monster. This little ceremony stamps the view, right at the start of Simon's life, that far from being his foe, God is his friend, and our friend, for ever.'

The sleepy congregation were spared any further musings as Sam clanked back through the door, the jug full with water swirling over the brim as he huffed and puffed. Bristling his moustache with great importance, he cut his way through the baptism party and sloshed the water into the font, which swirled round the lead bowl and splashed over the top. Deciding to delay no further, I tucked Simon's waist once again under my left arm, tipped his head over the tempestuous waters and christened him there and then: 'Simon David McGregor, I baptize you in the name of the Father, and of the Son, and of the Holy

Ghost. Amen.'

I then held on to him while I made the sign of the cross on his forehead. But the little lad had other ideas, and with his free arm scooped up a handful of water, with which he liberally showered the bystanders. He was obviously a bright little soul, because once he'd cottoned on to the trick he did it again and again and again as I stood there transfixed. Eventually I had the presence of mind to step down from the font and remove him from his source for mischief. However, his right hand and arm continued their quasi-bowling manoeuvre, which, no longer slowed down by the baptismal waters, shot up and gave me a resounding smack on the face.

With my cheek burning, I handed Simon back to Pam, who, despite the spots of damp which had liberally peppered her pale blue dress, gave me a broad grin. The rest of the congregation had been similarly drenched, hats sodden, hair damped down, light grey suits now suffused with darker spots. But no longer were anyone's eyes glazed over. The antics of a tiny child had brought them all to life.

'I really enjoyed that service, Vicar, I didn't realize the Church of England was so unstuffy,' a ruddy-faced professor lectured me at the christening party at Kirkwith Manor, immediately after Simon's baptism. 'What a lovely idea, getting little Simon to splash everyone as a reminder of their own baptism. I liked your talk too, about trying to see God as a friend rather than a foe. We all need to hear that.'

'Yes, I don't think you can tell people too many times that God loves them,' I agreed.

'Mind you, I used to be absolutely terrified of him as a child,' the professor confessed, 'what with pulpit-thumpers shouting "Thou shalt not this" and "Thou shalt not that", sending shivers down my spine. And the Almighty seemed to be such an absolute swine, positively insisting on his Son's bloody sacrifice, not to mention initiating all that Old Testament gore. There's one particular episode which always used to get to me as a lad: poor, confused old King Saul gets clobbered for sparing the Amalekites rather than massacring them. God gets cross with him for being too merciful. What do you make of that?'

'I think people were making God in their own violent image, projecting their blood-lust on to him, rather than seeing him as he really was.' I replied. 'Either that or, as biblical history progressed, God mellowed with age.'

'I like that,' the professor laughed. 'God mellows with age! Very good! When I was up at Oxford I heard some liberal cleric dismiss the idea of particular divine intervention, because, "If you believe in that," he said, "then God's a sod!" I remember thinking at the time, "Mm, I rather like that. God's a sod. That's what I've been brought up to believe." To be honest, I've never had much truck with God or the Church since.'

'Did you have to go to church much as a child?' I asked.

'I had to go twice every Sunday, without fail, Matins and Evensong, with daily Evensong compulsory when I was up at school,' he barked out. His views were all too familiar, since people were always telling me things like this, expressing the same sentiments, even employing the same words, as if they were delivering some anti-Catechism parrot-fashion. 'What with psalms you couldn't sing and which never seemed to end, coupled with interminable lessons read in an absolute drone of a voice, I don't know, it inoculated you against religion rather than sowed its seeds. And the sermons, don't talk to me about the sermons – bored out of my mind, I used to be. Mind you, going to church as a lad taught me something that has been indispensable throughout my academic life.'

'What was that?' I asked.

'How to yawn with my mouth tightly shut and to sleep with my eyes wide open! I've been able to survive many a dull depart-ment meeting because of that skill!

'Anyway, good to meet you, Vicar. Here's a little something for your organ appeal.' And with that he pressed a ten-bob note into my hand.

As I moved among the eminent guests that day, I heard many times how stuffy the church of their youth had been, and how they'd been put off religion ever since. I also had many ten-bob notes pressed into my hand to enable the present-day church to sing again, which I took as their sort of prayer, a commitment to the church's future, a yearning for a return.

'Do you know, I've collected twelve pounds from your guests for a new organ,' I informed George and Pam as Rebecca and I helped them clear up.

'We're not inviting you again, if you scrounge off our visitors,' Pam laughed. 'Just think how much money he'll collect at our wedding reception, George!'

'I didn't ask for a penny, honestly,' I protested, rising to Pam's teasing. 'They just kept pushing money on to me!'

'Oh, David, come on. That cultivated, wan look, those slightly tatty cuffs, the oil stains and cycle-clip marks on your turn-ups,' she teased. 'You're appealing before you even open your mouth. "Poor vicar," they'll think, "stuck out here in the middle of nowhere, so witty yet so overlooked. Let's give him some money. Let's assuage our guilt about neglecting the Church." "Just wan look, that's all you gave to me!"' she trilled, parodying a recent pop song.

'Pam, just behave yourself!' George chided. 'I'm really pleased that you've got the money, David. Let's strike whilst the iron is hot and get a replacement for that farting harmonium!'

'Where on earth do you start looking for one?' Pam asked.

'Oh, they're all over the place,' George said, expansively. 'I like to read the "For Sale" columns in the *York Evening Press*, gives me a bit of relaxation after studying some obscure Latin text. There are always three or four organs stashed away in Grandma's living room or Uncle's attic that some relative is trying to get rid of.'

'I didn't know they had organs in Roman times,' quipped Pam.

'No, in the *York Press* not in the Latin text, you dolt!' George laughed, grabbing Pam around the waist and tickling her. 'How you ever conned people into thinking you had the wit to be a teacher...'

'Yes, well, I got found out eventually, so they demoted me to be your housekeeper, good sir,' she mocked, as they both laughed delightedly. I coughed, feeling that Rebecca and I were intruding on their foolery.

'Let's have an organ expedition,' George suggested, positively bursting with enthusiasm. 'We've got next Saturday free if you have, David.'

'Yes, I don't think I've got anything on,' I replied. Weddings tended to be few and far between. Even if I married off every single inhabitant of the Withs, I'd still have a few Saturdays free.

'Great, perhaps you'd like to come as well, Rebecca,' Pam added. 'It would do you good to get away from this forlorn and faraway place, not to mention all that marking. We could take the estate, have the children with us as well, and make it a real family picnic...'

Saturday 25 June

Five days later, early on Saturday morning, a heavily laden Cortina crawled out of Kirkwith. George was driving, I sat beside him with a map and the *Evening Press* on my knee. Rebecca and Pam with the newly baptized Simon on her knee, squeezed into the back seat. Emma, Peter and Sally sprawled out with the picnic basket on the estate floor, looking out of the tailgate window at the sleeping village receding behind them. It was Emma's thirteenth birthday, so the trip was part of her birthday treat. She eagerly unpacked her presents en route, duly passing them over her shoulder for inspection by the adults. 'Oh Pam, that's simply wonderful,' she cried, unwrapping a gold necklace. 'How did you know that's just what I wanted?' She leaned over the back seat and gave her prospective stepmother a kiss, both spontaneous and genuine. It augured well for their future relationship that the children had fallen in love with Pam long before George had been smitten by her.

After an hour's drive we pulled up at Kirkham Abbey, just south of Malton, and breakfasted on marmalade sandwiches and boiled eggs in the summer morning sunshine. We had a reminder of home in that the ruined monastery nestles on the banks of the same River Derwent which flows by the Withs, but younger here by thirty miles. The place provided an enchanting stop, set in a wooded valley by a railway line with a level crossing and signal box. Little diesel trains frequently trundled through, packed with trippers bound for Scarborough, wishing away the minutes until they arrived at their seaside destination, oblivious to the beauty they were encountering on the way. The children fervently waved at the trains, and then ran up and down the abbey's drainage channels and tunnels, deep and wide and set in stone. 'Dad, are these channels still used?' Sally piped up.

'Mercifully not,' George replied, with his usual dry humour, 'otherwise you lot certainly wouldn't be travelling any further with us!'

'Yes,' Rebecca added. 'And since we live downstream, we can all be glad that the days have long since gone when they carried the monks' effluent into the river.'

'Pam, what's effluent?' Peter asked innocently.

'Waste water, dear,' answered Pam, well used to heading off primary children's embarrassing enquiries.

Much refreshed, we drove down into Malton for our first appointment. Despite the early hour there was already a traffic jam of cars bound east for the first day of their holiday, their passengers bright and cheery, as well as a traffic jam of cars bound west, returning home after their week away, their passengers looking weary and glum. We nuzzled through the town, past a thriving cattle market, and after driving up and down a few minor streets, found our first organ of the day.

It was in a terraced house pleasantly set above the town, with a gorgeous outlook which took in the whole span of the Wolds from their rising at Garrowby right across to their fall into the North Sea. 'What a wonderful view!' I enthused to the house-holder, a certain Mrs Ruswarp.

'Oh yes, I suppose so,' she said, casting the beautiful Wolds a perfunctory glance, as if she'd never really noticed them before, nor would bother to cast her eye on them ever again. 'You'll have to speak up, I'm a bit deaf.'

'Could Rebecca play the organ, please, to

try it out?' I shouted.

'Dry it out?' she bellowed. 'But it's not wet. It's lower down in t' town where they get flooded out, never up here. Never once in the sixty years I've been here. That organ's perfectly sound, so don't you try pretending there's something wrong with it just to try and beat t' price down.'

'No, of course not,' I replied, beaming an inept smile at her. It was a mannerism which I often resorted to, which went down rather well with a dog collar. Unfortunately I'd forgotten that today I was in civvies, so the smile by itself without the mediation of clerical attire sent quite the wrong signal.

'Is he not right in t' head or somert?' Mrs Ruswarp bluntly asked Rebecca.

'Oh, normally he's OK,' she replied, speaking slowly and deliberately. 'I think he's just suffering from motion sickness. We've had a long drive.'

'Well, don't let him be sick on my carpet, that's all I say. It's as good as new, only laid twenty years ago,' she shouted, fixing me with a queer look.

'No, don't you worry,' said Rebecca, reassuringly. 'Could I have a play of your organ, please?'

'Yes, go ahead, love, it makes a lovely

sound. It were me Auntie Jessie's and she passed it on to me when she died,' Mrs Ruswarp explained. I imagined the good Auntie Jessie rising up from the grave, struggling to carry the massive harmonium, a parting gift to her niece from the hereafter.

Rebecca pulled up a chair, sat at the console, pulled out a few stops and started pumping the pedals. If I wasn't a vicar, I would say that she carried off the whole manoeuvre very sexily. But since I am a vicar, I have to content myself with saying something like she performed the whole set of movements with a natural grace that made my heart miss a beat, and let the reader understand.

However, the harmonium didn't make a single sound, not a note, or a squeak, or a lovesick camel's honk, or a whale's call. Nothing. Rebecca pulled out a few more stops and pumped the pedals more quickly and tried to play again. But again there was nothing. She made a third attempt, pulling out every stop to its very limit and pumping the pedals faster than a cyclist shooting down Garrowby Hill. Still without a single sound.

Mrs Ruswarp gave us a smile that was

positively beatific. 'Lovely sound, absolutely lovely, don't you agree?' she shouted. 'I often play it of an evening. Such a sweet sound. Do you know, I've never had the neighbours complain.'

Despite her labelling me as not quite right in the head, I felt utterly sorry for her, confined by deafness to a near-silent world. And then pity turned to admiration as I realized that she had at least one advantage over us, in allowing things to sound as she wished them to sound.

'Thank you very much, Mrs Ruswarp. It's very kind of you to let us look the organ over,' Rebecca said diplomatically. 'If you don't mind, we'll have a think about it and get back to you if we decide to buy it.'

'Well, don't forget, it's only eight pounds seven and six,' she bellowed, as she showed us the door. 'An absolute bargain with a sweet tone like that. And not a bit of damp,' she concluded, fixing me with an icy stare.

We wended our way out of Malton, driving towards our next port of call at Hovingham, eight miles north. As we had a bit of time to kill, we turned off the main road and had our elevenses overlooking the magnificent house and park of Castle Howard, with a picturesque lake in the foreground. We worked off our coffee and KitKats with a walk around the lake. The children ran ahead, startling the ducks, who took off noisily, slicing the waters in two and rippling the lake's calm surface. Rebecca and Pam, with Simon in her arms, walked ahead of George and me, chatting happily.

'I always think this place would make a marvellous setting for Evelyn Waugh's *Brideshead Revisited,* if they ever made it into a TV series,' George mused.

'Yes, I see what you mean,' I agreed. 'Just the right atmosphere. But our society will have to defrost a heck of a lot before it can take the issues raised in *Brideshead*. I hear the BBC is planning to do Galsworthy's *The Forsyte Saga*. I guess that should be controversial enough!'

George stopped to give a few demonstrations to Peter on how to skim a stone successfully across the lake, and then we carried on walking together. 'I tend to connect this place with Sydney Smith rather than Evelyn Waugh,' I admitted. 'Have you come across him?'

'Not really,' George frowned, with that I'm-trawling-through-the-back-of-my-mind look.

'He was vicar here in the early 1800s and

was a great friend of the Carlisles who reigned here then,' I explained.

'Oh, a parson in his lordship's pocket, was he?' George asked, with a thin smile on his lips.

'Not really,' I explained. 'He actually moved very easily amongst the high and mighty, probably because he was a great wit.' As we walked back towards the car, I entertained George with a few examples. 'He was the one who said, "I never read a book before reviewing it, it prejudices a man so!"'

'Ah, most of the critics who reviewed my books must have taken their cue from him!' George chuckled.

'He was a great one for buildings as well,' I said, as we looked back to the house. 'He poured great scorn on the newly built Brighton Pavilion, claiming that it seemed like St Paul's had gone to the seaside and pupped!'

George giggled with the glee of a teenager. 'But tell me something,' he asked. 'Why did this witty fellow end up here, in this backwater?'

'It's a good question, and one which Sydney Smith was much vexed over,' I answered. 'Eventually he became a canon of St Paul's, but it was a long haul. I guess he'd wounded too many dull but influential people with his rapier wit, and they got their own back by not promoting him.'

'Oh dear, the Church can be a very cruel place,' George commented.

'Yes,' I agreed. 'But quite a lot of the time he was amazingly sanguine about it all, comparing ordination to a ticket in a lottery where becoming a bishop was the rare prize. He reckoned that remote though your chances were of ever being preferred, without that distant prospect no one would ever go to the tremendous trouble of being ordained.'

'That seems a fair assessment,' George shrugged, as he unlocked the car and summoned his children, who were still running around wildly, enjoying the sense of freedom that only a warm spring morning can bring.

We soon arrived in Hovingham, a tiny estate village sandwiched between the Howardian Hills and the North York Moors, which created stunning views to south and north. Pam took the children for a stroll while we called on Mr Eston, who lived in a tiny terraced house in the main street. Mr Eston, a plump and jolly old man, ushered the three of us into a small, low-ceilinged front room. Four adults would have made for a tight squeeze in that tiny place at the best of times, but the presence of a huge Wurlitzer-type organ meant that we had about as much room to manoeuvre as a rugby team in a telephone kiosk. Toes were trodden on, elbows dug into solar plexuses as we tried to edge around each other.

The situation was considerably relieved when the rotund Mr Eston removed himself from the scrum and sat at the organ stool. 'Let me give you a tune,' he cheerily announced, flicking several switches. The organ whirred into life, the console glided up out of its casing, surrounded by a row of gaudily coloured light bulbs, which started flashing on and off in time with the beat. He played a jaunty piece which sounded like a variant of 'The Raggle-Taggle Gypsies'; it was accompanied by an electronic cocktail of drums rolling and cymbals clashing. As the piece progressed, the drums and cymbals crashed ear-splittingly, with the lights like Blackpool illuminations, flickering on and off so fast that they made me feel giddy. The whole room positively reverberated with the cacophony, the candlesticks jigged on the mantelpiece, the china danced on the sideboard, the floorboards throbbed beneath your feet.

And then after the performance had come to its end, a merciful, palpable silence.

'Don't you think she's wonderful?' Mr Eston enthused.

'Er, yes,' I replied. The beat may have stopped, but my poor head was still pounding. 'Yes, truly wonderful. But perhaps not quite what we had in mind.' I shuddered to think of what Doris Harsley would do to the *Nunc Dimittis* when let loose on this monstrosity. The strains of 'To be a light to lighten the Gentiles' would take on new heights, as coloured shadows probed the dark, hallowed corners of Kirkwith Church and pillars which had stayed staid since the Normans were now conscripted into resonating with the beat of drums. 'No, indeed a wonderful instrument, but I don't think our purposes would harness its full potential,' I explained, trying to let Mr Eston down gently.

Pam and the children had exhausted the delights that Hovingham had to offer, and were waiting for us by the car, so we sped off to our final appointment in the market town of Helmsley, keeping our fingers crossed that this time we would find an instrument which was neither mute nor monstrous.

We descended a steep hill, the red roofs of Helmsley stretched out before us, the moors beyond, majestic yet with a dark threat about them even on this sunny day. 'It used to be called Helmsley Blackmoor,' I explained.

'Why?' asked Sally, naturally inquisitive.

'Because of the black moors behind it, silly!' Peter snapped, before I could get a word in.

'But then they dropped the Blackmoor bit when they started trying to attract the tourists,' I joked. 'They thought it might be a bit off-putting.'

'Oh, I don't know,' Rebecca responded, 'I think it sounds rather quaint. Just think of Blackpool: who'd go swimming in a place with a name like that? Or who'd go wandering in a creepy forest called Der Schwarzwald?'

'Yes, but Blackmoor?' George sneered, as he swerved over a winding bridge and dropped down into the town. 'It evokes memories of Heathcliff and all that dour Brontë sort of stuff. I can see why they scrapped it.'

'No, I agree with Rebecca, I think it sounds rather romantic, in a perverse sort of way. They should have kept it,' Pam said, casting her vote.

Having agreed to quit at deuce in our retaining v. dropping Blackmoor doubles match, we trailed up to the castle for a picnic lunch. Apparently the place had been half knocked down by cannonballs, fired by Roundheads piqued that it was a Royalist stronghold. Yet it still stood proud and dwarfed every other dwelling in the town. Except, that is, for the parish church, whose smoke-blackened tower vied with the castle's keep for supremacy, a cheeky golden cockerel pivoting on its roof, crowing the ultimate victory of Church over State. Or so it liked to pretend.

From our eyrie high above the town, we looked down on the blue pall of smoke which hung over the place. 'Look at all those chimneys!' Peter exclaimed. 'It's just like Mary Poppins, on the rooftops of London.' Like a budding Julie Andrews, Pam led a chorus of 'Chim, chiminy, chim, chiminy, chim, chim, cheree,' with George doing a mean impersonation of Dick Van Dyke at the end: 'The rooftops of Helmsley, cor, what a sight!'

During lunch Sally and Peter occupied themselves with counting the chimneys:

only those with wisps of smoke spiralling upwards qualified for the census, but even then they counted fifty-two pots pothering into the atmosphere beneath us.

And that on a warm summer day! 'Ee, it's good to breathe in this 'ere country air,' Pam jested, her eyes sparkling with fun.

Lunch over, we left the castle behind us and risked descent into the town's hazy plains. We wound our way to yet another terraced house, opposite the beck. Leaving Pam and the children to watch the dozen or so ducklings who paddled up and down stream, George and Rebecca and I stooped as we entered through a low door and were shown into a back room. There against the wall stood a nicely proportioned harmonium, thankfully not a Wurlitzer, with no hint of coloured bulbs or rising consoles or any other of the electrical gimmicks which had assailed us in Hovingham. The only odd detail was that fixed above the organ was a massive red firebell, at least a foot in diameter.

'It were me mother's,' Mr Norton, the organ's owner, explained. He was broad-shouldered and tall, an unfortunate impediment in a house with low ceilings and low doors. 'Apparently it started out life in

Australia, but then me mother's family had it shipped over here for her to practise on. She used to play t' organ at chapel up at East Moors.'

'Do you think my fiancée could have a play?' I asked.

'Fine, be my guest,' Mr Norton agreed, sliding back the lid.

George and I held our breath as Rebecca pulled out a few stops, pumped the pedals and brought her nimble hands down on the keyboard. We were treated neither to silence nor to an ear-splitting electronic timpani, but to a sweet if slightly reedy rendition of 'The Old Rugged Cross' which she then merged with 'The Green, Green Grass of Home'. As she played she gave me a minx-like grin. 'I thought this would bring back happy memories of the old people's home, David.'

'I think you've got the tune wrong, love. "T' Old Rugged Cross" doesn't go quite like that. Shift over and let me have a try,' Mr Norton suggested, excluded from our little joke.

Rebecca duly complied and Mr Norton took over, showing us what the harmonium was capable of. Strings vied with trumpets, tuba vied with piccolo to give a distinctly impressive performance. At last we were on to a winner.

'How much do you want for it, Mr Norton?' I asked as the hymn came to its merciful end.

He thought for a moment, scratching his head before eventually replying, 'I know it's old, but it's a bit of a family heirloom. So I reckon on four to five pounds.'

'That's very reasonable, very reasonable indeed. And the harmonium seems just the ticket. Will you accept four pounds ten shillings?' I asked, smiling because success seemed to be almost in the bag, at last.

'Four pounds ten shillings, four pounds ten shillings?' he growled, rising up from the organ stool and towering over us. 'Where the heck did you get that price from?'

'From you,' I stammered. 'You just said that you'd accept "four to five pounds."'

'I never did. I said FORTY-FIVE pounds not four to five pounds. I think you need your ears syringing out, sunshine!'

At that moment the large firebell went off, clanging so loudly that any wax in my ears would have instantly shifted. 'Bloody hell!' Mr Norton exclaimed. 'There's a fire somewhere. I'm an auxiliary fireman and that's station summoning me. I'll have to be off.

Me missus is in t' back garden, have a word with her if you want the thing.' Donning his jacket, he tore out of the house and hared down the road, shouting back at us, 'But it's forty-five pounds, mind you, not a penny less.' He rapidly disappeared into the distance, pursued by similarly muscular men sprinting to their fire duty.

We postponed summoning 'me missus' for a moment or two while we discussed the sharp inflation affecting the organ market. 'Well,' said George, 'a good harmonium in the hand is worth twenty-five in the *Evening Press* "For Sale" column. We could spend weeks traipsing round, getting nowhere. Let's go for this one, even if the price just went up ten times before our very eyes.'

Rebecca and I agreed, so we summoned Mrs Norton and made the deal there and then. We explained that the organ was to be installed in Kirkwith Church and put down a fiver as deposit. I promised to send Bill Everingham with the rest of the money when he came to pick up the thing in his farm truck later in the week. 'With just one condition,' I asked, as we prepared to leave.

'What?' said Mrs Norton, looking worried

'That you don't include that wretched firebell in the deal!'

My joke slightly backfired, in that it opened the floodgates. 'Do you know,' she confided, deadly serious, 'I've been trying to get rid of that wretched bell for years. Rest of t' firemen have telephones, but oh no, we have to have that antiquated thing spoiling our living-room wall and making enough noise to wake the dead. Are you sure I can't persuade you to take it away?'

'How much will you give to make it worth our while?' I asked, tongue in cheek.

'Oh, the going rate, about four to five pounds!' she replied, laughing.

It was our turn to look deadly serious. 'How did you know that that's the price we thought your husband said?' Rebecca asked.

'Oh, he's been trying that trick on for years, naming a giveaway price to whet people's appetites and then, when they were hooked, telling 'em they'd heard him wrong. He's an absolute so-and-so that man of mine, believe you me,' she admitted.

'Tell you what,' she continued. 'Seeing that it's for t' church you can knock ten pounds off t' price. Just get your church-warden to bring thirty pound when he calls.'

'But won't your husband mind? He was pretty adamant about the forty-five,' I replied.

'Well, I'll tell him you thought that included firebell, and I had to reduce t' price when you realized that wasn't part of t' bargain. That'll teach the bugger for hanging on to the outmoded thing all these years!'

She signed a receipt for us 'to make it all proper' and we hastily left Helmsley, before she had the chance to change her mind. We drove north, climbing up a sharp bank out of the town, and then dropped equally sharply into a hidden valley, pine trees clinging on to its steep sides by the fingertips of their roots. Another ruined abbey, but prouder than Kirkham, sprang out of the flat valley bottom – all three children gasped as we rounded the bend and saw it majestically poised there before us. Sally had trouble saying the name of the place, chanting 'Reevox, Rivers, Ryeforks, Rev. Forks,' but never quite getting her tongue around Rievaulx, its proper name.

Peter, like every ten-year-old, had just discovered vulgarity, and so was particularly taken with deliberately misreading the signs to the Fratery, having overheard his incautious father complaining about Kirkwith's farting harmonium. 'Did the monks have to eat a lot of baked beans?' he giggled, running off into one of Rievaulx's many distances before we could reply.

Emma, admirably aloof from the rantings of her younger brother and sister, wandered off alone and stood at the entrance to the long, roofless church, with a faraway look in her eye, a young girl teetering on the edge of adulthood, taking in the building's span and her life's span in one misty gaze.

Simon, with Pam holding on to his right hand and George holding on to his left, stomped around the Chapter House, disturbing the monks buried there, who had never once expected a child to invade their hallowed ground and shatter their slumbers.

Nor had they ever expected a priest to wander through the place arm in arm with his fiancée. 'Hallo,' I said, my lips brushing Rebecca's cheek. 'Good to have you alone at last!'

'Yes, it's a nice change to find a church building allowing us space for each other rather than driving us apart,' she replied, her eyes dancing with amusement.

'I'm sorry,' I answered, suddenly catching a glimpse of our married future: Rebecca sitting in church, alone, for months and months of Sundays, with every eye in the place fixed on her, Mrs Vicar, noting her every whim of fashion, her every grimace, her every smile. In my mind's eye I looked down from the pulpit and saw her trying to hush our children as the congregation tutted, resentful that a baby's cry prevented their minds wandering off during the vicar's sermon. In my mind's eye I looked down from the pulpit and saw her sitting there season in and season out, smiling at her husband's little jokes, jokes that she had heard a thousand times before, nodding at her husband's sage wisdom, for her so passé. In my mind's eye I looked down from the pulpit and saw her blonde hair gradually turning grey, her smooth face gradually crossed with wrinkles, getting old as I was getting old. I shivered.

'What's the matter?' Rebecca asked, concerned.

'Oh nothing, really,' I explained. 'They're weird places, these abbeys, with their ghosts of past and future. I was just thinking whether you realized what you were taking on, all that parish life and me to boot.'

'Mm, forty years in a moorland parish,' Rebecca quipped, quoting the title of a local tome. 'It sounds pretty grim, doesn't it, forty garden parties, forty Lents, forty

Circum, Circum, Circumcisions of our Lord...' she laughed. She had been there that fateful New Year's Day, and had added to my embarrassment.

'Actually it's fifteen times forty, er, six hundred Circum, Circum, Circumcisions of our Lord,' I corrected. 'I fear we're in for a painful life!'

'But we'll be together and we'll have such fun!' Rebecca breezed, swinging me round and round in sheer glee. 'Forty Easters and forty Christmases, forty Whit Sundays and forty Harvests, these are a few of my favourite things...' she trilled, parodying 'My Favourite Things' from *The Sound of Music*. 'And lives are always like that when you tot up what lies ahead. Just think of me, marking twenty thousand German exams and directing twenty thousand German policemen to York Minster!'

'All singing Beethoven's *Ode to Joy* as they merrily thronged the streets of York,' I laughed as her lightness of touch banished the morbid.

On our way back we called in at York to treat Emma to a fish and chip party. It was a birthday to remember, feeling as if we had taken in the whole of Yorkshire in one span, and most of its musical repertoire to boot.

And we were just some of the many to be saved by the fireman's bell, though not quite in the way the devious Mr Norton envisaged.

Wednesday 29 June

'He couldn't sing in tune, he couldn't read Latin very well, his writing looked like the trail of a spider who had had a wild night, fallen into an ink bottle and crawled home. In fact every job a monk had, he was useless at, absolutely useless. Yes, Sharon?' I was taking yet another assembly at Eastwith School, and before Sharon Dubbins' interruption, had been building up to my grand finale.

'I don't believe anybody would run away from the circus to work for the church,' the incredulous Sharon informed her schoolmates. 'I can see how someone would run away from the church to join the circus. I think you've got the story the wrong way round.'

'Sir, sir,' the ever-naughty Paul Broadley shouted, straining his hand so high that if it had had a brush at the end of it, he could have painted the school hall ceiling.

'Yes, Paul,' I said, trying to mask my impatience.

'We went to see the circus at York in the Easter holidays,' he blurted out.

'And did you see any acrobats?' I asked, attempting to recover my story's theme.

'No,' he admitted. 'But we saw some elephants. One did a poo in the middle of the ring. It were steaming and the pile was as high as one of t' dwarfs.'

'Paul!' Miss South shouted. And then for a moment she hesitated, uncertain whether to correct his bad grammar or chastise him for being indelicate. She bravely but perhaps unwisely opted for the former. 'It was steaming, not were steaming, Paul. All of you, for goodness sake, be careful to speak properly,' she stressed, in her best teacherly voice. Geoff Goodmanham's shoulders started shaking, and he blew his nose loudly to conceal his mirth.

'Sir,' Sally Broadhurst shouted. 'We saw an elephant when we went to the zoo which had five legs, two at the front and three at the back. And it was ever so lively. It kept trying to ride on the back of the other elephants.'

'It must have been his tail, dear,' Miss South informed her, unflustered. 'Now shall we all listen very carefully and hear the rest of this lovely story that Mr Wilbourne is telling us. Hands down please, children.'

'Well, as I was saying,' I continued, feeling a long way away from my original story, 'this acrobat felt very sad, because he wanted to give all his time to God, but could do nothing right. Every way he tried to worship God went wrong. And then he thought, "What I'll do is to offer God the thing I'm good at." So late at night he sneaked down to the monastery chapel, which was in darkness...'

'Oo, spooky!' Lee Moss wailed.

'Be quiet, Lee, or you'll get the cane,' Miss South barked, her renowned patience obviously under strain.

'And in front of the altar, he performed his acrobatics, offering God the very skill that he was good at. He tumbled and did handstands and cartwheels and somersaults, just like this...' This was to be my *pièce de résistance*. At my instruction, Geoff had placed a PE mat before me and I leapt up off my chair, sprang on to the mat and did a forward somersault, followed by a backward somersault, and then sprang up again and clapped my hands above my head.

The only trouble was, much as I had enjoyed this activity as a child, I had forgotten I wasn't quite as agile as I used to be, and sprang back up just a wee bit too quickly before the blood had had a chance to return to my head. Dizzy, I reeled around the front of the hall, careered into the piano and landed up in the lap of the redoubtable Miss South, sitting at the piano stool keeping an eagle eye on her charges. Surprised by an assault from an unexpected quarter, and not used to having clergymen, or any other men for that matter, perch on her knee, Miss South exclaimed, 'Good heavens, Mr Wilbourne, what on earth do you think you are doing?' as if I was some naughty child in Reception.

'I think the acrobat must have been at the Communion wine,' Lee Moss shouted out.

'Lee Moss, that's your last warning,' Miss South shouted, regaining her composure as she brushed out the creases in her tweed skirt. Geoff was busy blowing his nose once again.

I resumed a rather wobbly stance at the front of the school and brought my story to its conclusion. 'The acrobat did this night after night. Obviously he was far better at it than I am. Cartwheels, handstands, somersaults, tumbling...'

'You're good at tumbling, sir!' Paul Broadley interrupted.

'Paul Broadley, you'll be getting the cane too, if you don't watch out,' Miss South thundered.

'The acrobat did proper tumbling, not my kind of tumbling,' I continued. 'Night after night he performed his offering to God. But one night the Abbot, the head monk, came into chapel to get a book he'd left there and discovered him leaping about in front of the altar. "Disgraceful!" he thought. "Such things should not be allowed in our holy chapel." He was just about to tell him off, when a strange thing happened.'

'Did the acrobat land in his lap like you did in Miss South's?' David Harsley asked innocently. Geoff started blowing his nose loudly again.

'No, David. But the Abbot watched as the acrobat sat down to get his breath back. He was about to come out of the shadows and tell him off, but was absolutely amazed when a statue of the Virgin Mary, Jesus' mum, smiled at the acrobat and slowly came down from her pedestal, her stand. She took out her handkerchief and gently wiped the acrobat's sweating brow. The

Abbot realized that this was a sign that God was pleased with the acrobat for offering to him what he was best at, and so didn't tell him off after all. The lesson for us is that we can't be good at everything, but that each of us is good at something, and should offer that to God as a thank you for giving us the skill in the first place.'

'I'm good at carrying bales,' Sharon Dubbins, star of the Howden Agricultural Show, blurted out. 'But I can't see how I can offer that to God. Them lot as goes to church wouldn't be very pleased if I started luggin' bales into the place and gerrin' straw on their precious carpets.'

'Getting, dear, not gerrin',' Miss South corrected, back on form.

'No, Sharon,' I said, laughing at her straightforward manner, and also at her description of my clearly off-putting congregation. 'But if you're good at carrying, you could help people who are poorly, or too weak or old to carry much, and offer that to God.'

'I'm good at football,' Lee Moss informed us. 'But you wouldn't want me to play footie in church. A couple o' years ago I was playing near the graveyard and my ball accidentally hit one of them stained-glass windows. T' churchwarden came out and started 'ollerin' at me somert rotten...'

'Hollering at you something rotten,' Miss South translated.

'Well, it was,' Lee continued, unabated. 'You should have heard his language. I thought church people weren't supposed to swear.'

'I suppose the stained glass was someone else's offering to God, so we've got to be careful not to spoil other people's gifts,' I explained. 'Even so, when you play your football in a safer place, you can thank God for the tackling and the shooting and the saving, for all those skills, for being able to run, free and fast, as you whizz around the field.'

'I haven't got any skills,' David Harsley said in a very sad little voice. '"You're good for nothing, our David," my grandma told me. I'd got the wrong shoes on the wrong feet again.'

'David, that was very wrong of your grandma,' Geoff said, in a quiet voice. 'As you grow older you'll have lots and lots of things you're good at. For instance, I've never known a child as good at maths as you are. You just tell your grandma that, and offer all those sums to God, as Mr Wilbourne was saying.'

'Sir, if I offer all my sums to God, will he make them right?' Sharon Dubbins shouted out, stumping me with a real poser.

'I'm sure God will help you to think clearly,' I replied lamely. 'Anyway, let's leave it there. Miss South, we'll sing the hymn "All things bright and beautiful".'

'I know God pulled off some pretty big miracles, dividing the Red Sea, toppling the walls of Jericho and raising Lazarus and all that stuff, but really, David, getting Sharon Dubbins to think clearly?! You don't half have a lot of faith in this God of ours,' Geoff Goodmanham laughed as he took me over to the school house for a cuppa during break. 'But if you're into miracles, I wanted to try out an idea with you that June and I have been hatching for a while.'

'Fire away,' I said, as we settled around the kitchen table, Elizabeth asleep in her pram, June bustling around us, preparing lunch. The kitchen was standard antiquated, like almost every other kitchen in Eastwith. A pot sink, its original white stained with decades of limescale, lead piping which seemed to orbit the entire room, a free-standing electric cooker, the floor of stone flags, with a few mats scattered about, plasterwork crumbling, windows and back door ill-fitting. June worked hard to make the place hospitable, feel like home. But still, not a good place to bring up a child. 'I really ought to get the church to improve the place,' I thought, as I thought every time I stepped into their home.

I could hear my Texan airman's denunciations ringing in my ears: 'Reverend, you don't expect such a promising teacher to live in this squalor, do you? You should be thoroughly ashamed of yourself.' The trouble was, most homes in the parish were squalid and deserved renovation. I felt like the proverbial mosquito in a nudist colony: so much to do, I didn't know where to begin. At least we were making a beginning with the almshouses, although how we would raise the remaining £800 defeated me.

'David, you're miles away,' Geoff complained. 'You've got that faraway look in your eyes that the older lads in my class have when we try to get stuck into some maths problems.'

'Sorry,' I apologized. 'I was actually thinking that it was about time we had this kitchen done up, so I hope you'll be lenient with me over my mental lapse, sir.'

Geoff and June laughed, although I noticed her ears prick up when I mentioned home improvements. 'Anyway,' said Geoff, 'I was saying about the kids around here needing their experience of life broadening. It's obviously a lovely place to live, very secure, with the countryside offering lots of opportunities for play. But I'm worried that when they grow up and move away, the hustle and bustle of city life will overwhelm them. Just going to secondary school in Selby or York will be a tremendous shock, an ocean compared to this little pond of a school that the children have been used to.'

'Yes, I can see that,' I agreed. 'But I'm not sure whether we can do much about it.'

'Well, June had a marvellous idea about an end-of-term activity, didn't you, darling?' Geoff gestured to his wife, inviting her to take up the tale where he had left off.

'To cut a long story short,' June explained, barely able to constrain her excitement, 'we thought we'd take the older children to London for a week, let them see the sights, be excited by our swinging capital that is just a bit more lively than round here.'

'Wow, goodness me!' I exclaimed. 'You're certainly aiming high. It's a bit of a leap from the Withs to London. But I'm sure with the planning and the careful preparation you two are renowned for, you'll pull it off. When do you plan to go?' I expected them to be looking to the next year or even the year after.

'In the third week of July, the last week of this term,' Geoff answered. 'We thought London in the grip of World Cup fever would be just the ticket for the children. We might even have a trip to Wembley, although we'd be home before the World Cup final. We wouldn't miss your garden party for the world!'

'Well, you've certainly got high ambition, wanting to carry through a project like that so soon,' I replied. 'I hope you don't think I'm pouring cold water on your good idea, but I'm just a bit worried how these very, very rustic children will cope with the big city. You don't think it would be wiser to lower your sights a bit?'

'What alternative do you suggest?' Geoff asked, bringing his dry sense of humour to the fore. 'A day trip to Salvington, or Selby, or a couple of nights in Leeds? It's got to be London or nothing,' he enthused.

'Yes, I can see that,' I agreed. 'But I still wonder about the children coping. How many do you intend to take?'

'The fourteen from the top class as well as baby Elizabeth,' Geoff explained.

'And how many adults?'

'Just June and I,' said Geoff, smiling fondly at his wife. 'It'll be our little family.'

'Not so little, in fact quite a handful of children for the two of you, and a baby to boot. I can see how it could be a terrific success. I just don't want you to take on too much,' I said. I was beginning to sound like the murder board of my church council, although I didn't like the role of being a wet blanket one little bit. But my concern was simply that I was worried for a couple for whom I felt a great tenderness.

'That's why we're telling you about it,' June said, with an ominous edge to her voice. 'We were wondering if you would come along as well. We felt your experience in darkest East Hull...'

'and an even darker Cambridge...' Geoff added, mischievously.

'...would be terribly useful, and could bring a bit of urban common sense into areas where country kids were a bit naïve. What do you say?' she concluded.

'When did you say you were going?' I asked, getting out my *Parson's Pocket Book*, which as well as being a diary also included exciting things such as magazine subscription lists, visiting lists, sick lists with a column for ticks for successful visits, parish accounts, altar requisites, and daily Bible readings. It was a veritable Filofax before its time, but it so weighed down my jacket pocket that I invariably leaned to the right, a novel experience for socialist old me.

'Monday the twenty-fifth to Friday the twenty-ninth of July,' said the ever-efficient June. 'As Geoff said, we'd be safely back in time for the garden party. Do say you can come.'

I thought for a moment. 'Well, I've got nothing else booked for that week. And it would get me out of the cake-stall ladies' hair and all the last-minute panic about cream going sour and what to price the scones.' And then, adopting a more serious tone, I added, 'Actually, I'd love to come. It sounds as if we'll have a great week together.'

Geoff and June did a jig of celebration around the kitchen table, while I secretly wondered just what I had let myself in for.

JULY 1966

Tuesday 5 July

'Idol vice, idol vice, you look happy to see me,' Becky Ludlow trilled, as she sat beside me. 'Ee, Vicar, I'm right looking forward to seeing t' *Sound of Music*. Those songs are never off my lips, so it'll be nice to see how they set them in real life.'

'So you've heard them already?' I asked, rather stupidly. Alongside 'World Cup Willie', everyone in Britain was crooning the ballads from the Rodgers and Hammerstein hit musical. Although no one had adapted them quite as well as Becky Ludlow.

'I am sixty, going on seventy, I guess I'm quite naïve,' she warbled. Her performance was accompanied by the drone of Ron Ran Run's vintage bus as it wended its way towards Leeds. The twenty-nine-seater bus was packed full of women from the Withs, stalwart members of the Mothers' Union, out for their annual trip. It was a warm, humid summer's day, with the sun blazing on the bus's windows, frying us all. Every window in the sweltering bus was jammed shut and hadn't been opened in living memory. Close inspection of the windows revealed that it wasn't because of wear and tear that the openers didn't work – they had been deliberately screwed tight into the bus's coachwork, making a seal as effective as the window in a glass-bottomed boat.

When I first encountered the local bus service, I'd commented on this strange feature to Sam Harsley. 'Ay, Ron deliberately screwed 'em shut when he first acquired the bus in 1935,' he had explained. 'He runs the service on a shoe- string, so he tries to save money wherever he can. They gobble up the fuel, those old buses do, so he drives them as slow as possible and never puts the heaters on, even in the severest winter. In 1947 and 1963 there were icicles on your nose by the time t' bus got you to York, believe you me,' Sam had laughed. 'Our freezin' churches were warm in contrast with Ron's ice-cold bus.'

'But I still don't understand why he screwed the windows down,' I'd objected.

'Well, he's a bit quaint is Ron. He has this theory that a bus is like a storage radiator, which works over t' seasons. You build up a store of heat in t' summer which lasts you through t' cold winter. So you want to let as little of it out as possible. Hence the screwed-down windows.' Sam's moustache had bristled with pride, and he had looked as pleased with himself as a budding scientist proving the laws of thermodynamics from first principles.

Given the bus's hothouse effect, I had dressed appropriately for today's trip, just a short-sleeved clerical shirt, light flannel trousers, bare feet in sandals, but even then I boiled. The ladies of the Mothers' Union were all trussed up in their weighty woollen winter coats, fastened tightly, their garb completed by thick scarves coiled around their necks and substantial hats wedged over their ears. Not one of them shed a single layer. The face of every one of them was bright red. If you could see a brow under the massive brims of their massive hats, it positively glistened with perspiration. As the journey progressed, there was a definite and unmistakable bouquet, which put me in mind of the Lifebuoy soap advert: 'B.O.!' I felt like whispering to each Mothers' Union member. Not that it would have had any effect, since they always dressed like this, come rain or shine. Why on earth, when they knew what Ron's bus was like, they didn't don cooler garb, absolutely defeated me.

'High on the 'ill there's a lonely goat turd!' Becky Ludlow sang.

'She's not a proper member,' I heard someone behind whisper cruelly. 'She never had any children, you know. They only let her in 'cos the vicar said she needed a bit o' company.'

I seethed as well as boiled. Every woman on that Mothers' Union trip was well past childbearing age; in fact many of their children were well past childbearing age too, so if being an actual mother of young children was a qualification for being a member, none of them passed. And in my mind's eye, I saw hundreds and hundreds of children file past Becky Ludlow as day after day she served them with the most nourishing and delicious meals, and mothered every single one of them. In my book, she qualified to be a 'proper member' with flying colours.

As we chugged along to see *The Sound of Music*, my mind switched to another film, *Goodbye Mr Chips*, starring Robert Donat as a long-serving schoolmaster.

Nearly everyone in the cinema had wept as his wife had died in childbirth. Nearly everyone in the cinema had wept as he died. By his bedside, a colleague whispered, 'He never had any children, you know.' In the dream of death Mr Chips saw the myriad boys he had taught and fashioned, and as he breathed his last gave a smile which was positively beatific. Becky Ludlow was the Withs' Mrs Chips, and in my view had an honoured place on our trip that day.

Mrs Riccall – she of the haunted Landings and many children – had told me how she had bravely gone along to one or two Mothers' Union meetings in the village hall, dragging her children along with her. I had come across her, yet again, wearily making for home, weighed down with heavy shopping and children straggling across the road, and had stopped to lend a hand.

She had chatted on as we walked. 'We were a minute or two late the first time, Vicar. As I dragged my kiddies through the doors, every head in the hall turned towards us, their eyes boring holes in us, as if to say "What are you lot doing here?" I stared them out, because after all, you'd told me the Mothers' Union was there to support people like me, mums with their hands full.

My hands were a bit full that afternoon, keepin' the bairns quiet, I can tell you. The little ones were quite good, considering. They had this speaker, a woman who was barely audible, whispering about how to embroider church linen. Not exactly fascinating stuff for the under-fives, I'm afraid. I kept the baby quiet by feeding her, quite discreetly, mind you. But I heard someone tut, and a stage whisper, "Some women are so backward. You'd think she'd have progressed to bottle-feeding by now."'

After a couple of weeks one of the members, decked in the customary thick coat and hat, had taken her aside: 'Perhaps, dear, it would be better if you came when the children are a wee bit older. Some of our members are a trifle frail and a bit deaf, and can't hear the speaker when there are children around.' Mrs Riccall had called it a day after that.

I thought of the women who made up the Mothers' Union, people like Doris Harsley, Ivy Weighton, Hannah Everingham, individuals with characters that were absolutely golden. As a group they could be golden too, but so often this was tinged with an unconscious cruel streak that could wound people like Mrs Riccall and Becky Ludlow.

The bus queued for about half an hour in the customary jam in Selby, the traffic slowed up by the toll bridge over the Ouse. We crept slowly towards the river, Ron paid his 9d to a man standing in the middle of the road, the bus juddered as we drove over the rickety planks of the bridge, with even the welded window fastenings threatening to shake loose, and then we were across and speeding on our way.

Speeding on our way is perhaps a bit of an exaggeration as far as Ron's creaky bus was concerned, but even so we still had lots of time in hand to get to our destination, the Mecca Cinema in Leeds. Several hours in fact. 'Is it the matinee performance we're booked in to?' I asked Becky Ludlow. 'Otherwise, we'll have a few hours to kill in Leeds.'

'No, Vicar, er, David, er, Vicar, it's the evening performance,' Ivy Weighton shouted from across the aisle, confused as to how to address me in public. 'Haven't you had your programme? We've got a few other things planned.'

'No,' I confessed. 'I thought we were going straight to see the film and then coming home again.'

'No that would be far too tame,' Doris

Harsley shouted breathlessly, tuning in to the conversation from her perch at the front of the bus. 'We're going to look round t' pig factory first and then stop off at a café for fish and chips.'

'A pig factory!' I exclaimed. 'A pig factory? What on earth do we want to go there for?'

'Well, most of our husbands have kept a few pigs over t' years,' Hannah Everingham explained, putting in her sixpennyworth to a conversation which now involved the whole bus. 'They've either had 'em slaughtered at pig factory and then had t' cuts of meat back, or sold 'em to t' pig factory outright. We women thought it would be interestin' to see t' factory's workings.'

'Didn't you used to slaughter your own beasts, Ivy?' Ron shouted, as he steered the chugging bus around a hairpin bend over the A1. I was thinking that that would make one of the most original chat-up lines of all time.

'Ay, we did, but it was a while since. It made such a mess, and it was such a bother cutting everything up,' Ivy explained. 'Last time we did it was in t' war, the very day we heard that Fred's brother had been killed in t' Far East. Blown to smithereens by a landmine, poor lamb. T' vicar, to his credit, was round in a flash to offer his condolences. "We're just cutting up a pig to take his mind off it," I told him, as I let him into kitchen. Poor vicar didn't half go pale. Not that there was that much blood around – I kept wiping table down with t' teatowel. "Would you like a cup o' tea?" I asked him, wiping my hands on t' cloth. "I don't think I'll bother," he replied, goin' even paler. He was even more fussy about hygiene than this one,' she joked, nodding her head towards me.

The bus tittered to a Mothers' Union member as we turned in at the factory gates. Ron parked alongside sundry pig lorries, and as our bus disgorged its perspiring load, sundry pig men bellowed and swore as they drove their load of squealing swine into the massive sties which leant to against the factory wall.

As we hung around in the lorry park, trying to avoid being mistaken for pigs, a gum-chewing individual approached us, sporting a white hat and a white coat stained with blood. 'You'll be t' trip, I suppose,' he declared, looking down at the clipboard he was holding. 'Twenty-eight women and one vicar, is that right? Lucky old vicar, that's what I say!'

We all agreed that that was who we were, and he continued, 'Well, I'm Eric, and I'm goin' to show you round. Mind you, why anybody wants to tour this place, defeats me. None of you is squeamish, is you?' he asked. I was about to put up my hand, but then decided against it, not wanting to appear a wimp in front of my future mother-in-law. 'Right then, we'd better go to t' clockin'-in room, where you can put on your overalls and your 'ats, and then off we go,' he concluded.

Squeezing our way past herds of pro-testing swine and swearing pig men, we followed him into the building, and in the large cloakroom dutifully donned white overalls and hats. I guess the idea was that you took off your normal outdoor clothes first, before slipping the overalls on to your sylph-like figure. But the bell-shaped ladies of our Mothers' Union decided to buck the trend and put them over their own thick overcoats and woolly hats, which made for a certain tightness, to say the least. 'Ee these pig-factory workers must be thin Ivy,' a size eighteen Doris Harsley observed as she heaved herself into a size twelve overall, her usual breathless lack of punctuation forgivable under the circumstances.

'You're right there, Doris,' Ivy Weighton agreed. 'And this 'at won't stay on me head.'

'Perhaps you'd be better taking your own 'at off first, love,' Eric helpfully suggested.

' If you don't mind, young man, I'll leave it on,' Ivy Weighton responded huffily. 'I want a bit o' protection when you show us round t' deep freeze.'

Eric shrugged. 'Suit yourself, dear,' he said. 'I was only trying to 'elp, so keep your 'air on!' The last injunction was hardly necessary, since Ivy Weighton now had her hair firmly held in place by not one but two hats.

We set off for our tour. All twenty-eight women bulged under their overalls with their arms splayed out from their bodies. The tightness of fit made their gait awkward, and they wobbled around like astronauts on a space walk, and drunken astronauts at that. As we slithered along narrow gangways which were splattered with lard and offal, I held a handkerchief over my face to stop me retching from the stench. The rest of the party didn't seem to mind, positively relishing the fetid atmosphere. 'Ee, it takes you back, doesn't it, Hannah?' Ivy Weighton observed, drawing a deep breath and savouring every vapour.

'Ay, reek of a pig-killing, you can't beat it,' Hannah Everingham agreed. 'I remember that aroma from childhood as they cut up t' pig on t' kitchen table. It was a real party of a day, with every inhabitant of Kirkwith popping in and taking a bit o' pork home with them. We'd no fridges or freezers in them days, so we just had to share it out. And then, when one of our neighbours killed a pig, we got some of theirs. It certainly made for variety, since you were never really sure which bit of t' pig you'd been given.'

By now we had reached the abattoir and lined up in a long row along a catwalk, like members of the jury peering down on the accused below. Except that the accused weren't on trial, but were being summarily executed. With mouths agape, we witnessed a steady stream of pigs squealing plaintively for mercy, all strung up on a wire which passed them before our eyes. Then the wire passed each pig through a strong electric field, there was a loud and sharp hum as electrocution finally put them out of their misery, and their limp bodies jerked and twitched a highly charged dance of death.

'Well just look at that one with t' black

face,' Doris Harsley cried excitedly, nudging me to get my attention just when I'd been trying to avert my gaze from the sorry line-up. 'That'll make a juicy joint or two,' she lectured me. 'They always say that t' ones with t' black faces are the most succulent.'

'Nah,' Hannah Everingham chided, 'That's just an old wives' tale. It's ones with t' black trotters not black faces that are t' tenderest. I thought everybody knew that.'

'Never mind all that, by the time electrocution's done its work they all have black faces and black trotters,' Ivy Weighton quite rightly noted. 'You won't be able to tell a juicy joint from a tough one.'

'Ay, it were better in days when we just slit their throat in t' kitchen and collected blood in t' cauldron,' Hannah Everingham exclaimed. 'What do you think, Becky?'

'I think that I'll be giving pork a wide berth at Eastwith School for a few weeks after watching all this carnality, that's what I think,' Becky Ludlow replied, her habit of not quite getting the right word surprisingly introducing an element of the sensuous into our bloody proceedings. 'It's right put me off pig products, let me tell you!'

'What do you expect from someone who's not a proper member?' I heard someone whisper, probably the same malicious person who had done Mrs Ludlow down on the bus. This time I felt they were right to question Mrs Ludlow's qualifications for being a Mothers' Union member. Not because she wasn't sufficiently joyful, or peaceful, or caring, or loving, qualities one would reasonably expect from such an organization. But rather because she clearly didn't have it in her to be sufficiently brutal to relish the carnage that was going on before us. I found it utterly surreal that these stalwart members of my congregation seemed to have more bloodlust than a Colosseum mob on Garrotte-a-Gladiator Day.

We moved off the catwalk and followed Eric into the sorting hall. Some pigs' bodies were being loaded straight into vans to be dispatched whole to local butchers. Others were being chopped up, and as we were led through the factory we followed the process. We saw ham, pork and bacon joints being sealed into plastic bags: I could cope with that. Unmentionable parts of pigs were being ground up and piped into sausage skins: I started feeling slightly queasy. To top it all, there was a vat of evil-smelling stew, far fattier than Grandma Weighton's deluxe version with a couple of church candles thrown in for good measure, which was being distilled into pastry crusts: I felt that if I didn't get out of this place soon, I would throw up. 'It makes your mouth right water seeing those pork pies,' Doris Harsley confided to me. 'I wonder if they'll let us try one?' For the first time in my life, I found myself having massive sympathy for the Jewish and Muslim faiths, primarily for their laudable aversion to swine.

Doris Harsley's wish came true, in that Eric presented each of us with a carrier bag of the factory's products. 'They're a bit past their best,' he explained, 'so I wouldn't let them hang around too much. Maybe you can have a feast on the way home, girls!' Unwisely, I sneaked a look into my carrier bag. There was a joint of pork, dark red in colour, the fat deep yellow. On it nestled a couple of pork pies around which were coiled a string of sausages: 'Salmonella Surprise,' I thought.

Having prised the overalls off themselves, the Mothers' Union members positively bounded for Ron's bus with a spring in their step, like Victorian ladies liberated from over-restrictive corsetry. Once again we had to avoid being mown down by the pigs stampeding around the car park. Having endured the tour round the factory, I had considerable sympathy for the poor beasts, and could only applaud them as they had their last heady gamble before their inevitable and gruesome fate. As we chugged away from that house of death, never have I thanked my God more profusely that he'd made me a man and not a pig.

Our bus crawled through Leeds, pothering out blue exhaust, a vestige of another age in the midst of a concrete city which positively hummed with a Sixties' feel. As we parked outside a fish and chip restaurant, a small crowd gathered, and applauded as we disembarked. 'It's costume dress,' I heard someone say. 'No one ever wears those clothes any more. They must be the audience for The Good Old Days. Look, there's Leonard Sachs!' Someone rushed up to me and asked for my autograph, but went away disappointed when they realized I wasn't the presenter of the Edwardian music-hall TV show.

Twenty-eight ladies, still heavily over-coated and hatted, wound their way up the stairs of the restaurant, bearing their carrier bags from the pig factory. 'We didn't want to leave 'em on t' bus,' Doris Harsley informed me, 'in case we got confused about whose is whose.' She looked into her bag before continuing, 'I've got a good bit o' gammon in 'ere and I don't want to let it out o' my sight.'

We were shown to five tables that had been laid out for us in a corner of the restaurant's upper room. The area looked slightly cramped even before we invaded it, but our corporate bulk enabled it to evolve into a squeeze which would have made the Black Hole of Calcutta seem spacious. Twenty-eight women took off their bulky coats, elbowing each other in concert, and draped them over their chair-backs. The chairs threatened to topple over with the sheer weight of cloth, until they were counterbalanced by twenty-eight bottoms gingerly lowering themselves down on to seats that were too small for one buttock, let alone two. Twenty-eight hats were removed from twenty-eight heads and perched on twenty-eight sideplates. 'You see, Vicar, these bread plates were reluctant anyway, so we might as well make good use of them. We all puts us bread on t' main plates so we can dip up t' fat,' Becky Ludlow kindly explained to me as I raised my eyebrows at the forest of hats which had suddenly sprouted from the tables. Finally, twenty-eight carrier bags, their paper bottoms by now soggy and oozing pigs' blood, were stuffed under the tables, their contents massaged and compressed by twenty-eight pairs of feet, as keen to retain possession as a World Cup player his football. 'You're very unwise not bringing t' bag in with you Vicar', Doris Harsley pointed out. 'By the time Ron's driven round Leeds your pork will be rolling all over bus's floor.' I felt I could live with such a tragic loss.

Twenty-eight women placed their orders of twenty-eight jumbo cod and chips, a pot of tea and a bap. Still feeling decidedly unwell after witnessing the pig cull of the century, I ordered a child's portion. 'A child's portion?' Doris Harsley blurted out. 'You're as thin as a rail already,' she cackled, 'you'll disappear completely if you eat much less.' She shouted across the packed room, 'Ivy you want to get this vicar fed up other-wise he won't survive his wedding night!' I blushed as the whole room burst into laughter, exhaling gales of lardy breath.

Once they had placed their order, twenty-eight women decided they needed the lavatory, so all rose as one, taking their precious carrier bags with them, and stampeded over to the other side of the room, chairs toppling in their wake. I noticed that one or two of the carrier bags were in a really bad way, and were leaving a trail of blood between the tables and the toilets. 'There's only two lavvies,' Doris Harsley shouted out to the twenty-seven-long queue behind her, as well as helpfully informing the rest of the restaurant. 'We'll double up shall we Hannah?' she asked, loudly and perkily, like a child inviting her friend to hitch a ride on the crossbar of her bike.

Doris Harsley and the equally portly Hannah Everingham squeezed themselves into one tiny cubicle and mercifully passed out of our sight, leaving us to conjecture what precise advantage doubling up would have with only a single 'lavvie' between the two of them. I supposed one could be adjusting her dress while the other relieved herself, although I didn't allow my imagination to dwell on such a terrifying spectre. I already feared that for several nights ahead, my sleep would be haunted by those unforgettable horrors we had witnessed in the ham factory So the last thing I needed was for my rest to be further troubled with nightmares of two old ladies cramped into one lavatory.

Twenty-eight women sauntered back from the loo, dragging their carrier bags behind them, their return coinciding with twenty-eight massive portions of cod and chips being set before them, piled high on each plate, and crowned with a bap, evicted by a hat from its rightful place on the bread plate. Twenty-seven of the twenty-eight women tucked in, their appetites undiminished by the wholesale slaughter they had witnessed not an hour before. Only Becky Ludlow picked her way slowly through her meal, slightly queasy like me, for whom a child's portion was more than enough to be going on with.

'These fish and chips are very nice, Ivy,' Doris Harsley blurted out, 'but they'd be even better with a chaser.' Managing to contort her considerable body, she rummaged in the carrier bag beneath her feet and triumphantly brought out a pork pie, simultaneously unravelling the sausages that had got entwined around it and letting them fall back into the bag. 'This'll finish off things just nicely,' she commented, taking a bite out of the crust.

A black-suited gentleman, whom I assumed was the manager, had been observing the commotion, and bustled over to us from the other side of the room. 'Madam, you are not allowed to consume items that haven't been cooked on the premises,' he informed Doris Harsley in stentorian tones.

'But you need a chaser with fish and chips and you don't serve pork pies,' she shouted back.

The manager treated Doris to the full flood of his sarcasm. 'This being a fish and chip restaurant, Madam, and the finest fish and chip restaurant in Leeds at that, you would hardly expect us to serve pork pies, would you?'

'The finest fish and chip restaurant in Leeds and you only have two ladies' lavvies?' Doris replied. 'Finest fish and chip restaurant my eye!'

'The quality of our fish and chips, I am pleased to say, Madam, has nothing whatsoever to do with the quantity of our ladies' lavatories. But it has everything to do with not allowing people to bring their own food in. Will you put that pork pie away, or do I have to ask you to leave?'

'Don't you threaten me with your pettyfogging rules and regulations,' Doris protested. 'I always like a pork pie or something with my fish and chips – it makes them slip down a treat.' She looked around at the other Mothers' Union members, inviting support for her rebellion. 'Why shouldn't we be allowed to indulge ourselves on our annual outing girls?' Looking at the gaggle of grey heads stuffing themselves before me, I felt that girls was a bit of a misnomer.

'We hope everybody who comes here enjoys themselves, Madam,' the manager stressed, realizing he had the whole of the upper room as his audience. 'But they're not my rules and regulations, they're health and hygiene rules imposed by Leeds City Council. They'd close us down if we permitted people to bring in their own pork pies.'

Doris drew a breath before retaliating further. I took my chance and ignoring the injunction from the Book of Proverbs, 'He who interferes in another's quarrel is like the man who grabs a passing dog by the ears,' decided to intervene. On our last outing to Swaledale, Doris had got embroiled with an assistant at a cake shop in Reeth, and had needed me to bail her out before the event escalated into a women's wrestling match. 'I'm very sorry, sir, we don't get up to town much, so we hadn't realized about the regulations. But I notice on your menu that you serve Cornish pasties. I wonder if Mrs Harsley could have one of those to help her get her fish and chips down. Let it be my treat, Doris.'

The manager agreed to the compromise, and strode off to the kitchens to fetch Doris' chaser. Doris unceremoniously doubled herself up again and put the pie, with a bite taken out of it, back in her carrier bag. 'You needn't have bailed me out Vicar I'm quite used to dealing with his sort,' she protested. 'We didn't beat Hitler in the war to have to deal with his like in Leeds.'

'Well, I'm sorry, Doris, but I couldn't see the situation getting any better. And I didn't want us all being thrown out. Just imagine the headline in the *Yorkshire Post*, "Vicar and twenty-eight women evicted from restaurant for unruly behaviour!"'

'I know you were trying to do your best,' Doris conceded. 'I'll just have to eat t' pork pie in t' cinema.' I closed my eyes as I dreaded another confrontation. 'Provided Leeds City Council don't make rules about what you can and can't eat in the dark.'

The manager himself brought Doris' Cornish pasty, which saved the day since the meal passed without further incident.

Twenty-eight women left twenty-eight six-penny tips under twenty-eight saucers and then donned their coats and hats and inevitable carrier bags and bustled out. The manager watched us all as we left, obviously relieved that the visitation of the blessed Withs Mothers' Union had come to its end. He looked a happy man, still mercifully oblivious to the fact that along with a pork pie, several dismembered pigs had been brought on to his premises. Presumably the stains on his restaurant carpets would mean he would not be oblivious for long.

Wednesday 6 July

I woke up the next morning thinking I was reeling from a nightmare, until I realized that the nightmare was real and was called yesterday. Having been duly fed at Leeds' finest fish and chip restaurant, the good ladies of the Mothers' Union and poor old me made for the Mecca Cinema just across the road, picked up our tickets and were shown to our places by an usherette with a torch, since the trailer film had already begun. The cinema was fairly full, but a block of seats had been reserved for us in the centre of the stalls, so twenty-eight burly ladies, still clutching their carrier bags, clambered over the members of the audience who blocked their way. As one carrier bag was dragged over her bare legs, a mini-skirted girl screamed at her boyfriend, 'Oh, Rick, I felt something cold and clammy glide across my thighs!'

'You just keep your hands to yourself, Rick!' some wag shouted from behind.

The affronted Rick turned round. 'Do you want a punch on the nose, Mister? I never touched her!' Why was it that my Mothers' Union caused strife wherever they went?

After the brisk walk from the restaurant, the Mothers' Union ladies were clearly a little warm, so they discarded their coats and scarves, draping them over their seats. This activity effectively curtained off the film, *Andrea Goes to the Andes*, from the people behind, and there were loud shouts of protest. '*And now Andrea, with condors flying above her, is straddling the Andes, South America's mountain range, high above the snow line, searching for the lost home of the Incas,*' the posh-voiced narrator informed us, as a scantily clad Andrea strode over glaciers, oblivious to the sub-freezing temperatures.

'Look, will you lot sit down!' someone else

311

complained, as Doris Harsley struggled to remove her coat. 'You're like a bloody mountain range yourselves, and we can't see over the top of you.'

'I'd rather straddle Andrea than this lot,' the wag chipped in, laughing seedily.

'I'm only taking my coat off so keep your hair on Mister,' Doris retorted, more breathlessly than ever. 'And you,' she shouted at the wag, 'stop making smutty remarks or I'll hit you with this!' She swung her carrier bag threateningly, sprinkling her neighbours with drops of pig's blood.

'*And so we leave Andrea, dreaming of South America, inviting us, the audience, to join her in her dreams,*' the posh narrator tweely concluded.

'We've missed half of that film because of you lot,' the angry man complained. 'All we can do is dream of South America, because we've hardly bloody seen it.'

'Wow! I wouldn't mind joining her in her dreams,' the wag informed all and sundry. 'She wouldn't be dreaming for very long!'

As Doris Harsley again swung her carrier bag threateningly, I decided to intervene, for the second time that evening, to save the day. I placed my hand firmly on Doris' shoulders and forced her into her seat. 'Sit

312

down, Doris, the main film's just about to start. That's what we've come for, so let's not spoil it.'

'Bloody hell, there's a vicar blocking our view now,' a voice shouted out of the gloom. 'Will it ever end?'

'Yes!' I shouted back into the darkness. 'Just give us a minute and we'll settle down and be no further trouble. I'm sorry for all the inconvenience.'

My twenty-eight women duly seated themselves, using their coats as ample cushions, which raised them a few inches more than their normal height. They were still sporting their hats, so the overall effect was that they blocked off the sight-line of the audience behind us. 'Vicar, can't you get your women to take their hats off ?' the angry voice shouted again. 'It's like a wall of wool in front of us. We might as well watch the film with a blindfold on.'

'Ladies, I'm ever so sorry,' I pleaded, 'but do you think you could take your hats off so that the people behind can see? This isn't like church, where you have to shield the congregation behind from seeing my face!' I feared that it might take a heatwave of Sahara proportions to entice these Mothers' Union stalwarts to remove their precious hats. And even then I guessed we'd need the mediation of someone with the negotiating prowess of U Thant, the UN Secretary General, who was always popping up in the world's trouble spots. But to my surprise, my weak humour won them over. and they complied with my plea, perching their hats on their knees.

The opening strains of *The Sound of Music* echoed around the cinema and twenty-eight women fell silent and gawped upwards at the screen, entranced. 'Ee, Vicar, er, David, I never realized this was what they got up to at Thicket Priory,' Ivy Weighton whispered, as sundry tetchy nuns trilled *'How do you solve a problem like Maria?'* around their crowded cloister.

'Sh!' someone hissed from behind.

We watched enthralled as Maria hesitantly left the security of the nunnery perched on an Alp-top, and won the hearts of the von Trapp children and finally their frosty father. The film moved to what seemed to be its climax, Maria's wedding at the nunnery, with a cluster of piqued nuns peeping at Julie Andrews radiant in her wedding dress, silently voicing *'It should have been me!'*, the words of a hit surprisingly not included in Rodgers and Hammerstein's repertoire. The wedding bells rang, the Archbishop blessed the happy couple in the nunnery now miraculously changed into a cathedral, and all looked set for them to live happily ever after. 'Right girls let's get out before they play the National Anthem,' Doris Harsley piped up. Twenty-eight women shot out of their seats, plonked their hats at rakish angles on their heads, crumpled their coats under their right arms, and stuffed carrier bags dribbling pig's blood under their left arms. They bustled out, clambering yet again over the other members of the long-suffering audience. Even Job would have found his renowned patience severely tried by the members of my Mothers' Union.

'Oh, Rick, something hot and sticky's dribbling down my legs,' the teenage girl screamed, as she came into contact with another carrier bag from the pig factory.

'Just control yourself, Rick!' our wag shouted.

'Look, I've told you already, Mister,' Rick spluttered. 'One more word from you and I'll knock your teeth so far down your throat you'll have to brush them up your ar–'

'*How do you solve a problem like Maria?*' the nuns trilled, thankfully drowning out any

315

further obscenities. *'How do I solve a problem like my Mothers' Union?'* I softly sang to myself. I sighed with relief as we got to the gangway and followed my stampeding women into the cinema foyer.

There we surprised the cinema manager sneaking a crafty cigarette. 'Bloody hell, where did you lot come from?' he exclaimed. 'Oh, I'm sorry, your Reverence, I didn't see you there,' he added apologetically.

'T' film's finished so we're getting out before the rush,' Doris breathlessly explained, diplomatically not mentioning her aversion to the National Anthem.

'Finished? Finished? It had better not have,' the manager bleated. 'I'm just about to go up to the projection room and help the projectionist change the spool. We're only half way through.'

'But we've got to t' end,' Doris Harsley maintained, 'Maria's got married!'

'Ah yes, but there are a few surprises in store yet, ladies. That's not the end by a long chalk,' the manager explained. 'Back in you go, ladies!'

'Oh no,' I thought. 'We haven't got to go through all that again!' I would gladly have left the film there, whatever surprises it still had in store, rather than complete the assault course back into our seats. The dark voices would protest yet again, Rick's girlfriend would complain of being molested yet again, Rick would threaten the wag yet again, Doris Harsley would stand up for her rights yet again. I could hardly bear to think of what lay ahead. 'Lord, take this cup away from me,' I prayed, and not entirely flippantly.

Miraculously my prayer was answered, because as we sauntered back in, the lights went up for the interval, and we were able to return to our places with the minimum of disruption. The other punters had vacated their seats in search of the ice-cream lady, so there was hardly anyone left to clamber over. There was, however, one minor emergency. As her eyes became accustomed to the light, the mini-skirted girl howled as she realized that the hot sticky stuff running down her legs had been blood. 'Darling, I'm bleeding,' she cried out to Rick, who shot to his feet, shouting out in panic, 'Help, help, she's bleeding!'

'Don't worry, I'm a midwife,' a large woman cried out reassuringly, moving towards the couple from the other end of the row. She helped the girl out of her seat, cleared a way through the crowd and laid her down in the main aisle. She then gave her as discreet an examination as possible under the circumstances, while interested *Sound of Music* fans looked on. 'I don't think it's you who's bleeding, love,' she concluded. 'The blood on your legs must have come from someone else, or something else.' The girl started shrieking hysterically.

'Or maybe its not blood at all,' I added, trying to calm things down yet again. 'Maybe it's tomato ketchup, somebody might have had a leaking bottle in their shopping bag. Look, it's all over the carpet...' I hadn't actually lied, but I hadn't actually told the truth either, so I prayed that the same God who caused the interval at his whim would also forgive me. I noticed that all twenty-eight of my ladies were sitting sheepishly, with their offending carrier bags tucked out of sight beneath their seats. I think it was the first time that day that all twenty-eight of them had been perfectly still and quiet.

Rick helped his girlfriend to her feet and wisely led her to another part of the cinema, safely out of harm's way. The lights dipped, and we saw the encore we never expected. How could we have lived with ourselves if we'd missed the Anschluss, the music festival, the escape from the Nazis? Not to mention the von Trapp family soaring unfettered into the heavens as they scaled the Alps, accompanied by the ever-musical Maria! Even a brisk mountain climb and Nazis breathing down her neck could not stop this woman dispensing her nauseatingly homely wisdom set to song.

This time we didn't rush out at the end, just in case there was more, and the film explored how even the heady freedom of the von Trapps wasn't all it was cracked up to be. But the National Anthem struck up and assured us that this was definitely the end, so we, together with the thick overcoats and the hats and the carrier bags, stood to attention out of respect for our monarch. I hope the Queen was touched by such devotion.

Ron was waiting for us outside the cinema, so we boarded the bus. This time there was no crowd intrigued by our exploits, since the rest of the cinema-goers stayed well clear, glad to see the back of us. I found my seat, my carrier bag in pristine condition in contrast to the other twenty-eight, which by now were in the death-throes of a carrier bag's life. As we headed for home, several of the women slept, giving me space for thought. I looked at Doris Harsley, breathlessly fierce in her defence of her rights and the rights of her cronies. I looked at Ivy Weighton, a generous, homely if unhygienic soul, grieving for her German farm-hand, taken for granted by her men-folk, but adored by a daughter who was soon to be my wife. I looked at Hannah Everingham, a sensible Yorkshire head on her shoulders, who kept her slow-witted churchwarden husband on track. I looked at Becky Ludlow, no husband, no children, these women who despised her barrenness her only friends.

They were all lovely women, yet sometimes they displayed a corporate mean streak which saddened me. I thought of a talk I'd heard by the Bishop of Birmingham, Leonard Wilson, who had been tortured by the Japanese during the Second World War. He had resisted cursing his tormentors by seeing behind their cruel and sadistic faces the children they had once been, secure in their parents' love. He also tried to imagine what they could become if they allowed their cruel, dark selves to be shaped by the light of Christ. The exercise helped him in his torment, since it was impossible to hate either children or those who shone with Christ's light.

As I gazed on the Dorises and Ivys and Hannahs before me, I imagined them as little girls, slim little girls, rather carefree before the Great War had cast a shadow over them, well-dressed and well-fed, their village a cosy, tight-knit community with even the closest town seemingly a world away. As brothers and fathers and uncles and cousins proudly left to serve in the trenches, never to return, I saw their lips begin to curl downwards, their bright eyes dull. In the years between the wars I imagined them newlyweds, soon with children of their own. As they struggled to make ends meet through the Depression years, I saw their shoulders hunch with the worry of it all. Even the dullest coat and the most shapeless hat was better than nothing in those lean times.

And as to what they could become with Christ beside them? I imagined Jesus stroking faces which no man had touched for years. His fingers smoothed out the wrinkles, eased away the worry lines, teased the sagging lips into a smile. He made them laugh again as they rediscovered the toys of their childhood, as they felt their heart race with the first flush of love, as they held close to their breast the children they thought were no more. The light came back into their eyes as they walked with Him beside them into a golden sunset, their shoulders bowed no longer.

As these thoughts raced through my mind, I smiled with a real fondness for them all. But I was suddenly brought back to earth with a bump as I heard Doris Harsley pipe up, 'What's a matter wi' vicar?' she shouted. 'What's he beaming like that for?'

'I don't know, he's a mystery to me,' I heard her friend reply. 'Perhaps he's got dyspepsia wi' fish and chips, or maybe he's got a crush on Julie Andrews. They're partial to nuns, these vicars are, you know.'

Monday 11 July

'Oh, Vicar,' Ivy Weighton walled, 'I just feel so awful, so very wretched.' She broke off, sobbing uncontrollably. Though uncontrollably is an unnecessary word – as if the sobs of deep grief could ever be controlled. Her unease reminded me of when she had visited me during my first few days in the Withs. She had stumbled across a grieving

Sally Broadhurst and had asked to see her mummy, unaware, as we all were at the time, of the massive tragedy the family were nursing. Disturbed by the little girl's tears, Ivy Weighton had come to me, to see if I could make some sense of it all.

We had sat in my study then, books partially unpacked and piled like towers around us, and we sat in my study now. This time the room was ordered and tidy, but inside I felt the same as I had done on that first occasion. I still felt unsettled, uneasy, like a new boy at school, unsure whether I had anything to offer. And even if I did manage to summon up a few crumbs of comfort, I was unsure whether they would be of any use to the woman more than twice my age sitting before me, whose unexpected visit had disturbed a neatly planned afternoon of sermon-writing.

'Grief is a strange process, Ivy, and takes its own time,' I heard myself saying. 'It's not like a cold which you can get over in a few weeks. You're talking about a far longer time span. Nor do you recover from it gradually like you do an illness. Some days will be fine, with memories sweet, other days will be, be, well, wretched is your word and sums it all up very aptly, so very aptly.'

'But it's months now since he died, and it's just getting worse and worse, darker and darker,' she cried. 'I put on a brave face, I make conversation, I smile, even crack a joke, yet it's all a front, underneath I feel, I feel...' She struggled to find the right word. 'Underneath I feel simply terrified.'

It was an unusual word, not one my parishioners normally used to describe their grief, not that many of them put it into words at all. 'Why terrified, Ivy?' I asked softly. 'What are you terrified of?'

Ivy looked away from me, stroking my sheepdog, Dewi, who had nuzzled up to her. Like so many dogs, he was acutely alert to sorrow. There was a long silence and then she turned her head back towards me and fixed me with her gaze, the same gaze as Rebecca, the same steel-blue eyes, but their light filtered through a pool of tears. 'There are so many things I'm terrified of,' she confessed.

'Take your time,' I encouraged her. 'It'll help to talk, to get them out in the open, to check whether the terrors are rational or irrational.'

'I know that, I know that,' she agreed. 'And it had to be a priest. I couldn't really trust anyone else with what's worrying me.

Not that they would have gossiped – people like Hannah Everingham are the dearest and discreetest of friends. It's just that I couldn't load them with what I'm carrying, it wouldn't be fair.'

'Are you happy talking to me, Ivy?' I asked. 'Would you prefer to see another priest who isn't so personally involved?'

'I've thought about that,' she replied. 'It takes some getting used to, having a vicar who's also marrying your daughter – though I guess you marry every parishioner's daughter,' she added, a glint of humour breaking through her gloom. 'But I felt that precisely because you were "so personally involved", as you put it, that at the end of the day you were the only one I could talk to. You know so much about us, you took Hans's funeral, you've been alongside us through it all...'

'I feel very privileged that you should want to talk to me, Ivy,' I said. 'So tell me what things you find so terrifying.'

'I suppose it's the missed opportunities,' she began. 'So many missed opportunities. You fool yourself, thinking that you'll get around to them one day, and then a death happens, and you know they're gone, gone for ever.' She began to cry again.

'I suppose life is a process of coming to

terms with all the lost opportunities,' I replied, sounding rather pompous as I filled the silence, 'coming to terms with the certain fact that we can't do everything. But having to be selective about what we are able to do, doesn't have to stop us being sensitive. You're a sensitive person, Ivy, immensely sensitive. That's a great treasure. Your grief at all the missed opportunities just shows your real quality.'

'But I don't feel I've got any quality, I feel I'm just, just rubbish, worthless. So much I could have done, I should have done...' she trailed off, weeping again.

'I often wonder whether heaven will be an eternity of revisiting all those missed opportunities and redeeming them,' I said, trying to find something to comfort her. 'We'll have to find something to fill our time. To be honest, spending millions of years singing "Holy, holy, holy" around God's eternal throne doesn't grab me very much at all.'

'Even if from round 'ere it would be "'Oly, 'oly, 'oly",' Ivy joked, a smile breaking through once again. A lovely smile which her daughter had inherited.

'Yeh, even then,' I agreed, laughing with her. 'I like to think our life is a bit of a trailer for heaven, sets an agenda for eternity, giving us the space to explore each and every one of the opportunities we so much regretted missing on earth.'

'I like that idea,' she admitted. 'Although it sounds a bit complicated. Especially when it comes to revisiting all my missed opportunities.'

'I believe God can cope. Complications are his stock-in-trade!' I replied. 'But all these missed opportunities; do you want to tell me about them? Or some of them, if they're as complicated as you reckon.'

'Well, how about this for starters? Hans was Rebecca's father,' she blurted out.

'Good heavens, Ivy!' I exclaimed, utterly and totally stunned.

'So you didn't have an inkling? Didn't you wonder why she's so different from her brothers?'

'Not really,' I replied. 'I just assumed the boys had taken after their taciturn dad and your daughter had taken after you.'

'But her interest in German, didn't that make you suspicious, even down to the way she speaks the language with a Transylvanian accent, "Vere the vampires come vrom"?' she pressed, doing a perfect impersonation of Hans.

'Well, no. She'd obviously got on well with Hans ever since being this high, so I thought nothing of it.' I paused to consider for a moment before adding, 'In many ways I'm more easy about Hans being Rebecca's father than him not being. In many ways I feared such a close relationship between an older man and a younger girl was a bit unhealthy, if you know what I mean.' Even so, I felt rather strange that I was talking about my fiancée in this way, that having such a conversation at all, speaking of her as a third party, was a sort of betrayal.

Another long silence fell between the two of us, with me feeling awkward, out of my depth, not knowing what to say. 'How did it all come about, Ivy?' I asked eventually.

'As you know, Hans was stationed on the farm as a low-risk prisoner of war. He was a hard worker from the start, but was bullied by t' other workers something awful. I felt so sorry for him, he was such a gentle soul compared to t' other men round here.'

'Including Fred?' I asked.

'Well, Fred's all right really, from good farming stock, he gets right on with t' job rather than doing much talking. A man of few words. But sometimes a woman needs words. Though still a young girl, I was weighed down by two bairns to look after, with a decrepit farmhouse to run and a resident mother-in-law to cope with, and a husband who hardly talked to me. Hans talked to me, in his broken English, about everything, his fears, his hopes, the life he had left behind. I was entranced by it all.

'One day he'd been in a terrible fight with one o' t' farmhands. I was cleaning his little cottage, as I did for all the men we employed who weren't married, when Hans limped in, a nasty cut on his face, his lip broken. He looked absolutely wrecked. I sat him down at the kitchen table, poured out a bowl of water and began to clean the blood off his face. Well, one thing led to another, before we knew it we were in each other's arms and I was in his bed. I know I did wrong, Vicar, er, David, I've been thoroughly ashamed of what I did every single day of my life thereafter. Yet I would be untrue to myself if I didn't add that I'd never known such passion before and never known it since.'

'But were you having normal relations with your husband at the time?' I asked, feeling my blushing face burn red.

'Well, yes,' she admitted. 'Yes, if you can call what we did normal.'

'What do you mean?' I asked, steeling myself for her reply.

'Er, well,' she hesitated before continuing, 'it was just so brief and loveless, I felt we were like Fred's animals *mating* rather than two humans in love.'

'But if you were, erm, if you were having normal relations with your husband at the same time as you er, er, committed adultery with Hans, how do you know that Rebecca's his child and not Fred's?'

'I just know Vicar, a woman's intuition you can call it, if you want. She has the look of Hans about her, has a lot of Hans' mannerisms, even talks German like him. Surely you noticed.'

I remembered Hans and Rebecca singing the carol '*Stille Nacht*' together after an eventful Christmas dinner at the Weightons', in perfect harmony, like a father and his beloved daughter, so I could fully see what Ivy meant. But I also recalled the first time I had met Rebecca, how Mr Weighton had broken his surly silence and introduced her to me as his 'pride and joy', his face beaming with rare pleasure.

'But you don't know for sure, Ivy, whether Rebecca is Hans' daughter. At the end of the day you just believe that she is.'

'But you have to admit the proof is pretty strong,' Ivy replied.

'Yes, but you can't be one hundred per cent sure. And from the proud-father act that Fred puts on from time to time, he obviously believes that Rebecca's his child. Presumably he has no suspicions?' I asked.

'None. Hans and I were together just that once. I realized that it was wrong, very wrong, so we hardly ever touched after that night. I know it sounds wicked, Vicar, but now Hans has died, I no longer regret what we did. I regret what we didn't do, all that tenderness that I turned my back on.'

She began weeping again, really uncontrollably, the sobs wracking her body.

I waited until the crying was over, and then asked, 'Ivy, you've told me all this. What do you want me to do?'

'Do you think I did wrong, Vicar, do you think I'm a very bad woman?'

I doodled with my fingers on my desk for a few moments before answering her, trying to work out what words I could respond with. At college we used to sit ethics exams where test cases much like this were presented to us to solve. It was so different in real life: there were never, ever any easy solutions.

'I think, Ivy, adultery is wrong, very wrong, since it is a betrayal of faithfulness. Yet we're not discussing something that you're contemplating, but something that happened over twenty years ago and so is definitely in the past. What's more, it happened in wartime, when people were very frightened, and felt brutalized, with love seeming a wonderful refuge from all the terrible fear that was swirling around. You've opened your heart to me, Ivy, you've made a sort of confession, and I believe God loves you, the God who is tender to all his children and the wrong turnings they so bitterly regret. If God's prepared to wipe the slate clean, how can I think you're a very bad woman?'

'Really?' Ivy asked anxiously, clutching at my straw of consolation. 'As I said, every day since I've felt so guilty.'

'Well, I'm deeply sorry that you've had to carry that guilt for over twenty years,' I commented. 'But I'm also deeply impressed that you resisted further temptation when the man you obviously deeply loved was working on your farm and eating at your table. You deserve a medal, Ivy, not my condemnation.'

She looked so touchingly grateful. Her

face lit up, until a further storm crossed her brow. 'Do you think I should tell Fred?' she asked.

'No, I don't,' I replied. 'What good would that do? If he thinks Rebecca's his, and she well might be, why disillusion him? And I'm getting to know these Vale of York farmers – they can be an unforgiving lot. I guess that telling him at this stage would fuel resentment for the rest of your lives together.'

'And Rebecca?' she asked.

'I think you have to tell her what you've told me, and let her make up her own mind. She was clearly very fond of Hans, and she's clearly very fond of her father, er, of Fred, when he's not being too chauvinist. I think she's the only other person who has to know. Tell me,' I added, 'did Hans know?'

'Oh yes,' Ivy replied, flushing at the mention of his name, 'he knew. Can I ask you just one more thing, David?'

'Fire away,' I said, smiling because her spirits had obviously lightened.

'When you said earlier about heaven being a place to revisit all our missed opportunities, did you really mean it?'

'I like to think so, yes,' I replied.

'That's good, very good. I only hope I can meet Hans in heaven and atone for all those years I kept him at arm's length,' she said, her smile positively beatific.

I had the feeling that Ivy had put her finger on a flaw in my neat theory, but I said nothing. I suddenly realized how Jesus must have felt when the Sadducees asked him which husband a woman who was married seven times would have in heaven. I also realized that had it not been for Ivy's indiscretion, the love of my life would never have seen the light of day. I watched Ivy walk down my drive, a spring in her step for the first time in months, bound to tell her daughter and my future wife the facts of her life.

Tuesday 12 July

At about ten to nine last night Dewi started barking, interrupting my favourite bit of *The Saint*, which I was watching on my minute TV. It was the resurrection scene: Simon Templar was bound and surrounded by a group of thugs who would have made the burly dockers of East Hull look genteel. The statutory beautiful and scantily clad girl was tied up beside him, with the thugs' diabolical laughter hinting that the most exquisite torture was about to begin. Then Roger Moore, with no more than a flick of his eyebrow, snapped the ropes that tied him to a chair, and waved them triumphantly at the thugs. Only minutes before, the very same ropes which Simon Templar had so easily broken, had been lifting two-ton crates of gold bullion. Gold that the thugs had thought they had stolen undetected until the Saint rumbled them.

Now a fight of fights broke out, Roger Moore lashing the crooks with the aforementioned ropes, smashing the chair and other sundry furniture over their heads, dodging the supersonic bullets by darting to the left and to the right, pulverizing more thugs en route, and laying a dozen of them flat before gliding over to the heroine. It was at that point that Dewi started baying excitedly and made me miss the final chaste kiss.

'OK, Dewi, there's someone at the door, I know, there's no need to tell the whole world,' I grumbled as I made my way to the porch, with Dewi taking no notice of me whatsoever, circling my legs and continuing his high-pitched barking. As a vicar I was always on standby, always on call, could never even watch my favourite piece of TV escapism without cocking an ear for the telephone or the doorbell. Any resentment evaporated in an instant as I opened the front door and saw Rebecca on the doorstep, looking totally dishevelled. The Saint's noisy carryings-on had meant that I was totally oblivious to the thunderstorm which was raging outside, a cloudburst which had drenched Rebecca in the short walk from her car to my door. 'Darling, come on in, you're totally soaked,' I cried, putting my arm around her sodden shoulders and drawing her in out of the rain. As I kissed her, I noticed the red eyes, tasted the salt tears, tears which mingled with the drops of rain which ran down her face.

'Let me make you a cup of tea to warm you up,' I said, leading her to the kitchen, my arm around her waist. I remembered the first time she had called here, and how nervous I had been. In my clumsy state, I couldn't even make a cup of tea, boiling the kettle dry, scattering tea-leaves on the kitchen floor, and finally hurling the tray of tea and biscuits at Rebecca's feet as I caught my jacket on the living-room door. Through it all, Rebecca had been so calm, so assured, so encouraging that I doubly fell in love with her.

Tonight the roles were reversed, I was calm, she was agitated, highly agitated. I made the tea without boiling kettles dry or showering tea-leaves like confetti, while Rebecca, between the sobs, tried to piece back together a happy world that had been shattered by her mother's revelations. 'Oh David, I just feel so lost, so utterly lost, as if I don't know who I am any more,' she blurted out. 'I knew there was something that was dragging Mum down, I knew it wasn't just grief, that there must be something else, but I never expected this, never in my wildest dreams.'

I merely listened, adding only the odd word or two to her torrent of words. She continued talking, following me as I carried the tea tray into the living room. 'If only I'd known earlier, if only I had known as a child that he was my father, I could have said the things I never said, I could have...' As we sat down, her words trailed off and she wept bitterly.

For the second time that day I waited until the crying abated, waiting which seemed like an age. In a strange sense, I felt as if I was poised on the brink of eternity. 'Actually, I think it's rather marvellous,' I heard myself saying, 'that you loved him for what he was, listened to him for what he had to say, rather than the loving out of duty and the listening out of duty that any child is obliged to bestow on a parent.'

'Yes, I can see that,' Rebecca agreed. 'But for the moment I feel so shocked, so very shocked, as if I've got to reassess the whole of my life.'

'You're a Pip in *Great Expectations*, who's suddenly realized that your sponsor, the person who's enabled the whole of your existence, isn't the fabulous Miss Havisham, but the outlaw Magwitch,' I piped up. 'And that takes a lot of coming to terms with.'

'Yes, that's it exactly,' she agreed, 'although I can't quite see Dad in the role of Miss Havisham!' I was glad to see that her humour, like her mum's, had survived. And then the smile gave way to tears again as she said, 'Dad? Dad? What can I call him now? Who is my dad?'

'We don't know, love,' I replied. 'We don't know. It could be the man you've called Dad ever since you learned to speak. It could be the man who taught you to speak in the language you fill your working day with. We don't really know. That's the frustration of the situation. And...' I added, after pausing for a moment's thought, '...the beauty of the situation too.'

'Beauty? What do you mean, beauty?' Rebecca asked, furrowing her brow.

'Well, today is all shock, with so much to take in. But not really knowing whether Hans is your father or Fred is your father doesn't necessarily make for a terrible confusion. What I mean by beauty is that it can actually give you space to hold on to both men and retain your own integrity,' I explained slowly.

'Go on,' Rebecca said, drying her eyes with her handkerchief, 'I'm with you so far.'

'Well, you gave Hans the attention of a beloved daughter and treated him like a beloved father, so if he was your actual father, where have you fallen short? And for all your life you've called the man who's brought you up Dad, as well he might be, so there's nothing there that's been changed by your mum's revelation either. All of a sudden you're having to reckon with having two dads while most of us spend a lifetime resolving the hassle of having only one,' I concluded.

I was grateful after my time with Ivy earlier in the day that I had had the space to stand back a bit and think one or two things through. Now I could share my comparative calm with Rebecca, who was still reeling from the shock. Not that I was very calm. Beneath my composed words I too was reeling, trying to resolve a confusion of roles. What should I be doing in this situation as parish priest, as friend of the family, as Rebecca's fiancé? Where were those roles overlapping, where were they eclipsing one another, where were they in tension with each other? I felt torn within as I tried to be scrupulously fair in a terrible situation, worried lest my advice be flawed by my conflicting levels of involvement. In many ways it would have been better if the family could have dealt with a priest they didn't really know. But the rub there was that if the priest hadn't really known Ivy, she would never have taken him into her confidence as she did with me.

We sipped our tea, the silence between us communicating far more than my inadequate words. 'I feel so abnormal, so unsure of myself, so guilty that I'm the result of something that never should have happened. What would your Archdeacon say about me now? He'd certainly think I was unfit to be a priest's wife,' Rebecca whispered.

340

'Oh, I don't know,' I replied. 'When Cardinal Wolsey was Archbishop of York he had the audacity to make his illegitimate son his archdeacon, so with a precedent like that, I don't think our Archdeacon has a leg to stand on.'

'Is that what started off parish priests complaining "The Archdeacon's a bastard"?' Rebecca quipped, with a mischievous grin. Again I felt that for her terrific sense of humour to have survived the trauma augured well.

'Seriously though, darling,' I continued, 'You mustn't feel abnormal because of what your mum did all those years ago. My guess is that when this permissive society which everyone is talking about really takes hold, the majority will have family arrangements which are so very complex, yours will pale into insignificance.'

'I hope not. I wouldn't wish upon anyone what I've gone through today,' Rebecca replied, speaking from her broken heart. 'I wonder if we ought to postpone the wedding?' she added, suddenly making my heart miss a beat.

'Why?' I asked.

'Because I don't think I should get married until I've worked out who I am, and I feel thats going to take a long time. I don't want to lumber you with all my uncertainty.'

'You wouldn't be lumbering me with anything,' I replied. 'For better and for worse, for richer and for poorer, in sickness and in health. It's not for better and for better, for richer and for richer, in health and in health. If only perfect people could get married, then no one would ever marry. We all come to marriage with deep flaws, which our partner is there to heal, not to shirk or feel they're being lumbered. But we must marry when we both feel it's right to marry. It would be foolish to make any decisions, to go ahead or to postpone, tonight when you're still reeling from it all. Let's give it a week, and then take stock.'

We wept a little, we hugged a little, we talked a little, we sat in silence more than a little, Rebecca left after a little, I slept very little, and woke up feeling so very wretched.

Wednesday 13 July

I was moping through, catching up on administration, completing returns, trying to write a sermon when my heart just wasn't in it. I feared I was losing Rebecca. I feared that we would never raise the £800 or so to renovate the almshouses and that Flo and Edna would be in squalor until the end of their days. I was ashamed of the state of the school house. How could I expect the best teacher I had ever come across to live with his wife and child in such a slum? Yet how would we ever find yet more money to improve it? I felt thoroughly glum.

Today I decided to get out and do some visiting. When I was first ordained, my boss advised me that if ever I was down, then visiting folk would lift my spirits. Other people would either cheer me up, or their woes would put mine into perspective.

I cycled the winding mile to Beckwith, the sky cloudless, the view clear, right across to the Wolds, and felt my woes lifting from me, even before I called on Captain Dunnington, a delightful old fellow who had been an officer in the Merchant Navy in the last war. His ship had been torpedoed by a U-boat and he had bravely co-ordinated the rescue of his men, manning the lifeboats with a fellow officer, pulling injured sailors from the high seas, taking the oars himself and rowing through slicks of burning oil to retrieve a couple of men from the flames. He had then rowed his boat three hundred miles to the nearest friendly coast, and had ultimately been awarded the Victoria Cross for his gallantry.

Now this wartime hero was in a sorry state. Diabetes had wreaked havoc with his body, gnawing off one leg, nibbling at the foot of the other, near blinding him. He sat all day in a wicker wheelchair on the veranda of his spacious home in Beckwith, overlooking the Derwent and the Ings, imagining that they were the sea on which he could no longer sail, the veranda the bridge he could no longer command.

I was met at the door by Mrs Dunnington, a pumpkin-shaped lady who bustled around her husband, fluffing up his cushions, putting a glass of water to his lips, moving his chair out of the sun if she felt he was too hot, moving his chair into the sun if she felt he was in a draught. She absolutely doted on him, her care was constant, would have smothered me, but Captain Dunnington exuded the deepest gratitude for her every act of kindness. 'Thank you, my dear, that's so very good of you,' a sentence he uttered repeatedly when often just a couple of words must have been a strain: a true officer and a gentleman.

Mrs Dunnington greeted me at the door.

'Oh Vicar, how good of you to call,' she fussed. 'Do you want to take your bicycle around the back or are you happy to leave it there? You can trust no one these days. And shall I hang up your cycle clips for you?'

'No, the bike will be just fine, and I'll leave the clips on if you don't mind, otherwise I'll forget them,' I replied. In my time I had left too many cycle clips behind on my visits, a novel sort of calling card. 'How is the Captain?' I asked.

'Oh, he's out on the veranda, as always. But he's not been too good – he's coming out of hypo and he keeps on having bouts of delirium. He's been calling for his charts, as if he were still at sea. I keep telling him, "You don't need them, love, we've been on dry land these twenty years," but I can't get through, and poor dear, he loses his temper. This morning he thought I was his First Officer – "Get me my charts, Mr Peters, or I'll clap you in irons!" he barked. I think he's even confused about which war he fought in.'

She led me through the house and on to the veranda where her husband was sitting, a wool blanket tucked over his legs, or what remained of his legs. He still wasn't with us. 'My charts, my charts, we should have brought my charts. How can we find land without them?' he cried. Clearly his mind was revisiting the rescue yet again, condemning the poor captain once more to be hopelessly adrift at sea, with little hope of survival. I often marvelled about the sheer enormity of the task of rowing all those men such a vast distance. That they made it was a miracle. Little wonder that his wandering mind now dwelt on the alternative, the grim reality for so many sailors who perished in that wartime sea.

'You sit down here, Vicar, and I'll go and get you a cup of tea,' Mrs Dunnington said, positioning a garden chair so I could sit beside her husband.

I sat in silence as he raved. 'My charts, why didn't you bring my charts, man?' he cried, looking straight through me, with terror in his darting eyes. And then they seemed to mist over, clearing again after a few moments. 'Oh hallo, Vicar,' he said calmly, as he came to. 'It's good of you to call. I was miles away.'

'Dreaming of wartime?' I asked.

'I'm always dreaming of wartime,' he replied, a gentle smile crossing his lips.

'It was a strange dream, this time, though. I think I'd got the Second World War mixed up with Captain Bligh and Mr Christian and we were lost in the Pacific. In the last twenty years I thought I'd dreamt every possible variation of my time at sea. But clearly not,' he said, smiling again.

'Why do you think it so haunts you?' I asked.

It was a stupid question, one I blurted out just to make conversation. But Captain Dunnington, ever the gentleman, treated it respectfully, as if Id put my finger on a key that had hitherto eluded him. 'I don't know, really. It was pretty bad, Vicar, we didn't expect to survive. As it was, we lost two of the men in our boat. I'd hauled them from a flaming sea, but they'd been so badly burned – their skin came off in my hands as I pulled them on board. They lived for a day and then died before our eyes, twenty-eight pairs of eyes watching their mates die a horrible death, twenty-eight pairs of eyes watching the fate which the sea had in store for them.'

'So very dispiriting,' I commented, not really finding the right word, my conversation still inept in the presence of this man's great drama.

'Yes, yes, that's very true,' he said, with an inflexion to his voice as if he had never thought of it like that before. 'Many of them were dispirited, not surprising, considering what they'd gone through. It had the opposite effect on me, though, made me determined not to be beaten, stirred me to row and row and row. I don't know where I got the energy from, I really don't. It was a superhuman strength that came to me in those days, a strength from Him above, I've always thought that.'

I smiled and nodded. Modestly, the Captain did not mention what his wife had told me on a previous visit, how, when he had pulled his burning shipmates from the water, his own hands had been severely burned. Somehow he'd torn his shirt into strips and bandaged them to give a little protection from the cruel friction of the oars. Given that further detail, the achievement came across as doubly superhuman. 'You deserved your Victoria Cross,' I said.

'They all deserved it, all those merchant seaman,' he replied, a hint of bitterness invading his gentlemanly voice. 'Their bravery kept Britain fed. But you don't hear much about all that now. And look at the way we treat our sailors today - underpaid, undervalued, is this the honour due to a body of men who daily risked their lives for us?'

Tears came into his eyes and we sat quietly for a while, my eyes fixed on the scarred, gnarled hands which rested on the top of his blanket. 'But enough of me, Vicar,' he piped up, breaking the silence. 'What about yourself, how are you getting on adrift in these faraway places?' A smile came to his lips again. 'They tell me that you're going to have the garden party on World Cup final day. They say I'm a brave man, but I'd never be brave enough to run the garden party side by side with that event!' After the sea, Captain Dunnington's other great love was football.

'Who do you think will win, then?' I asked.

'I don't really know,' he replied. 'So many teams have got such good form. I was disappointed that England could only manage a draw with Uruguay. I suppose it was only a friendly to start the competition, but even so, the match was so scrappy, and we needed a bit of oomph. Where's our bulldog spirit gone to?' he laughed.

'What about the Bulgarians?' I asked.

'Well, they're solid lads without a doubt. I wouldn't like to meet them down an alleyway on a dark night, certainly not in this state,' he said, patting his blanket.

'But you need flair as well to come

through, and I don't think they've got that.'

'So who do you put your money on for the final?' I asked.

'Well, it's a lovely contest really, with so many stars. Argentina, Italy, Russia, Portugal – that captain of theirs, Eusebio, he's one to watch. But you see, unknown teams like Korea, if they've got this far, then I can't see them letting go easily. But at the end of the day, I reckon England will come through, find their form on their home ground, and that it'll be us versus West Germany. I can't see anyone stopping those Germans, I really can't.'

'So it'll be the Second World War all over again?' I quipped.

'I suppose so,' he replied, that inflexion to his voice again, as if he hadn't thought of my obvious comparison. 'I bear no grudges, mind, it was dog eat dog twenty years back. I think of the terrible losses we had, I think of the terrible losses they had, and weep with the waste of it all. Too many young men and women have died this century in old men's or mad men's wars. Too many, far too many have been brutalized. I'd have been far happier deciding it all with a game of football than going to war, and that's a war hero speaking, lad,' he concluded, his eyes twinkling.

Mrs Dunnington brought our tea, and we continued chatting until Captain Dunnington drifted back into his maritime dreams and nightmares. 'He so enjoys your visits,' Mrs Dunnington said as she showed me back through the house. 'You really cheer him up. He finds what you have to say so interesting.' Apart from a few ums and aughs and the odd inept question and comment, I hadn't said anything interesting at all. It was Captain Dunnington who had made all the running. 'Good, it's still here then,' she said as I walked towards my bicycle. 'I tried to keep my eye on it for you. You have to be so careful these days, don't you?' I waved back to her as I wobbled off down the road, finding it rather sad that the wife of a man who had braved torpedoes and the chill Atlantic now lived in fear of having things like bicycles stolen.

I pedalled back to Kirkwith and dropped in on Edna and Flo, and found them even more of a twitter than usual. 'Oh, Vicar, we were so hoping someone would drop in. We had a letter, a letter from America in this morning's post,' Edna told me excitedly. I smiled at the way she said 'this morning's post', as if she and her sister had a massive

351

mailbag to sort through each day. 'Trouble was, the writing was too small for me to make out, as you know, my eyesight's not what it was. So we were hoping someone would drop by and read it to us, and here you are, a real angel from heaven. I'll just nip up and get it. I took it up to our bedroom hoping the light would be better there, but I still couldn't manage to read it, not even the name of the person who sent it.'

'Let me go up and get it for you,' I offered.

'No, it's all right, Vicar, I can manage,' she replied. I watched her with my heart in my mouth as she struggled up the ladder which ran up from the side of the kitchen through a trap-door in the ceiling. My horror as I watched her ascent paled into insignificance compared to the deep dread I felt as I watched her come down, a handbag in one hand, holding on to the ladder with the other, her feet hanging in mid-air as they felt their way towards each rung. 'That pilot was right,' I thought. 'I should be ashamed of myself allowing them to live in such conditions.' I wished with all my rapidly beating heart that I could be a real angel from heaven and raise the money needed to rebuild the place.

'Here we are,' said Edna, puffing as her

feet touched safely back down on the firm stone flags of the kitchen floor. She took an airmail letter out of her handbag and passed it to me, handling the thing with the greatest reverence, as if it were immensely precious. The envelope's edge was jagged and torn, the contents stuffed back inside. 'There seem to be two letters, Vicar, but that's all we could make out,' Flo explained.

I slowly unfolded one of the pieces of paper, turned it over and screwed up my eyes as I tried to make out the signature at the end. 'It's someone called Jimmy something,' I said. 'I can't quite read the surname.'

'Jimmy Benson?' Flo asked.

'Yes, that's it, I can make out the B and the "son". Now where have I come across that name before?' I puzzled, racking my memory.

'Why, Vicar, you can't have forgotten already,' Edna chided. 'That was the name of the Texan whose parachute landed in our garden.'

'Of course,' I said. 'How stupid of me to have forgotten! Now let's see if I can read what he has to say. Forgive me if I can't quite manage the Texan drawl: "Dear Flo and Edna, my ladies of mercy..."'

'Oh, he was such a flatterer, such a flatterer,' Edna and Flo twittered.

'"...I am sorry I have taken so long to thank you for your tremendous kindness that night I 'dropped in' to your home. Nothing was too much trouble for you, I really feel that you brought a battered pilot back from the grave!"'

'Oh, we did hardly anything, hardly anything at all, Vicar. All we did was to make him a few mugfuls of our special Bournvita,' Edna interrupted.

'Well, you clearly made an impression,' I replied. 'Shall I continue?'

'Oh please do, Vicar, please do,' the two women pleaded in unison.

'"You will be pleased to know that 'the drop' caused no ill-effects, other than a slight headache I had the morning after I returned to base. 'It must be a hangover from that wild party you had in the quaint old English countryside with those ladies you've been telling us about,' my commanding officer joked. He was always pulling my leg about me being a teetotaller, never let up, he did."'

'Well, I think that's wicked of him,' Edna chipped in. 'Jimmy was such a clean. upstanding boy. I think it's terrible that someone who was supposed to be a superior officer should make such fun of him. I really do. He should have known better.'

'Oh don't take on so. I'm sure the officer didn't mean any harm,' snapped Flo. 'Let the vicar continue, you, or we'll never hear the letter through.'

I read on. '"But seriously, ladies, my commanding officer was extremely grateful for all you did, and asked me to send his thanks and kindest regards."'

'See!' interrupted Flo. 'I told you the officer was a good sort!'

'"As I say, ladies, I am truly grateful for your kindness,"' I read, moving on to the next paragraph. '"I don't quite know how to put this, and I hope you won't be offended, but I was totally appalled by the terrible condition of your little house. I talked to that nice guy who called on you, the Reverend Whatever-He-Was, who agreed with me that something ought to be done. It seemed there was some money in the kitty, but that you were about two thousand dollars short, and couldn't start work until that was raised."'

'Oh, you shouldn't have talked to him about our predicament, Vicar, you really shouldn't. This place has always been like this, we don't mind, do we, Flo?' Edna commented.

'I mind the fact that it takes you longer and longer to clean it up these days,' Flo complained. 'My lunch was an hour late yesterday, you were so behind.'

'Flo and Edna, listen to this,' I said excitedly, reading on. '"I hope you will accept the enclosed check as a thank you for caring for me."' I hesitated for a moment as I looked in the envelope for a sample of tartan, until I realized Americans spell our 'cheque' as 'check'. I picked up where I had momentarily left off. '"My daddy owns a big oil firm over here, Benson's Gas Products, and when he heard about your plight, and what you'd done for me, he positively insisted that we try to help you out. The money's just peanuts to us. 'Let's put it to good use to help our poor cousins in the old country,' my daddy said. So please pass on the money to your Reverend friend, and I hope the work will soon begin."'

'How very, very kind of him,' Edna said. 'So very kind. But he needn't have sent us anything at all. He was such a nice young man. We were just glad to have his company.'

'How much is the cheque for?' asked the

356

more mercenary Flo.

I slowly unfolded the other piece of paper, and then I sank on to the kitchen chair as my knees gave way. 'Phew,' I said, staring at the cheque, unable to believe my eyes.

'You'd think it was for as much as a hundred pounds, the way you're reacting, Vicar,' Edna joked.

'How much is it for, then?' Flo demanded. 'How much?'

'Eight thousand dollars,' I said.

'Eight thousand dollars?!' the two sisters cried in unison. 'Eight thousand dollars?'

'What on earth are we supposed to do with all that?' Edna asked.

'Hang on a minute,' I said, picking up the letter again and trying to find my place. 'Yes, here we are. "Your Reverend friend mentioned the possibility of a third residence, a new bungalow, to be built on the site of those rat-infested sheds around the back of your cottage, but thought you would never find the money to do up your house, let alone build a new one. Please use the money to make your cottage and the slum next door absolutely tip-top, and then build the bungalow. I would be absolutely delighted if my dropping in on you enabled three sets of old people to end their days in decent homes." It's signed "Your ever respectful Texan friend, Jimmy Benson,"' I concluded.

'Just think, Edna, we entertained an oil-rich Texan, and never realized it. What do you think of that?'

But at that moment Edna could not reply to Flo's questions, because tears were filling her eyes and she was too choked to say anything. After a few minutes she dabbed the tears with her handkerchief, recovering sufficient control to speak. Her words, dammed up for a moment or two, now came in floods. 'Oh, I'm so sorry Vicar, for making such a spectacle of myself. Whatever must you think. It's just that I feared we'd never get the money to do these almshouses up, never in a hundred years. I know you've been wonderful trying to encourage people to give, but they're a tight lot around here, even begrudging the pennies for my lavatory in York. I just thought we'd never make it, and though I was putting on a brave face, I really am finding it harder and harder to look after the place, and if I couldn't keep up, what would become of Flo and me?' She began crying again; uncontrollable weeping was breaking out in the Withs like wildfire.

'Don't worry, Edna,' I replied. 'We'll get

on with the building straight away now. We can do up next door first, and then move you and Flo in there whilst we do the same with this place, so as to limit the upheaval for the two of you. And I've seen the architect's plans; once the work is completed, it'll be a lovely little home, deliberately designed to be easy to care for. For instance, there'll be no more coal fires. All the heating will be clean electric, and more than adequate.'

'But I like a coal fire,' complained Flo. 'I can't be doing with anything else.'

'Ay, but you've never made a coal fire yet, nor cleaned up after one,' Edna rejoindered, showing her mettle. 'I'm going blind too, Flo, so you can't expect me to continue doing what you've never done. It'll be lovely to see out our days in comfort and not have to work my fingers to the bone.'

Flo was stunned into silence by her sister's rare display of temper. I looked away from them both, embarrassed by the confrontation. Letting my eyes fall back on Jimmy's letter, I realized there was more. 'Ladies, there's a PS I haven't read to you. "As soon as I was able to get away from the base, I bought a can of that Bournvita which you plied me with when I was with you. But I'm sorry to say the taste was nowhere near as heavenly as when I drank it at your cottage. Do you make it in some special way? Please let me know, because I've never ever tasted anything so divine. Love, Jimmy."

'We must send him a bottle of the finest malt whisky to mix in with the milk,' Edna declared. 'That's the very least we can do to thank him for such stupendous generosity.'

'That would be very kind,' I added. 'Just promise me one thing, ladies.'

'What's that, Vicar?' they asked eagerly.

'That you don't send him the whisky until we've well and truly banked his cheque!'

I came away from their home on cloud nine. My boss had said visiting would lift anyone's spirits, and he was right. I also thought of Bill Everingham's words on the evening before the jet crashed: 'We need an ang-el to drop the mon-ey in-to us laps.' And I also thought of my joke to Rebecca as we saw the white parachute fall, later that same night, that that must be Bill's angel come to our rescue. Never a truer word spoken in jest.

Sunday 17 July

The service at Kirkwith was full for the

dedication of the new organ, delivered safely from Helmsley on the back of Bill Everingham's farm truck, mercifully sans the firebell. Doris Harsley was decked out in a new black woollen coat, complete with a mock fur black collar, and a new red hat which, unlike all the other hats routinely sported by the members of my Mothers' Union, still had some shape. Sam Harsley, her husband, stood proudly by her side. Although he hadn't had new clothes for the occasion, his black suit had been dry-cleaned, and his verger's gown washed. 'Ee it were absolutely filthy Vicar,' Doris had announced to me loudly just minutes before the service began. 'I had to wash it three times and still water were absolutely black – I can't imagine what he's been getting up to in it!' She directed a suspicious look towards her husband before catching her breath and continuing. 'I gave it a good starch like I used to do to children's surplices,' she informed me.

I looked again at Sam in his slightly faded verger's gown, dye squeezed out of it by a wife obsessed with cleanliness. I had already thought that he looked rather stiff, but had just assumed that he had been doing too much gardening. But then my suspicions were aroused, because at that moment he sneezed. It was just a mild sneeze, a delicate 'atishoo' caused by pollen from the flowers that festooned every nook and cranny of the church. Nothing out of the ordinary, just one of the many coughs and sneezes which regularly punctuated my sermon. What was unusual was the ear-splitting crack which accompanied it.

Bill Everingham shot out of his church-warden's seat and hobbled towards me. 'Did you 'ear that crack, Vic-ar? I reckon tim-bers in nave roof are go-in'. I've al-ways feared they 'ad dry rot.'

'I think the cause is more at ground level,' I replied, nodding towards Sam.

'Ay, sorry Vicar, sorry Bill, it were me,' Sam confessed, his face turning red, as if he had been an embarrassed child owning up to a bad smell. 'T' missus has starched this gown so stiff that every false move I make it goes off crack, like a bullet from a gun. Come to think of it, every proper move it goes off crack too!'

Bill returned to his seat, and the service began. For the dedication, George had invited back his university colleagues, who had pressed their ten-bob notes upon me following baby Simon's baptism and had

362

thereby launched the new organ fund. Once again I prayed that nothing would go wrong; not that my prayer had worked last time. But at least this time we could count on the organ behaving itself.

We started the service in silence while I said a blessing over the new harmonium, Doris Harsley perching proudly and massively on the stool, Sam standing to crisp attention by the organ's side, ready to man the pump as soon as the dedication was over. 'Praise him upon the sound of the trumpet: praise him upon the lute and harp,' I began, having cribbed most of my home-made prayer from Psalm 150. 'Let everything that hath breath, praise the Lord. And so, Father, let this organ dedicated in your name, enable the praises of your people. Amen.'

I then announced the opening hymn, and our new organ made its first official sound in Kirkwith's church. 'O praise ye the Lord, praise 'im in the 'eights,' the congregation sang heartily, in unison with the confident and sonorous notes of the new instrument, with not even a whisper of a single lovesick camel to be heard. But by the third verse the volume of the congregation's contribution had waned as they strained their ears, puzzling over the loud cracking sound which accompanied each note, which had the effect of splitting up the syllables like a musical version of Bill Everingham. 'Loud - *crack* - org - *crack* - ans - *crack* - his - *crack* - glor - *crack* - y - *crack* - forth – *crack* - tell - *crack* - in - *crack* - deep - *crack* - tone...'

The punctuated hymn eventually came to its end, with everyone in the packed congregation sporting a look which had become increasingly puzzled as the verses had progressed. Apart, that is, from Bill Everingham and me, who knew the cause of the disruption. And the red-faced Sam Harsley, who was its cause, as his verger's gown cracked with each action of the organ pump. 'It must have a built-in garden gnome,' I overheard Becky Ludlow whisper to Geoff Goodmanham.

'Metronome, I think,' Geoff corrected her. To mask the congregation's titters, I started the liturgy. 'In the name of the Father - *crack* - and of the Son - *crack* - and of the Holy Spirit - *crack* - Amen.' Sam Harsley was High Church and so crossed himself at every opportunity.

As the service progressed, the cracking diminished as Sam's gown was run in, and the congregation relaxed. There was no other hitch, but by irony of ironies the Gospel reading set for the day was about the woman taken in adultery. The religious leaders of Jesus' day, tabloid readers to a man, entrap some poor woman, engaged in the very act of adultery. They drag her off to the temple courts and throw her at the feet of Jesus. 'Moses says that such women as this should be stoned, Master,' they sneer. 'What do you say?'

Shy Jesus averts his gaze from the scantily clad woman thrown in front of him, and doodles in the sand. He then looks her accusers in the eye and says, 'Fine, let the one of you without sin throw the first stone.' Realizing their own culpability, one by one they go away, leaving the woman alone with her Lord. Jesus looks at her and says, 'Has no one condemned you? Neither do I condemn you. Go, do not sin again.'

The sheer force of that story of unconditional forgiveness always made me want to cry. Doubly so this morning, with Ivy Weighton and my Rebecca in the congregation. I mounted the pulpit steps, determined to keep my sermon short and sweet; a few words was all my heavy heart could manage. Yet at the same time I had the sense that they were words on which three lives in that congregation would hinge. 'In the name of the Father - *crack* - and of the Son - *crack* - and of the Holy Spirit - *crack* - Amen,' I began. I prayed that Sam Harsley would now sit down and be still.

'The Israel of Jesus' day was a very tight community, full of gossip, and accusations, and counter-accusations, full of hypocrisy, full of people pretending to be whiter than white when their hearts were actually black as coal. It wasn't a fairytale land, it wasn't out of this world. It was a place much like anywhere. A place much like round here.' Mercifully, Sam's gown stayed quiet as a holy hush descended on the congregation.

'There are two things that the Gospel story doesn't tell us,' I continued. 'The first is how Jesus looked. I like to picture him smiling as he said those words to that poor woman. Not leering at her, nor sneering at her, but giving her a lovely smile, eyes twinkling, as he pronounced the words of her liberation, "Neither do I condemn you." And if the Lord of heaven and earth didn't condemn her, none of us can condemn her. And no one has the right, any right at all, to condemn us.'

Every eye of every person in that congregation was moist, as they thought of their own need for forgiveness, their own call to be forgiving. 'The second omission is that the story stops there, doesn't tell us what became of the woman, how she used what remained of her day after Jesus had smiled on her. The Gospel leaves us to write the end of that story with our own lives, as Jesus shyly smiles on us, today, and what remains of our day on earth. "Neither do I condemn you. Go, do not sin again."

'In the name of the Father - *crack* - and of the Son - *crack* - and of the Holy Spirit - *crack* - Amen.' I came down from the pulpit steps, sat in my stall, and fought to hold back the tears.

Monday 18 July

The night was close, very close, after a hot, humid and sticky day. A night to spend out of doors, seeking every cooling breeze. Definitely not a night to spend in the Dettol-permeated haunts of Eastwith School. The hall was packed with the parents, grandparents, relatives and friends of the fourteen children we were to take to London the following week. It seemed that every member of each child's extended family had turned out for the occasion, which we could have entitled 'What's our so-and-so going to get up to in the big city?'

Geoff and June and I sat behind a well-worn table, carved by countless generations of naughty children who had immortalized their initials while their teacher's back was turned. Baby Elizabeth bounced up and down on her mother's knee, happily chortling at the vast crowd, who sat uncomfortably before her gaze on tiny infant chairs. Because of the large number of people, the chairs had to be arranged closely together, coming right up to our table's edge, the chins of the people in the front row actually resting on it, like coconuts on a fairground shy.

Geoff rose up, sporting his usual Harris tweed jacket, seemingly oblivious to the evening's heat and the baking, fetid atmosphere of the full hall. 'This will be the trip of a lifetime,' he began, his enthusiasm in direct proportion to the miserable looks that the crowd returned our way. 'We'll make sure every child comes back home with a real flavour of our Swinging Sixties' capital. We'll take in all the sights, breathe in the air, eat the food, even sail on the river. It'll give them a feast of memories that will certainly fuel the rest of their childhood and probably their adulthood as well.' June looked at her husband adoringly. I admired the man too for his unbridled and seemingly inexhaustible enthusiasm. But the crowd remained unmoved, positively tight-lipped.

Geoff breezed us through the five-day trip, the visits, the hostel where we would stay, who would sleep where, how the menu could be adjusted for each child's fads and crazes, how we would cope with the tube, the crowds. At the end of his talk, he suddenly strode around the tiny hall, his Harris tweed flapping, leaping over sundry chairs and legs, drawing the flimsy curtains. 'Ee he's a bit premature,' commented Doris Harsley, there because her grandson David was coming on the trip, 'the sun hasn't even set yet.'

'Perhaps he wants to keep the cold out,' explained Becky Ludlow, there to serve the refreshments. 'It can be a bit chill on these summer's evenings.' With the curtains drawn, the atmosphere in the hall became even more airless and stifling: even the tiniest hint of Becky Ludlow's feared chill would have been more than welcome.

The curtains might have kept out the cold, but they certainly didn't exclude any light.

The sun, low but still brilliant over the Ings in the west, shone straight through the curtain material as if it wasn't there. Which somewhat spoiled Geoff's finale, a slide show of the capital's sights to whet the appetite for the forthcoming trip. We all peered at the first picture, a ghostly image of Big Ben. 'What's that?' Becky Ludlow hissed to her neighbour. 'I can't make it out. I think I've got catamarans in my eyes.'

'Oh it's obviously an obelisk,' Doris Harsley explained, airing superior knowledge. 'You tell her Sam!'

'Oh yes, that's definitely an obelisk,' he agreed, 'I know one of those things when I see one. I was a Desert Rat, you know. They were all around us when we were stationed in Egypt during the war, sticking up all over the place.' His moustache bristled with pride as he recalled his wartime memories.

'But what are they for?' Becky Ludlow asked.

'Well, erm,' Sam replied, shuffling on his chair, twiddling his moustache round his finger, not wanting to admit he hadn't much of an idea. 'Well, there was a young lad who was an officer stationed with us, who'd read Classics at Cambridge. He said they were, er, oh, I can't rightly remember what he said,' Sam's voice trailed off. Even though everyone in that hot room was highly coloured, I noticed his face went a deeper hue of red.'

'Well don't ask me I wasn't there,' Doris replied.

'Oh, I remember now,' Sam cried out. 'He said they was fertility symbols. That's it, fertility symbols!' His face went even redder; he'd obviously decided he'd rather be embarrassed than seem ignorant.'

'Ee these exotic practices you came across,' Doris commented. 'Going to war really broadened your mind.'

'Well, isn't it nice of Mr Goodmanham to show us erotic slides,' Becky Ludlow piped up, nearer the truth than she reaized. 'It'll make a lovely end to the evening.'

Everyone in the audience screwed up their eyes as they peered at faint pictures which blended nicely with the interior brickwork of the hall, painted shiny-yellow. I was just about able to make out Buckingham Palace, the Houses of Parliament, the Tower of London, Tower Bridge and Wembley Stadium. But there again, I had seen them before, so had an unfair advantage over the rest of the company, who saw anything they wanted to imagine in poor Geoff's slide show. Virtual reality was born in Eastwith, thirty years before its time.

We came unstuck with a shimmering image of St Paul's Cathedral. 'Now that's the Taj Mahal,' Sam Harsley shouted out. 'After we'd cleaned the Jerrys out of Egypt, we went on to guard India from the Japs. I'll never forget that Taj Mahal, as long as I live. An absolute wonder of the world, it was. The picture will stay in my mind until the day I die.'

'I think that's enough slides for now,' Geoff announced, deciding to quit while he was losing. 'I've told you about all our plans for the week, you've seen a few of the things we'll see, I'm sure you'll have lots of questions, so fire away.'

Mrs Dubbins rose to her feet, with drops of perspiration on her brow. She was a large woman from a family of large women, their bale-throwing frame specially developed through generations of careful breeding. And she had a voice which sounded as if she had swallowed a megaphone. 'Mr Good-manham,' she boomed, the sound reverberating around the tiny hall.

'Yes, Mrs Dubbins?' Geoff replied sweetly, the epitome of eagerness. The hall too was poised. What cunning question about the trip's detail was she going to floor the head teacher with?

'Mr Goodmanham, can you tell me whether our Sharon is going to pass her Eleven-Plus next year or not?'

'It's a little early to say, Mrs Dubbins,' he replied, hiding well his disappointment that his brilliant presentation had gone totally over her head. 'In my experience, children develop a lot over the summer holidays, so things will be a little clearer in the autumn term. Come and see me then, and we'll have a chat about it.'

I admired his diplomacy immensely. Never mind about developing over the summer holidays, Sharon Dubbins' IQ would have to make a quantum leap for her to come within a mile of passing for grammar school. 'Now, any more questions?' Geoff asked.

' Yes,' said Mrs Moss. 'When's t' church going to stop all these bricks on t' school building flakin'? Our Lee's always coming home wi' a cut head, cos someone's thrown a bit o' brick at him.'

'I have to say, Mrs Moss, that Lee gives as good as he gets,' Geoff replied, quite firmly. 'Only today, two of the infants had to have cuts dressed because of your Lee throwing pieces of brick at them. But the school rule is that no one throws anything at anyone. I hate caning children, but if all this brick-throwing goes on much longer, it'll be a cane-able offence.'

'Never mind caning t' children,' Mrs Dubbins boomed. 'Why doesn't t' vicar get t' building repaired?'

'It's on our list of priorities,' I assured Mrs Dubbins. 'It's just a case of finding the money for every worthy cause. And that means raising it from you.'

'Finding the money, finding the money?' she shouted. 'Finding the money? Why don't you use the Church Commissioners' millions, instead of always fleecing us ordinary folk?'

'Let's not get sidetracked by the Church Commissioners,' Geoff pleaded. 'Now, any more questions? Anything you would like to ask about the trip, perhaps?' Which after all, was the sole reason why we were all there on this scorching summer's eve.

Since the audience had exhausted themselves with Eleven-Pluses, decaying buildings and the Commissioners' hoarded millions, there wasn't a single question about the London visit, so a disappointed Geoff adjourned the meeting for refreshments.

Quite a few of the mothers cooed over baby Elizabeth. 'Oh, isn't she coming on! Is she out of nappies yet?' Mrs Dubbins boomed.

'No, I think we still have a few months to go,' June Goodmanham assured her. 'And even then, it'll be a year or two before we have a dry night.'

'Maybe more than a year or two,' Mrs Moss informed her. 'Our Lee's still wetting t' bed at night, and he's nearly twelve!' she declared nonchalantly to all and sundry. I pitied the child next week who had the lower bed with Lee the Pee on the top bunk.

Sunday 24 July

It had taken longer than a week for Rebecca to take stock. I didn't force the issue, but as the days went on the subject of Hans and whose daughter she really was loomed less large as other items invaded our agenda. I was preparing for the exodus of the children of the Withs to London. She was in the middle of the exam season, with five hundred scripts to mark.

'No *Odes to Joy* then?' I quipped, as she came back with me to the vicarage after

Evensong, the night before Eastwith School's departure for London.

'Well, yes, just that one girl never gives up,' she admitted. 'There was a question in the fourth-form exam, "Describe what you would see if you visited the Ruhr."

'Our friend wrote *"Ich möchte Freude im Ruhr finden..."* - I would like to find joy in the Ruhr – and then off she went with her Beethoven's Ninth, *"Freude, schöne gotter-funken"* and all that.'

'I would have thought the industrial wastelands of the Ruhr were the most joyless place on earth,' I quipped.

'Yes,' she agreed. 'But I actually gave her full marks. First, because her German construction was perfect, and second, because of her sheer determination to see joy everywhere. If you could find joy in the *Ruhr*, then you can find it anywhere.'

Rebecca was quiet for a moment before continuing, as if she were carefully selecting her words. 'Actually her obsession with *Ode to Joy* brought me up short about my own situation, and helped me come to a decision.'

My mouth immediately went dry, my heart started pounding in my chest. 'Really?' I heard myself squawk.

'Yes,' she continued. 'It was like a big idea suddenly springing on an inventor, a light suddenly switched on at the end of a dark tunnel.'

'The big idea being?' I asked.

'Simple really,' she replied, her smile breaking through. 'Voting for joy, whatever life throws at you. I realize that bad things happen to everyone, and good things too. No one is immune to either the bad or the good. But how you react to them is up to you, you can greet them with joy or with misery.' Though obviously rehearsed, it was a fine speech, clearly from her heart. 'It suddenly dawned on me what I had, Mum, Dad, or the man I call Dad, this place, my job, the best job in the world, memories galore of a man who gave me so much time, taught me so much, seemed so close. I decided I should be thankful about all those things, not mope about them. And finally, and most of all, you,' she said, looking straight at me with those steel-blue eyes. 'If you'll still have me, I'd love to marry you.'

'But what about the space you wanted to work out who you were?' I asked. 'Rebecca, I love you enough to want you to have that, rather than rush into things.'

'Yes, well, I'm sorry about all that angst,

and I'm really, really sorry about putting you through it all. I guess there's always the temptation to run away to some desert island and sort yourself out...'

'Stop the world, I want to get off!' I quipped.

'But you can't, can you?' she argued. 'The world is the only show in town, and it's in that world where you'll find yourself, or by definition you won't exist at all. I decided that it was in relating to those around me rather than avoiding them that I'll find myself, and most of all in relating to you. So will you marry me, darling?'

'Of course I will,' I replied. 'How about Saturday August the twentieth? – I've already got that date clear for something or other.'

'So have I,' she laughed. 'So have I. But just one thing, though,' she added.

'What?' I asked.

'Do not allow Doris Harsley under any circumstances to starch Sam's gown. I couldn't keep a straight face making my vows in the name of the Father and of the Son and of the Holy Ghost with him cracking like a whiplash.'

'I'll see what I can do,' I agreed, taking her in my arms.

Monday 25 July

'Please, sir, the train won't go without us, will it?' Sharon Dubbins anxiously asked. She was sitting hunched in her seat on Ron Ran Run's vintage bus, a rucksack on her back the size of a small bale. Clearly her mother was training her to be a prizewinner at the Howden Show, yet another generation of champion bale-hurlers. The bus was crawling into Selby, held up as usual by the queue of traffic at the toll bridge.

While I shared Sharon's concern about whether we would get to the station in time to catch the 8.30 London train, my apprehension was tinged with relief that we were travelling slowly rather than quickly. Sid, the ill-sighted one, was driving. Happily no parked cars had marred our path on the journey from the Withs. Sid was now in his element, in that all he had to do was to idle along behind the vehicle in front, which was easily in his myopic range of vision. We had encountered a slight problem when he'd followed a lorry into the flour mill on Selby's outskirts. That, however, had soon been overcome as Sid had reversed back into the traffic's stream with a confidence that far exceeded his ability. Fortunately he was well known in these parts, so other drivers knew it was in their best interests to take avoidance measures without delay, when they saw Sid hurtling backwards towards them.

Geoff Goodmanham was sitting at the front, hair ruffled as usual. Beside him sat June with baby Elizabeth on her knee. Geoff was keeping amazingly calm. 'Now don't you worry, Sharon,' he cooed reassuringly. 'We've got plenty of time. Even if the toll bridge is up to let the *Evening Press* barge through, then they'll have to swing the railway bridge open as well. Which means the train will be kept waiting on the wrong side of the Ouse as well as us.' His cool, matter-of-fact analysis put Sharon, and us all, at our ease.

After what seemed an age we rumbled across the dreaded bridge and chugged alongside Selby station just as the London train was pulling in. Fourteen youngsters rushed on to the platform, their duffle bags and rucksacks bouncing on their backs, seemingly as excited as their owners. We hurried along behind them, with June and Geoff each carrying a handle of Elizabeth's carry-cot as they ran. The three of us must have looked like Sherpas, about to trek up Everest, loaded as we were with bags and cases in every available hand, under every available arm and over every available shoulder. Elizabeth's need of supplies was out of all proportion to her size.

The train, already delayed, was held up for a few more minutes when Elizabeth's carry-cot got wedged in the door. A perplexed June, still on the platform, pushed with all her might. The ever-calm Geoff, safely on the train, pulled with all his strength. Elizabeth wailed her protest with the full force of her lungs. 'You'll have to get that bloody cot shifted, we've got ten minutes to make up before Doncaster,' an over-officious guard complained loudly, as if June and Geoff had contrived to have their precious daughter travel to London with her legs dangling out of the express. I treated the whole situation like an interesting mechanics problem from my A-level days, persuading Geoff to stop pulling and June to stop pushing, instead encouraging them to turn the cot on a horizontal as well as a vertical plane. I had always known that arduous years spent studying rotational dynamics would come into their own one day.

Soon we were all safely aboard. The guard's whistle blew and as the train inched out of the station, the white limestone of Selby Abbey, caught in the summer sunshine, beamed its farewell at us. We were London-bound, at last.

Elizabeth howled, fourteen hyped-up children shrieked, Geoff, June and I got our breath back, the rest of the passengers in the carriage cursed their luck at being holed up with a school party. I only hoped the three hours' journey sped by as quickly for them as it did for the children, who excitedly pointed out landmarks in successive towns: the tall tower of Doncaster Parish Church to the left; the equally tall spire of Grantham Parish Church, also to the left; Peterborough Cathedral sprawling like a crab, again to the left.

While the trip broadened the children's education no end, it left them with the unfortunate misapprehension that there was nothing notable in England to the right of that railway line. 'It's obvious there's nowt over that side and that it's all over this side,' Lee Moss pointed out, with thirteen junior heads nodding in agreement. Lee was a bit of a bully, so it was in their best interests to go along with him. 'On that side it's all wasteland falling into t' sea.'

'You're wrong, there, Lee, I'm afraid,' I butted in. I simply had to intervene, otherwise these children would be left with a warped geography of the British Isles for the rest of their lives. Which was hardly the intention of this mind-expanding trip. 'There's some delightful places in the west.'

'Such as?' Lee demanded, his voice surly.

'Well, Cornwall, and Devon and Somerset, for instance.'

'But what about places?' he persisted. 'They're just counties, names for t' wasteland that falls into t' sea, like I said.'

'There are lots of places,' I replied, racking my frozen brain to recall a few. 'There's Gloucester and Bristol and Birmingham and Exeter, for instance. I could go on and on.'

'Ah, you're just kidding us,' he protested. 'You don't really know. Me dad always says, "Don't take any notice o' them parsons, they'll spin you a line." You've only got to look owt of t' train window to realize it's obvious that there's nowt on that side.'

'No, Lee,' I said firmly, slightly irked by his precocious anti-clericalism. 'You just have to believe me.'

'But how do you know?' he persisted.

'What about that tractor yonder, what make is it?' he asked, pointing out of the window. It might have been a small help to my cause if the tractor had been on the right-hand side rather than the left.

'Er, er, a Massey Ferguson,' I replied.

'A Massey Ferguson, a Massey Ferguson?' Lee cried out, giving a hollow laugh, which was immediately copied by the rest of the children. 'Why, it's a David Brown, it's obvious. Fancy not being able to tell the difference between a Massey Ferguson and a David Brown! If you don't know t' simplest things, like names of a tractor, how can you know what's over there, or not over there,' he concluded, tipping his head to the right of the train.

Fortunately the train juddered at that moment, making the omniscient Lee spill orangeade down his front. He therefore became preoccupied with other things, most notably wringing out his sodden T-shirt and then licking the precious orange juice off his fingers. Though I was grateful to be let off the hook, I had the funniest feeling that there had been an undercurrent to the discussion, with issues more important than the existence of the West Country and even the make of tractors at stake.

By the time we pulled into King's Cross, the atmosphere was highly charged. The children's excitement was, not surprisingly, at fever pitch. The anxiety we three adults were experiencing was at a similar level, because ahead of us lay the Underground. None of the fourteen children had ever been to any large city before, let alone London. None of them had ever been in a single tunnel, let alone a labyrinth. None of them had ever encountered a crowd larger than that which attended Kirkwith's carol service - a hundred people seemed a stupendous multitude to them. All these factors had demanded considerable strategic thinking. Like those German generals with their Schlieffen Plan on the brink of the Great War, we were now poised to put our carefully laid designs into action, nervous in case they should all come to grief.

June carried Elizabeth with two of the eldest girls assisting her. Geoff and I then marked six children apiece as we all approached the Underground. Despite their severe misgivings about such a long staircase, let alone a moving one, we coaxed each of our six on to the escalator, and then headed for the Piccadilly Line. Each of my six charges whiled away their time on the platform by asking me in turn why a pigeon could stand on the central rail without being electrocuted. Their incessant questioning was silenced by the *whoosh* of the approaching train. I stood against the doors while they squeezed into the carriage with their luggage, checked not once but thrice that there were six heads, and only then moved away from the doors.

At Holborn I counted six children out, and we made our way to the Central Line for the tube to Holland Park. We had given each of the children an Underground map, and now we had managed one leg of the journey successfully, were encouraging them to use a little initiative of their own. The only near-casualty was David Harsley, who had had the same instructions as the others, to keep to the left and board the down train. He turned right and was about to board the up train, but I managed to extract him before he was whizzed away to the East End, simultaneously keeping an eye on my other five charges. I was beginning to feel like a very amateurish shepherd assigned to a very wayward flock of sheep.

Even though the children had treated their first Underground ride as a tremendous adventure, I noticed a tangible relief as we re-emerged into daylight, even the daylight of a London whose horizons were far more restricted than the open plains of the Vale of York. They were so thrilled to be out in the open that they almost skipped the mile to our youth hostel in Holland Park, despite the fact they were still laden with luggage. We arrived, booked ourselves in, and did a recce of the dormitories, one for June and Elizabeth and the six girls, the other for Geoff, me and the eight boys. The lads ran upstairs, keen to claim the top bunks. Geoff and I trudged behind them, wearily. I was already feeling ready for bed, and we hadn't even had lunch yet.

I had to admire Geoff's tact and diplomacy. Lee Moss was taller and stronger than the other boys, and was the unchallenged leader of the pack. For that reason he had been the natural spokesman on our journey down, putting ignorant vicars to rout. The kingpin, he sauntered behind everyone else and so was the last boy to arrive in the dorm, by which time the much-sought-after top bunks had all been claimed. However, such was his power that one look brought several offers from younger boys, suddenly keen to exchange with him for a lower bunk. But as Lee proudly enthroned himself on his lofty perch, Geoff went over to him and said, 'I think I'd better sleep there, Lee, so that I can see everyone.' He then lowered his voice to a whisper so that none of the other boys could hear: ' Anyway, perhaps it would be wiser for you to have a lower bunk, what with your little problem.' Lee meekly complied, his honour still intact.

Having unpacked, we headed off for lunch at the nearest Lyons Corner House. The children all savoured Mrs Ludlow's school dinners, where the only choice around was to have seconds or thirds, or to push the cabbage around your plate in preference to eating it. In the Lyons Corner House there was choice unlimited, and the children hesitated, unable to make up their minds, while impatient customers tutted in the queue. 'Can I have some taties with that meat?' Lee Moss asked a harassed assistant, slaving behind a counter of steaming vegetables.

'Some what?' she replied. 'We ain't got any of them, dearie.'

'I think he means potatoes,' I interpreted.

'Well, why didn't he say so?' the assistant complained. 'We've got 'em mashed, boiled, chipped, roasted, or in their jackets. Which is it to be? Don't take all day about it, we've got a lot of people waiting behind you for their meal.'

'Er, er,' Lee hesitated. 'What does Mrs Ludlow usually give us, Vicar?' he asked.

'He'll have them mashed,' I instructed the assistant.

'Hear that, girls?' she shouted to the other assistants further down the counter. 'We've got a vicar in today. We'd better stop effing and blinding for half an hour, and refrain from winking when we ask the customers if they want stuffing!' She turned her head towards me. 'Hey, if you're a vicar why haven't you got a dog collar on?'

'Because I'm on a sort of holiday,' I replied.

'Well, it's jolly well not fair, leading people astray like that, being all undercover like. When a vicar wears a dog collar, we knows where we are, where we stand. But if you're going to start popping up without one, who's to say what you'll come across, what saucy things people will say to you without realizing that you're a man of God. You really will have to be more careful.'

'Do they all talk in London like that woman?' Lee whispered to me as we queued to pay.

'Oh, they're renowned for it,' I replied, my

face mock serious. 'It's called Cockney banter.'

'Well, I don't like it, I don't like it at all,' Lee went on, grave beyond his years. 'Up north we call a spade a spade and then shu' up. That woman went on and on for ages, yet when she'd said it, she'd said nowt.'

After lunch we headed off to the newly built Post Office Tower. The children entered the massive lifts with the timidity of Yuri Gagarin on his first trip into space. 'Ee, I've lost me tummy,' they all shrieked in concert as the lift took off and we soared to the top. We climbed above the restaurant to the public gallery and stood still for twenty minutes as London revolved around us, a trailer for the visits to come. Lee peered over to the far west, guided by the compass provided. 'See, Vicar, nowt over that side at all. Absolutely nowt.'

'Sure, Lee!' I replied.

'Did you hear that, Burt, that man's a vicar,' a woman standing by blurted out. 'You'd think they'd wear a dog collar, wouldn't you, just to warn us to watch our language...'

We wandered back to the youth hostel via another Lyons café and then turned in for the night, a hot and humid London night, the boys talking until the early hours despite our encouragement to them to get some sleep. In the courtyard below a student with a guitar struck up the strains of 'Ave Maria'. His guitar was out of tune, his voice was off key, yet it caught the essential strangeness of our plight, hundreds of miles away from the Withs, where the only sound of human origin that ever heralded the dawn was the sugar beet dryer.

Tuesday 26 July

We rose early and stampeded down the stairs for a breakfast of underdone, anaemic-looking bacon, an overdone and fatty egg whose yolk was dark and hard, finished off with fried bread saturated in lard. The children picked at their meal and one or two shed a tear as they thought of home. More than one or two envied baby Elizabeth, gurgling in her high chair, enjoying a breakfast of mashed banana spooned into her by an adoring June.

'What's a matter, Flower, never seen a cooked breakfast before? Don't they have them where you come from?' the cook shouted at Sharon Dubbins, who was staring at the plate before her.

'We keep us own pigs,' the sobbing Sharon replied. 'Bacon we have never looks like this stuff.' She pushed a rasher around her plate, with a look of disgust on her face.

'Now don't take on so, it's proper bacon that is. I cooked it myself and it's none of your rubbish. It'll have come from a good, clean hygienic pig. Not the sort you have rummaging around in a filthy back yard.'

'Our back yard isn't filthy, it's lovely,' Sharon wailed.

'Thank you, I'll see to her,' I said, dismissing the cook as I strode over towards Sharon.

'Oh, Vicar, I never thought I would miss home so much,' Sharon confessed, the tears streaming down her face.

'Did you hear that, girls? We've got a vicar staying with us,' the piqued cook shouted to her assistants in the kitchen.

'You'd think he'd wear a dog collar, wouldn't you, just to warn us to watch our bloody language...' she cackled as she shuffled back to her fatty den.

Following breakfast we had our chores to complete, making beds, sweeping the dorms, washing up. The girls set about their tasks with a zeal which put the boys to shame. 'My dad's never done a day's washing up in his life,' Lee Moss complained, up to his arms in soapy water. '"That's woman's work," he always says, "You just keep clear of it, son." I feel, I feel,' he groped for the right word, 'I feel I'm betraying him, doing all this,' he concluded, as if he were breaking some Levitical code honoured by generations of Moss males.

Every other boy on the washing-up rota agreed with their hero. 'It makes perfect sense,' David Harsley blurted out. 'Men do the work outside the home, women do the work inside it. You know where you are with all that.' I must admit I had some sympathy with his point of view, if only because his involvement had set us back somewhat. Being told to dry the washed dishes on the right of the sink, he had proceeded to dry the dirty plates on the sink's left. We were then held up five minutes while the grumbling cook fetched clean tea-towels, which were obviously a precious commodity and held under lock and key in some underground vault.

Eventually the chores were completed, and we set off on the tube for our first jaunt of the day, to the BBC Television Centre at Shepherd's Bush, to see a TV programme being recorded. As we queued outside the studio, the children were high with excitement. Clearly hitherto they'd allotted TV some sort of divine status, with programmes beamed to the Withs direct from heaven. To have found the site of that heaven on earth made for a heady time.

The theatre doors were opened and we galloped in and claimed our seats. A man with a posh voice stood at the front and told us when to clap and when to laugh, and the show began. *Mr Pastry* was a silver-haired, silver-moustached geriatric who spent half an hour engaging in pure farce and utter slapstick, acting out a script (if there was a script) devoid of any intelligent content whatsoever. The children simply loved it, and laughed wildly, their homesickness banished.

Once the show had come to a merciful end, we sped across London to peer at Buckingham Palace. Eager to take a photograph with his Brownie camera, David Harsley stuck his head through the railings to get an unimpeded view. Unfortunately the little lad had jug-ears, and once he had successfully taken his photo, try as he might, he couldn't get his jammed head back through, despite the well-intentioned advice offered by the growing crowd around him. 'Try and twist your head around, and I'll give it a tug,' Lee Moss counselled, but the more Lee pulled the more David yelled and the more jammed his swollen head became. The whole episode was degenerating into a farce of *Mr Pastry* proportions.

June rummaged in baby Elizabeth's changing bag and took out a pot of Vaseline which she proceeded to smear on David's ears and head, but even then the well-greased David refused to budge.

The increasingly large crowd attracted the attention of the burly, red-faced policeman on duty. 'Hallo, what have we 'ere then?' he barked, as if he was delivering a much-rehearsed line. The rest of the children looked at him adoringly. Not only had they been privileged to watch *Mr Pastry* in the flesh; it now seemed they had walked on to the set of *Dixon of Dock Green*. 'Oh, a little boy with his 'ead stuck in the railings, is it? Don't worry, son, we'll soon get you out,' he declared as soon as I had explained the situation to him.

However, having sounded so reassuring, he seemed to lose interest and glanced towards the road. He strode over to the kerb and flagged down a passing motorist. 'Excuse me, sir,' he addressed the driver of a battered Morris Minor. 'Would you mind if I had a look in your boot?'

'No, no, no, not at all, officer,' the driver of the car stammered, with the nervousness of a smuggler who suddenly realized he had been rumbled by Customs.

The policeman flung open the boot and rummaged in it for a few seconds, before yelling triumphantly, 'Good, just what I was looking for!'

The white-faced motorist shuffled from foot to foot, and I suspected was about to deliver the time-honoured line, 'I can explain, Constable.'

'If I can borrow this for a minute or two, sir, it'll do just fine!' the policeman announced, saving the hapless driver from voicing his confession. Pulling out the car jack, he marched with an important air back to the railings. He took off his tunic, folded it and folded it again and placed it over David's much-greased head. He then jammed the jack over his tunic, and frantically levered it, prising the railings slowly apart. 'Try it now, son,' he exclaimed, wiping his brow after such an impressive display of physical fitness that it made me feel tired just watching. David sprang free, toppling back, butting his head into my solar plexus.

'Oh, I'm sorry, Vicar,' he apologized as I tried to catch my breath.

'Did you say vicar?' the policeman asked. 'I do apologize, your Reverence, for not addressing you properly. You want to be careful, you know, surprising people incognito like that. Just imagine what it would be like if I went around out of uniform. People wouldn't see me coming, and they'd have to be good the whole of the time.'

'David, say thank you to the kind officer,' June prompted. I guess she was addressing David Harsley rather than me, since I wasn't over-fussed with the policeman for blowing my cover in front of such a large crowd.

'Thank you very much for releasing me, sir,' David said, in the sweetest of voices.

'Ah, think nothing of it, son,' the policeman replied, as he jacked the railings back into their parallel position. 'We get one or two incidents like this a week, and there's no harm done, apart from buckling the fence a bit.'

'And giving guilty motorists near-heart attacks,' I thought.

'And I understand,' he whispered confidentially to David Harsley, 'that Her Majesty's quite sympathetic, what with her

397

eldest lad having ears just like yours!'

Wednesday 27 July

After Buckingham Palace, the logical follow-up was the Tower, with jokes galore en route about David Harsley being sent there for damaging Her Majesty's railings.

A Beefeater acted as our guide, all fourteen children staring at him throughout the tour, goggle-eyed at his garb. 'Any questions?' he asked.

'Those ravens that you said have never left since William the Conqueror's time, how old are they?' enquired Lee Moss, used to putting people in authority on the spot.

'They live for a good few years, son,' the Beefeater replied.

'But not for nine hundred years,' Lee asked.

'Oh no, son, no, none of them lives as long as that,' the Beefeater chuckled rather patronizingly.

'So they have left then?'

The Beefeater looked puzzled. 'I don't know what you're getting at, son.'

'Well, if they die after a few years, then they do leave in a sort of way, don't they, going off to raven heaven or wherever? So they have left and Britain hasn't been invaded, so that story you told about us only being safe as long as they stay just isn't true,' Lee concluded, like a prosecuting counsel who had never lost a case.

'If you say so, son,' the Beefeater agreed, not the first person to be floored by Lee's logic. I guess he wouldn't be inviting questions so freely in the future.

The memory I took away from the Tower was of the Crown jewels, or rather of two little girls who feasted their eyes on these magnificent glittering specimens. Sharon Dubbins had looked at them and then promptly burst into tears. 'What's the matter, Sharon?' I asked. 'Is it that they're so lovely?'

'No, it's not that,' she replied. 'My mummy's got no jewels at all, not even an engagement ring. I wished she could have jewels like these, but I know she never ever will.' It was the saddest speech I had ever heard, and at the same time the loveliest, made more poignant because it was delivered by an unbecoming girl with a distinctly unbecoming mother.

'She's got you, Flower, the best jewel in the world,' the Beefeater quipped when he saw her tears.

Sally Broadhurst started crying after that. 'What's the matter, love?' I asked, fervently hoping that mass hysteria wasn't going to break out in our party.

'It's just that I wished I still had a mummy to give jewels like this to,' she sobbed.

June came over and put her arm around her. 'Sally, would you like to carry Elizabeth for a while? I'm feeling a bit tired,' she said soothingly.

'Oh, yes please,' Sally replied, as the thrill of new life eclipsed her grief over life that had been lost.

'And perhaps you'd help, too, Sharon?' June asked.

'Of course, Miss, I'd love to,' replied Sharon, flexing her muscles. Clearly, after months of practising bale-throwing, carrying a baby would be a piece of cake.

I looked from Sharon to Sally and from Elizabeth to June, and thanked my God that we'd be smuggling these four crown jewels back with us to the Withs.

Thursday 28 July

As the week went on, the children's excitement abated, and by the third night, most of them managed to have a good sleep, the midnight conversations having been exhausted both of their novelty and content. So we were well rested for our long walk through the City. Even with their good night's sleep and even temper, nearly every child moaned over something or other as we trudged from landmark to landmark. Instead of gasping at Big Ben striking noon, Lee Moss informed me repeatedly that he had a stitch.

BONG!

'Do you think it's appendicitis, Vicar?'

BONG!

'No, Lee.'

BONG!

'But it doesn't half hurt and it's on my right side...'

BONG!

'It's just a stitch, Lee. Don't worry about it.'

BONG!

'Oo, Vicar, it's killing me!'

BONG!

'Did you hear that, Ethel, that man's a vicar...'

BONG!

'...in disguise. Perhaps the Church is going...'

BONG!

'...undercover to keep tabs on us ordinary folk.'

BONG!

'How do you know it's just a stitch? You...'

BONG!

'...can't even tell a Massey Ferguson from a David Brown!'

BONG!

Merciful silence!

BONG!

David Harsley was as bad, informing me at every stop that his feet were hurting. Instead of looking up in awe at St Paul's, he never so much as raised his head to the sky, but rather looked pointedly at his feet, as if his gaze would dissolve the blisters. 'Look, David, don't worry. All our feet are hurting. We've been walking a long way on concrete when normally we walk on the soft turf of the countryside, so they're bound to throb a bit. Now forget about your feet and look at that wonderful dome.'

'But, Vicar, my feet are just killing me,' he protested.

'Did you hear that, Jackie, that guy over there is a vicar? Perhaps the canons at St Paul's have got new trendy uniforms which he's trying out!' I decided it would have saved the tourists and the locals a lot of trouble if I'd sported my dog collar for the whole trip.

Our walking tour ended with a river trip on the Thames. Lee Moss sat on a bench on one side of the little tripper clutching his aching stomach opposite David Harsley shuffling his tired feet. 'Look at him,' Lee suddenly shrieked, pointing at David. 'He's got his right shoe on his left foot...' He then paused for a moment before his quick brain reached its logical conclusion, '...and what's more, he's got his left shoe on his right foot. Fancy not knowing his left from his right at his age!'

Poor footsore David Harsley, still fragile after getting his ears stuck in the Queen's railings, broke into floods of tears, as nearly the whole class started taunting him, taking up Lee's lead. 'Nah, nah, nah, nah, nah, who can't tell his left from his right?' they all chanted.

I had never seen Geoff so angry as he put the ringleader sternly in his place. 'Lee, he may not be able to tell his left from his right, but we all have things which it takes us a little longer than others to master, don't we?'

The deeply ashamed Lee went bright red,

shouting in contrition, 'Leave off him, everyone, it's an easy mistake to make.'

While all this was going on, David was distraughtly tugging his shoes off to swap them around. Unfortunately he pulled at one too vigorously, sending it catapulting through the air. The glancing blow it gave Lee Moss was much deserved, but its trajectory was sadly not at an end. Instead it bounced off him, and flew over the side of the boat before splashing into the Thames.

A horror-struck silence descended over the whole company, making the rest of the river trip markedly subdued, which at least had the advantage that we were able to see the sights without children moaning about some ailment or other. Fortunately it was the last event of the day, so David was able to hobble, one shoe off and one shoe on, off the boat and on to the tube and then back to Holland Park. The warden there had a spare pair of plimsolls in Lost Property, which, though a little larger than David's size, had the advantage that they wouldn't pinch if sported on the wrong feet.

When we eventually returned to the Withs it transpired that David was due a new pair of shoes anyway, so the loss didn't bring the financial calamity on his family I feared. The final note of encouragement which sounded out of the tragedy was when I saw David hobbling along down the stairs at Westminster tube station. At least he had his one shoe on the right foot: he'd twigged the difference between his left and right at last.

Friday 29 July

The lights started coming on again, the lights in the children's eyes. I had noticed that though every day of the week had been exciting, with new sights to see and new experiences to be had, as our time in London went on, the children looked dulled, had a weariness about them, were lacking the liveliness and *joie de vivre* which was their exhausting trademark. They coped with the bustling capital just fine, proved themselves eminently streetwise, but by Thursday had a distinctly dried-out look. And then as the tube juddered towards King's Cross, and the train home, the lights started returning.

Their excitement reached a peak on the train ride north. 'Have you missed them then, Lee?' one child asked the leader of the pack.

'Nah, not a bit,' Lee replied. 'I got me mum a present, though. I guess she'll expect a bit of something or other. Do you want to see it?'

'Go on then.'

Lee took out of his rucksack a gaudy model of the Tower of London in a cheap perspex case, and handed it to his friend. 'Go on, shake it up,' he encouraged.

The child shook it up and the mini-Tower of London was engulfed in a snowstorm. 'It's even got the ravens in – the detail is very impressive,' Lee explained, sounding adult beyond his years. 'It cost me five shillings – I hope she'll like it.'

There were displays of presents and conversations like this going on up and down the carriage. Tacky souvenirs which were like treasure to them, not because of what they were, but because of what they were trying to say through them. They were attempting to make these cheap gifts voice their thanks, their love, their gratitude, towards their parents, emotions which, even at their tender age, they were too proud to put into words. Their obvious frustration was that what was on offer didn't even remotely fathom their depth of feeling. Those fourteen children and their frail little gifts brought tears to my eyes.

It was only when Ron Ran Run's vintage bus crossed the Derwent and Kirkwith's avenue of poplars came into sight that I realized how London had drained me too. The Ings, the ripening fields, the Wolds with their patchwork quilt of crops, all soaked into me like rain watering a thirsty land. It dawned on me, as it hadn't dawned on me before, that I was truly coming home.

Saturday 30 July

'Don't worr-y, Vic-ar, we'll still draw a big crowd,' Bill Everingham had assured me last night, as we moved the trestle tables from his barn to my garden. 'Most wom-en can't stand foot-ball, so they'll be real glad to have an ex-cuse to miss gogg-ling at it on tel-e-vis-ion. And they'll prob-ab-ly drag their men-folk al-ong too.'

'But surely no man will miss the chance of seeing England in the World Cup?' I asked. 'It's a historical first, the first time in history they can all watch it in their living rooms.'

'Ay, and the first time in his-tor-y they can all die in their liv-ing rooms,' Bill quipped, as he lugged a ten-foot trestle off the back of his tractor.

'What do you mean, Bill?' I said, intrigued by his line of argument. We huffed and puffed with the trestle and laid it end on at the side of my house.

'Ee, just look at them house mart-ins' nests und-er your eaves,' Bill commented, distracted as he looked up. 'I've never seen so man-y of them. That's a good sign, that is. Not just for to-morr-ow. You and Reb-ecc-a will be rich-ly blessed, believe you me. Rich-ly blessed. "Hap-py the bride whose new home har-bours a house martin," say-in' goes. You must have more than a doz-en of 'em!'

'Yeh', and their constant chattering so near my bedroom window keeps me awake at night, so I must say I find it a funny sort of blessing,' I replied, laughing. 'But never mind the house martins, what do you mean about all these men dying in their living rooms?'

'Well, they'll all have heart att-acks if t' Germ-ans win,' he explained. 'They're a pre-ju-diced lot round here, can't for-give t' Germ-ans for two world wars.'

'But what about Hans?' I asked. 'Every-body liked him.'

'They did-n't to start with. Loc-als gave

him hell. And then they on-ly liked him cos he'd changed sides, as it were. And he were-n't reall-y from Ger-man-y, any-how, but Trans-yl-vani-a, they could just a-bout for-give him for that.'

'But surely all that war stuff is forgotten and forgiven now. We're a new Europe, with a Common Market we can't wait to join. Surely Germany is seen as our ally in the Cold War rather than a foe?'

'Not ar-ound here. They've got long mem-or-ies and take a long time to change their minds. Take your Reb-ecc-a, for instance. When she started study-in' Ger-man as a lass, all the sec-on-dar-y school kids on t' bus used to rag her som-ert rot-ten. Man-y a night I used to come ac-ross her, walk-in' home in tears. They'd pulled her hair, torn her un-i-form, thrown her school books all ov-er t' coach. "Naz-i-lov-er," they'd taun-ted her.'

'Oh dear, oh dear, I never realized,' I said, my heart wrung with pity.

'Don't wor-ry your-self. She sur-viv-ed them and won through in the end. She's a tough lit-tle nut, your Reb-ec-ca, bel-ieve me. Rich-ly blessed, you'll be, rich-ly blessed,' Bill assured me.

'So you think the women will drag their

menfolk along just in case Germany wins?' I asked.

'Ay, I do. If their men did-n't have a heart att-ack, they'd go wild and smash t' house up. T' gard-en part-y'll be a posit-ive God-send, you mark my words.'

'So you think Germany will win, do you, Bill?' I asked, trying not to swear as I impaled my finger on a splinter from one of the dilapidated trestles. 'I'm afraid I've been a bit out of it this past week or two, what with the London trip and a few other things.'

'Well, I hope Eng-land will win, but I'd put my mon-ey on Germ-an-y,' Bill admitted. 'We've had a bit of an eas-y time of it. We on-ly had to play ag-ainst ten men in t' quarter fin-al, when t' Arg-ent-in-ian cap-tain was sent off, and I reck-on t' Port-u-guese in sem-i-fin-al were tired out. Playin' those pluck-y Kor-e-ans in t' quart-er fin-al had real-ly knack, er, er, had really tak-en it out of 'em. That Eus-ebi-o, their cap-tain, had to run ar-ound t' pitch to turn that match a-round. They were three-nil down, but he changed it into a five-three vict-or-y. So I reck-on when they came to play us they were shat-ter-ed. T' Germ-ans won't be so eas-y to push ov-er.'

'Why do you say that?' I asked, feeling a real ignoramus as far as events in the World Cup were concerned. I recalled the advice in the Archdeacon's book, *Good Practice for the Pastoral Parson*: 'A priest should be at one with his people; their interests, their concerns, should be his interests, his concerns.' And here was I, totally out of it, with hardly a clue about a subject that the rest of the country were besotted with.

'Well, they beat t' Russ-ians, did-n't they?' the ever-patient Bill explained. 'I watched t' Russ-ians play in their quar-ter fin-al on t' tell-y. They were a blood, er a blum-in' good team, ab-sol-ute-ly sol-id. If t' Germ-an's could beat them, then I reck-on they-ll make mince-meat of us.'

'Anyway', it'll all be over this time tomorrow,' I pronounced, trying to sound sage.

'Ay, and gard-en part-y will be ov-er too,' Bill pointed out. 'How much do you think we'll make?'

'I don't know,' I admitted. 'I hope we make enough to do some work on Eastwith School and make Geoff and June Good-manham's house a bit more comfortable. At least we don't have to worry about the almshouses ever since our generous

411

American friend dropped in.'

'Ay, did-n't I tell you we need-ed an ang-el to drop the mon-ey into our lap?' he guffawed. 'By the way, Hin-der-wells the build-ers are start-in' on first t' alms-house on Mon-day, so that should be read-y by end of t' sum-mer.'

'So Edna and Flo will never have to cope with winter in that damp place ever again,' I concluded. 'I have to say, I'm really, really glad about that, a bit of a miracle considering what an impossible project it seemed just a couple of months ago.'

'Ay, that's true en-ough,' Bill had agreed, as we propped up the last trestle and decided to call it a day. 'But we'll need a far big-ger mir-ac-le than that tom-or-row if Engl-and are goin' to win and t' sun's go-in' to shine on our gard-en part-y. I know you've had a long day Vic-ar, trudg-in' back from London an' all, but be-fore you turn in, you'd bet-ter get on your knees and 'ave a word with t' Boss. See if he can grant us a doub-le!'

Certainly the second part of the double miracle was granted, in that the day had dawned bright and clear. Despite our protracted deliberations at the church council, Doris Harsley and Ivy Weighton decided to set up their cake stall under the sycamore tree. 'We've thought about it long and hard, Vicar, er, David,' Ivy Weighton informed me.

'Not that we weren't grateful for everyone's views,' Doris Harsley chipped in, ''cos we were very grateful indeed.

'But at the end of the day we thought we'd like to be nearer the centre of the action. It's been a hot, dry summer, so we didn't think we'd have any trouble from your sycamore spitting at us,' Ivy declared, making my sycamore sound more like a bad-tempered and erratic camel rather than a tree.

They spent over an hour and a half arranging their produce. Clearly every parishioner in the Withs had baked something or other, because their three trestle tables were soon groaning under the weight of sundry confectionery. There was a tremendous crack as one of the trestles, worm-eaten and rotten from being stored in Bill Everingham's damp barn, snapped at its midpoint, catapulting various goodies around the lawn. Ivy and Doris waddled around, retrieving a cake here, a bun there. 'Don't worry, Doris, I've brought my tea-towel with me,' Ivy said consolingly.' We'll wipe 'em down and no one will know. A bit o' dirt won't hurt anyone, anyway. Especially vicarage dirt.'

'I think I'll use my own tea-towel if you don't mind Ivy,' Doris declared. 'It's freshly ironed – yours looks a bit mucky.'

'You can say that again!' I thought. Still, it was good to see Ivy so cheerful and on such good form.

Bill and I were dispatched to fetch a more durable trestle, and then I stood transfixed as the tricky job of pricing the cakes began. 'I don't think anyone will pay ninepence just for ginger biscuits,' Doris opened the bidding, stroking her chin.

'Well let's charge sevenpence ha'penny then,' Ivy responded irenically, paving the way for a trade. 'Now I think you've priced that cream cake too high at three shillings – it'll never sell at that. Let's reduce it to half a crown and get it shifted before the cream goes sour in this heat.'

'All right if you say so,' Doris agreed grudgingly. 'But what's that mark on that chocolate log?'

'Ee, well would you believe it, that blessed tree's started spitting. Look, it's speckled grandma's mince pies that were left over from Christmas too. I think we'd better move it all.' Bill and I lent a hand as we shuffled the heavily laden trestles to the site underneath the horse chestnuts, the one we'd agreed on to begin with. By now Herbert Wykeham and his wife had set up their white elephant stall there, and were none too pleased at being evicted. 'Why can't we just have the two stalls side by side?' Herbert Wykeham protested.

'Because we don't want the manky old things on your stall spoiling the look of our high-class produce,' Doris pronounced.

'I'll have you know, they're not manky,' Molly Wykeham countered, her face red, a vein throbbing in her temple, a woman ready to do battle. 'Most of the stuff we cleared from my mother's house after she died. It's the best quality, no rubbish, so don't you go calling it manky, Doris Harsley. When it comes to that, one or two of your cakes look as if they've seen better days. Been wiping 'em with your tea-towel, Ivy?' she asked, cruelly.

'Now don't you go casting aspersions on Ivy's cleanliness,' Doris objected, conveniently forgetting that she'd been doing precisely that a few moments earlier. 'Her daughter's getting married to the vicar and we all know that cleanliness is next to godliness.'

I felt her logic was somewhat flawed, but all arguments in the Withs turned out like this, with people trying to score points off each other, like schoolchildren in the playground, not really thinking through what they were saying. 'Come on, Hubert and Molly,' I coaxed, 'Bill and I will give you a hand and carry everything to where the cake stall was under the sycamore. You'll be more in the centre of the action there.'

'Don't you think we ought to mention about that sycamore spitting?' Ivy whispered to Doris.

'Nah I don't,' she replied. 'Sycamore spit can only improve the rubbish that they've got.'

In theory a garden party is supposed to be the Church's shop window, presenting the community at large with a happy social occasion where the Christian virtues of tolerance, love and forgiveness can all be displayed and enjoyed. In practice it invariably turns into a fierce feud between warring factions, who take no prisoners, their tongues like razors, with sharp intakes of breath and cutting remarks filling the air. It's on days like these that I wonder why on earth I ever left off working in Martins' Bank. Even the bitter battles and infighting of the financial world were nothing compared to what Christ's Church could lay on.

Just before noon everyone rushed home for a bite of lunch, leaving me to guard about a dozen fully laden stalls. After the morning's hustle and bustle and succession of arguments, I enjoyed the breathing space and the chance to wander around my *Marie Celeste* of a garden in the sweetest of silence. Not that I was without a job. Doris Harsley and Ivy Weighton had given me strict instructions to guard their stall against sunlight, saboteurs and marauding bargain-hunters. 'We don't care whatever was said at t' church council,' Doris Harsley boomed at me. 'We don't want a single bun selling off our stall until after the opener's speech.' She fixed me with the sort of gaze a hanging judge would give to the quivering convict in the dock before him. 'So you're not to flog anything while we're gone!' And there was me, just itching to play shop assistants in my lunch hour.

The garden didn't stay quiet for long, as people thronged in. The summer sun beat down so fiercely that the women of the Withs had discarded their traditional garb of thick woollen overcoats and shapeless hats in favour of cotton dresses, which had

417

no doubt been first sported in the balmy summers before the war, and the Great War at that. The men rolled up their shirt sleeves, unstudded their collars, knotted handkerchiefs over their bald heads and grumbled at their wives. 'Why couldn't I stay at home and watch telly? What do I want with vicars and cake stalls and Punch and Judys and white elephants and Mrs MP blatherin' on when there's match o' t' century on TV?'

'Shu' up, I'm not leaving you at home swigging your ale and shoutin' your foul language at t' ref and muckin' t' place up.'

'Well, you could 'ave stayed with me!'

'Stayed with you, stayed with you? What on earth would I want to stay with you for, in your sweaty string vest and reekin' o' beer? And I 'ate football, absolutely 'ate it, twenty-two grown men kickin' a ball up and down a field all day. How daft can you get!'

'It's not half as daft as prancing about in t' vicar's garden, pretending you're interested in white elephants and havin' to listen to some borin' woman with a posh voice. Oh, hallo, Vicar, I didn't see you there behind us.'

'Hallo, Mr Sledmere, it's a lovely day, isn't it?' I said.

'Yes indeed, Vicar, absolutely bootiful. It's just good to be out of doors. I wouldn't have missed this for the world,' he lied as Mrs Sledmere narrowed her eyes at him fiercely.

'Are you a football fan?' I asked.

'Not really, Vicar. If I ever come across it on t' box, I'll give it a look, but I'm not fanatical about it. I can't see the point,' he replied, looking as if butter wouldn't melt in his mouth, while his fuming wife made the sound of a overheated steam engine letting off a head of steam.

'Well, if you were interested in the final...'

'Is there a match on, Vicar? Well fancy that, I never even realized!'

'If you were interested in the final, I've opened my living-room window and put the television against it, so people can check up to see how England are doing.'

My Georgian windows reached to the ground, so proving just the ticket for this sort of thing, a purpose for which they were never even remotely intended when they were first installed.

'Well, if I'm passing, I might give it a glance,' Mr Sledmere conceded.

As the crowd assembled, I heard scores of men grumbling like Mr Sledmere, and had similar conversations with each of them.

Every single one was shifty-eyed, and pretended he only had a fleeting interest 'in t' match'.' Every single one of them promised to give my TV a glance, 'but only if I 'appen to be passin', mind.'

By two o'clock the crowd was fully assembled. Or should I say two crowds. One of women, strategically positioned by the cake stall, ready to strike at the most tempting bargain as soon as Mrs MP had done her stuff. The other crowd, consisting entirely of men, lurked by my living-room window, primed for the kick-off which was still an hour away.

Mrs MP made a posh opening speech from a prepared text, which reflected her husband's brand of highly traditional politics. 'Ladies and gentlemen, you, the members of the Church of England, are the rock on which our glorious nation is built. I bid you, with all your heart, to resist the temptations of this permissive society, the sex and drugs and rock and roll which is taking our nation by storm.'

I looked around at all the old dears, mostly over sixty. 'Mm, I reckon you're preaching to the converted here, love,' I thought, very unworthily.

'Support your local church in its stand for

decency. Support your vicar as he battles against corruption and perversion,' she hectored, making corruption and perversion sound positively attractive. 'Finally,' she boomed, as a sigh of relief went around the garden with the women poising themselves to strike at the cake stall, shaking like cats about to pounce on a mouse, 'finally, I charge you, ladies and gentlemen, to empty your purses and your wallets for this worthiest of causes. I give you this toast: here's to your local church and the Queen!'

She seemed to have forgotten that she wasn't at the Mansion House dinner but in a humble vicarage garden, where none of us had a single glass we could raise. There was a weak round of applause, before Mrs MP corrected herself. 'Sorry, I meant to say, I duly declare this garden party open!'

The men stayed put around my living-room window, the women stampeded around the cake stall, which meant they missed a rather touching ceremony. Sally Broadhurst had been commissioned to present Mrs MP with Grandma Weighton's flower arrangement, which resembled a psychedelic hedgehog. In contrast to the flower arrangement, Sally looked a picture, decked out by Pam in a frilly white dress, her curly hair immaculately arranged, held together with the reddest of ribbons. At the last moment, the little girl took fright, no doubt terrified by the fierce speech, and wouldn't let go of her daddy's hand, dragging him and Peter, who unwisely happened to be holding his father's other hand at the time, on to the stage. The two males turned a deep shade of purple as Sally did her stuff, presenting the bouquet, and concluding with a curtsey which yanked her father down to Mrs MP's knee height.

Mrs MP wasn't cowed in the least by this novel procession which filled the tiny platform, keeping her smile fixed as if no garden party could be complete without a family reunion on stage, topped off with a professor sprawling at her feet. 'Thank you so much, my dear. Perhaps now you'd like to tour the stalls with me and hold that beautiful bouquet,' she sniffed, speaking to Sally as if she were a lady-in-waiting. Sally clearly relished the job, and followed Mrs MP around, still dragging a highly embarrassed George and an equally embarrassed Peter behind her.

Mrs MP graciously spent sixpence at each stall, each time making the same comment in ringing tones. 'Do you know, I never spend less than sixpence per stall when I open a garden party!' Her much-proclaimed policy hit problems when she got to the cake stall, because the only item still left for sale was priced at a shilling. 'What a delicious-looking cake,' Mrs MP enthused. 'I can't understand why it hasn't been snapped up!' I could, since it was Grandma Weighton's infamous walnut cake, to which the locals had given a sensible wide berth. 'But haven't you got anything else left for about sixpence?' Mrs MP quizzed a disgruntled-looking Doris Harsley, worn out by frantic trading.

'No we haven't,' she snapped. 'We're absolutely sold out.'

'Perhaps we could cut Grandma's cake in two,' Ivy Weighton suggested, sensing a sale on the cards for the stall's most unsaleable item, 'and make it sixpence each piece.'

'Fair enough,' Doris Earsley agreed, sawing the cake in two with the effort of a lumberjack faced by a piece of particularly tough mahogany. Mrs MP breezed off, thrilled to bits with her half, while I took pity on the remaining bit and coughed up my own sixpence. Pro-Weighton as I was, I not only bought the other half, but even ate it in the days following. Actually it proved delicious, absolutely saturated with walnuts. When I met a somewhat-green-at-the-gills MP a week later, I gathered that he and his wife had drawn the short straw, or to be more accurate, the tallow-saturated half, and had been laid low with food poisoning.

I counted my deliverance on a par with the children of Israel being led dry-foot through the Red Sea while their pursuers perished.

It might not have been that particular cake which poisoned them, since Mrs MP won the Guess the Weight of the Cake competition and so was treated to a double dose of Grandma Weighton's culinary delights. She balanced the cake in her hand, weighing it up and looking at the other entries on the list. 'People must be very bad at estimating weights around here,' she proclaimed, looking at the guesses: 3 oz; 2½oz; 1¼oz; 42lb; 45lb; 87lb. 'Put me down for four pounds two ounces,' she ordered, and won the thing outright.

As the afternoon progressed, we heard cheers and groans from the crowd of men standing in front of my living-room window. At a little after 4.30, as we were clearing up the garden party remnants, they all made a stampede down my drive. 'They're 'avin' to play extra time, so we're bugger, er headin' off to watch t' rest at home,' one of the men breathlessly explained to me as he rushed past.

Rebecca nearly mowed the posse of men down as she drove up to the vicarage. She had been marking GCE scripts all afternoon, but had agreed to come and help her mum and me tot up the day's takings, so we settled ourselves in my living room, turned the TV around and watched as we counted. Ivy Weighton spread her tea-towel over my new oak coffee table to offer some protection against the coins we piled up on it.

I was so thrilled when England scored their third goal that I accidentally knocked over a tower of shillings that Ivy had been building for ages. 'Ee, Vicar, I mean David, just control yourself otherwise we'll never get all this money counted. Has someone scored?' she asked, hardly interested in the piece of history that was being played out in front of our eyes.

'Yes, I think they have,' I replied, as the referee checked with the linesman whether the ball had actually gone into the goal-mouth.

We continued counting as the final minutes of the match rolled by. 'They think it's all over,' the worried commentator shouted as the spectators invaded the pitch. He was interrupted by a fuzzy Geoff Hurst shooting the ball into the back of the West German goal. 'It is now!' he concluded triumphantly.

'We've won, we've won,' I exclaimed, giving Rebecca a hug and hugging Ivy too for good measure. 'We've won, Ivy!'

'I know we've won, Vicar, don't take on so. I make the total a hundred and eighty-nine pounds ten shillings and fourpence, which includes the one and threepence collected in the box you put on top of your telly. We've never made anything approaching that amount before. We've really won. You'll be able to do up the school at Eastwith grand with all that.'

I should have remembered what Bill Everingham had said the night before about women's total aversion to football.

Sunday 31 July

Rebecca came for supper, and we ate from a tray in front of the TV as we watched the umpteenth re-run of the final, with the umpteenth post-mortem and the ump-teenth discussion about that goal. For the umpteenth time we saw the ball power off Geoff Hurst's foot, and hover tantalizingly over the goal-line as history itself was weighed in the balance. For the umpteenth time we saw the referee hesitate and look towards the linesman. For the umpteenth time we saw the linesman frozen in between decisions, and then his arm shot up, the flag flew, and for the umpteenth time you heard the crowd roar and felt your own heart swell.

'Who did you really want to win?' I asked Rebecca, as I tucked into my fourth bacon sandwich. I had managed to overcome my aversion to pork following our gory trip to the pig factory. And anyway, on Sunday evening I always had a massive appetite: crawling away from church after the last service, I could quite happily eat a horse without any repugnance.

'I don't know, I don't know,' Rebecca replied, genuinely in two minds. 'I'm glad England's won and that everybody is so thrilled – even the sleepy Withs has got a buzz about it today. And I'm glad England had a fight on their hands and it wasn't a pushover. But I'm sorry for the German team when they got so far, and their supporters – they must feel so deeply disappointed. Although I suppose Germans have got used to having their hopes dashed by now...' she trailed away.

'And do you think that goal should have been allowed?' I asked, the question which was on everyone's lips.

She shrugged her shoulders. 'I don't know,' she admitted. 'Who does? It seems funny that all these celebrations are based on a victory that was so vapid.'

'I suppose the fourth goal made it more of a certainty,' I replied, taking an enthusiastic bite out of my sixth bacon sandwich while Rebecca still nibbled at her first.

'Yes, but would we have got that goal if the Germans hadn't been so demoralized by our third?' she pressed. She paused for a while before continuing. 'It's queer, but in a funny sort of way, that match catches my own condition...' She broke off and cried. I put my arm around her and hugged her as she sobbed.

'I'm sorry,' she said, as the tears dried up. 'I'm all right, really. Just tired with all this extra marking I've taken on.'

'You're coping with a lot,' I said gently.

'And I've missed you like hell, this last week,' she added, smiling through the tears. 'Talking through things with you at the end of the day holds everything together. It was horrible when you weren't around.'

'Well, I'm going to be around for a lifetime, so don't worry. Although, keep quiet about it – I don't offer this service to every parishioner. Only the one. Only you.'

'It is funny, though, isn't it?' she asked.

'What, having a priest as your personal chaplain?'

'No, you idiot!' she replied, punching me playfully. 'This feeling that we build all our splendid castles on nothing at all really. The whole country's wild with excitement over a goal that never really was. Just because we've decided to go for it. And that's where the parallel with me comes in. My origins are so murky, I don't really know who my father is, I don't really know my nationality, whether my genes have a bit of Transylvania in them, "vere the vampires come vrom,"' she grinned wickedly. 'And yet, even with all that uncertainty, I go for it, and go for it with all my body and soul, mind and strength.'

'That seems a fair analysis of the whole human condition, really, love. Although you're a bit of an acute case with your Dracula streak. When we're married I'll make sure I always have some garlic under my pillow!' As I said that, she punched me again, not all that playfully. I could see I would have to keep a careful eye on this potential husband-beater.

AUGUST 1966

Saturday 6 August

If everything after the day England won the World Cup was just a postscript, then today would be a very honourable postscript indeed, the wedding day of George Broadhurst and Pam Thorne. There was a *Sound of Music* feel to the whole relationship, the sad widower in the big house with so many children to manage, rescued by a perky young woman who enables their hearts to sing once again. Doris Harsley caught that mood as she played 'Edelweiss' on the harmonium before the wedding. 'Idol vice, idol vice,' Becky Ludlow trilled softly from the fifth pew back.

George sat in the pew at the front, rubbing his collar nervously, turning around from time to time and smiling at friends and relatives as they clattered in. I noticed the smile had a slight quiver to it, symptomatic of the emotions of sadness and joy that were warring within him. After all, it was only just over a year since his wife had died so tragically.

Beside George sat his best man, Geoff Goodmanham, who had been prised out of his Harris tweed for the occasion. During our London trip, June had dragged him off down Oxford Street and had decked him out in the trendiest blue suit. His hair was still ruffled though.

I stood at the lychgate and watched Pam as she approached along the half-mile track to the church, followed by her bridesmaids who had their work cut out for them, keeping her train from sweeping the dusty road. At least there was no mud around after the long dry spell.

My mind switched back to a dark, wet October night, my first service here, after I had been installed by the Archdeacon as the parish's new vicar. Despite warnings from Sam Harsley, the Archdeacon would not be told, and slithered his car along the quagmire of a road, mud up to his axles, having a collision en route with an angry cow which had driven an outraged hoof through his car door.

My imagination also revisited my first Sunday, a train of gypsy caravans slipping and sliding along the same mud, gypsy children darting in and out and underneath the wheels, no strangers to danger. They'd just turned up, wanting their babies christened, and I had done the deed there and then, the church packed with yellow-faced gypsies and their yellow-faced babies, the hush the most reverent I had ever encountered. The leader of the pack had looked up at the baby Jesus, depicted in the stained glass of the east window, another baby with a yellow, weather-beaten face. 'We believe in Him, sir. We believe in Him,' he said softly to me.

I remembered another day, a windy day in March, when local farm-hands had walked the long half-mile along the church track, bearing Hans' coffin, carrying him to his final resting place, a place he had travelled to from Transylvania via Rommel's campaign in the Sahara desert, and made his home. I recalled Ivy's tears and Rebecca's tears, thinking at the time that they were grieving as if for a husband and father.

My mind snapped back to the present as Pam arrived at the church gate, the radiant bride. Her arm was held by Bill Everingham; he was taking the place of her father, who had died at home three years before, nursed to the end by his loving daughter.

Her chief bridesmaid was Emma Broad-hurst, decked out in a pretty pink dress, completely in control, with all the calm assurance of a girl on the brink of woman-hood. I led them to the church door and waved frantically at Doris Harsley, who hurriedly brought her rendition of 'Climb Every Mountain' to an end before it had even reached base camp, and struck up the chords of Handel's 'Arrival of the Queen of Sheba'.

We walked slowly down the narrow aisle. George shot out of his place and strode over to the chancel step, Geoff Goodmanham striding after him. George turned his head and looked at his bride, a broader smile on his face than the one he had greeted his guests with, but the same quiver to his lips.

Once we had reached the chancel steps, I separated Pam from Bill, who seemed welded to her arm. 'You can let go, now, Bill. You've got her here safely,' I whispered.

'Ay, well, I had to hold on to her tight. I did-n't want her fall-in' in ditch,' he shouted out in his usual ponderous voice, much to the amusement of the congregation. Once again I was singularly failing in trying to impress George's university crowd.

I announced the first hymn, 'All creatures

of our God and King', and then read the preface to the Marriage Service, while George's daughter Sally, second bridesmaid in command, whiled away her boredom by twirling her bouquet around and around. She was clearly intrigued by the centrifugal action which made bits of fern and flower petals spin off, following their trajectory eagle-eyed, jumping up and down with glee if they caught any member of the congregation a glancing blow.

'It was ordained for the increase of mankind, according to the will of God, and that children might be brought up in the fear and nurture of the Lord,' I read, as a chrysanthemum landed in Hannah Everingham's hair. Peter Broadhurst, normally as good as gold, competed with Sally in the naughtiness stakes. He looked so sweet dressed as a page in a crisp white shirt, black bow tie and shiny black suit, complete with a suede waistcoat. My guess was that he was all too well aware of how sweet he looked, and was uneasy because he feared the taunts of his school friends should they spy him dressed as such a toff. He shuffled from one foot to the other, fiddling with his tie, and pulled faces at any child who caught his eye, as if to say, 'You just watch it, chum.

435

Beneath this polished exterior lurks a real hard case!'

When she wasn't being bombarded by chrysanthemums, Hannah Everingham was attempting to nurse baby Simon, who roared in protest, wanting to be held by Pam and resolutely refusing comfort from anyone else. He made successive attempts to lurch out of Hannah Everingham's arms, and howled in protest each time he was restrained. His shrieking threatened to bring the whole proceedings to a halt, until in between the first set of promises, I had a quiet word with George, suggesting he extract his son from Hannah and make the rest of his wedding vows with a babe in arms. This act enabled the child, who was now near enough to his beloved Pam, to calm down.

'Who giveth this woman to be married to this man?' I asked, solemnly.

'Ee, Vic-ar, I do,' Bill Everingham blurted out, taking Pam's hand with great aplomb, and giving it to me, as if we were acting out some complex Highland reel.

I was about to place her hand in George's when baby Simon intervened, grasping her hand tightly with his own, and refusing to let go. This was obviously a child who liked to intervene in the Church's sacraments. I recalled the little mite taking control at his own baptism, scooping up the water from the font and drenching everyone with the same hand with which he now gripped Pam. I made a mental note to make sure he was always a good way from the altar when I was celebrating Communion, otherwise he'd be splashing communion wine around and I would be tempted to call on the services of the Blessed Consuming Sisters of the A1 yet again.

'Oh, just put your hand over Pam's and sandwich his in between the two of you,' I instructed George, sotto voce; in return he gave me one of those hapless looks for which professors are famous. Since the little boy was well under the legal age of consent, I felt that we could safely assume he wasn't entering into the marriage contract.

George was so very nervous, Pam so very composed. As he said his vows, he very nearly broke down as he came to the words 'Till death us do part'. That short phrase summarized it all, marking a death so sudden, so tragic, so much grieved over. But paradoxically, without that very same death, the love George and Pam were celebrating would never have blossomed. Little wonder

George almost wept.

Every wedding I take, a lump comes in my throat as I wrap my stole around the right hands of the couple kneeling before me and declare, 'I pronounce that they be man and wife together, in the name of the Father, and of the Son, and of the Holy Ghost.' The words are few and commonly used, so they shouldn't in themselves move me so mightily. The way they are put together has a certain poetry about it, but there again, a rhythmic economy shouldn't in itself make the tears well up. I suspect it is the timelessness of that moment which fills me with such awe. Stretched before me in an instant I see the years, the decades ahead, all the joy, all the heartbreak, all the love, all the children, all the grandchildren, all the generations yet unborn. I see one watching the other die, eyes so deeply sorrowful. The immensity, the sheer seriousness of it all, catches me, and I want to cry. I never do, but at a cost. At the end of every marriage I feel wrung out; the emotions warring within have drained me.

By the end of the marriage vows both George and I were distinctly the worse for wear. We were put to shame by Pam, who still retained that composed look, clearly relishing every second, radiating the impression that this was the day for which she was made.

We launched into the second hymn, 'Now thank we all our God'. I noticed that Emma choked up on the line 'Who from our mother's arms, hath blessed us on our way', which made three of us fighting back the tears. I led the couple to the altar steps for further prayers, including invoking the Almighty that Pam would be a follower of holy and godly matrons, which made it sound as if she was aspiring to the Hattie Jacques part in Carry On Doctor. Then, following the blessing, we adjourned to the vestry to catch our breaths and sign every register we could find.

I put my head around the vestry door and waved frantically again at Doris Harsley, who set to playing Widor's 'Toccata', or rather a reduced version somewhat limited by the harmonium's narrow range. George emerged from the vestry with Pam his new wife on his left arm and the ever-wriggling Simon held by his right, with their three children following dutifully behind, or reasonably dutifully in Sally and Peter's case. The whole congregation burst into spontaneous and hearty applause, an accolade which even Julie Andrews, warbling her highest notes, would have been proud to achieve.

Ron Ran Run's vintage coach took us the winding fourteen miles to York University's banqueting hall, where a lavish reception was laid on. Late into the evening, George and Pam departed for a brief honeymoon, entrusting their children to the Goodmanhams for a few days. 'These teachers have too long school holidays,' I heard Doris Harsley comment, 'so it'll do them good to have something to do.'

As Pam climbed into the wedding car, she threw her bouquet in the air. It was boldly caught by my Rebecca, certain now that she wanted to get married.

Friday 19 August

In the warm twilight of an August evening I decided to have a last wander around my garden, or at least my last wander as a bachelor. My eyes scanned the trees, their leaves grey in the half-light of dusk, their greens already jaded and fading in the full light of day, heralding autumn, the season where I came in. I was searching for the owl, whose sharp screeching so often disturbed my sleep. I don't really know why I looked for him with such a desperate longing. I guess I just wanted to nod to him in passing, to salute this bird so wonderfully made.

When Dewi had been a tiny puppy, I used to take him out last thing at night to stave off a puddle on my kitchen floor the next morning. One night the owl had swooped down upon him, mistaking him for a rabbit kitten, and when Dewi had yapped at him, realized his error and wisely aborted the snatch. I heard the slow beat of his wings as he fixed on his prey, and even though it was my pet which was threatened, I stood transfixed: in homage. Tonight, after peering at every tree, I saw his silhouette high in the elm, and stood still for several minutes, simply watching him watching.

I turned my head as I heard a car draw up along my drive, and caught sight of a Hillman Imp. A few months back, Herbert Molescroft would have been the last person I would have wished to see on the eve of my wedding. And yet tonight, I was strangely glad when I saw his familiar car trundle up the drive. So much had happened in these past few months, with Herbert Molescroft playing a pivotal role in so many situations.

We'd been through a lot together, and I actually welcomed this chance to see him and tie up some loose ends before my big day.

'I hope you don't mind me calling around on tonight of all nights, but I thought I'd pop over with a small present for you and Rebecca for your big day tomorrow,' he said as he climbed out of his car. He was bearing in his arms a large parcel, immaculately wrapped in silver paper and tied with a red bow.

'How very kind of you,' I replied. 'I'm very, very touched. Come in for a few minutes. I'll put the kettle on and we can have a cuppa and a bit of a chat. I realize I haven't seen much of you for a week or two.'

'Well, if you're sure that's no bother, but I really didn't want to trouble you. I only called to drop the present off,' he said meekly.

'It's no trouble at all,' I assured him. 'You'll have had a fair drive over, and the least I can do is get you a drink before you return.'

'Well, in that case, I will have a cuppa. It's a hot night and my throat has got rather dry,' he admitted, so I led him through the house into the kitchen.

'I'm rather glad you've come,' I said, as I put the kettle on. 'I've been thinking a lot about all those weeks you had following in my footsteps. It'll be good to hear your views about it all.'

'Yes, I've been thinking a lot about it too,' he agreed. And then suddenly he blurted out a neat little speech: 'I'm very grateful to you for all your efforts, and for sharing so much of yourself. The more I've thought about the things you did and said, and I didn't half react to some of them at the time, the more I've realized the good sense in them all. So sorry for being so stuffy.'

'I didn't really think you were stuffy,' I replied ('Oh yes you did!' a voice shouted inside my head). 'I sensed it was more that you had a theoretical view of ministry which needed defining by what was possible in practice. And we certainly had plenty of practice for you to bounce your theories off!'

'But it wasn't just that,' he replied. 'You actually were prepared to roll your sleeves up and get alongside folk. Like when you helped rescue that churchwarden's cow, while I stayed safe in my car, thinking that sort of thing was beneath me.'

'Oh, I'm not sure that's anything to do

with ministry,' I smiled. 'It dates back to my first day in Martins' Bank, when the manager's assistant took me aside and said, "Look here, lad, we all muck in here, from the manager to the junior, we all lend a hand. None of us is too important not to roll up our sleeves and help get the job done. You just remember that!" And I always have.'

'But that seems the essence of the Incarnation, God mucking in through what he did in his Son, Jesus,' he commented, clearly still prone to use churchy language.

'Well, yes, I can see that.' I agreed. 'Although I don't think my manager's assistant at Martins' would have quite put it that way.'

'Did he pass any other gems on to you?' Herbert asked.

'Well, yes,' I said, smiling as I reminisced. 'A favourite quote of his was, "As a customer gets nastier and nastier, you must get nicer and nicer, and then when he's gone, go behind the counter and kick the hell out of a desk!"'

'But that's pure Jesus, turning the other cheek,' Herbert exclaimed, once again lapsing into churchiness.

'Yes, well, part of the fun of ministry is

recognizing the Christian practices people live their lives by, even if they would never give them a Christian label in a million years,' I suggested.

'So is that why you spend so much time with non-Church folk?' he asked.

'Yes, it really keeps me going, being surprised by Christ in the most unlikely of places. It helps me cope with the disappointment when sometimes he doesn't seem to be around in the most likely places, like the Church,' I replied, being deliberately provocative.

But he wouldn't be drawn. He seemed like a man who had come with something he had to say, and was not going to be thwarted by me from saying it. 'And another thing,' he continued. 'Despite all the farcical situations we ended up in, you always carried on, never let it get you down, even with me moaning about what a mess we'd made of the show.'

'I've told you before,' I stressed, 'how real ministry takes place, not when we're at our peak of expertise and prowess, but when we sense we've failed and made a real pig's ear of things. At times like that, when we're forced to stop feeling yours truly is a real shining light, God's light can shine through.

In my book the only qualification for ministry that really counts is that someone should have promising weaknesses through which God's strength can flow unimpeded.'

'Mm, promising weaknesses, promising weaknesses,' Herbert said, rolling the words around his tongue. 'I like that. I suppose when I started here I thought that I had promising strengths for ministry. Watching you has taught me otherwise!'

'So what are you going to do now?' I asked.

'Well, next month I'm seeing the Bishop of Pocklington again,' he replied. 'I've stopped trying to map out my future. I'll just tell him about my time here, how I've changed, and see where he thinks we should go from there.'

'I'll drop him a line, put in a good word for you, tell him about your displaying a surprising talent for dance at the old people's home!'

'Oh, please don't do that,' Herbert pleaded, blushing a deep red as he recalled his ordeal.

'Don't worry. When the Bishop visited here last March, you should have seen the dance he performed at the Weightons' farm, when one of the sheepdogs bit his heel!' I exclaimed. 'And a few minutes later, he peered into Grandma's pot to admire her stew – bishops have to be pastoral like that – and accidentally dunked his pectoral cross in the stuff. You should have seen the dance he performed when the cross swung back and Grandma's scalding concoction trickled down his chest!'

Herbert laughed and laughed. If nothing else, his time in the Withs had enabled him to defrost and see the funny side of things. We chatted for a few minutes more, and then he made his excuses and departed. As I waved him off, my friend the owl swooped down over his car, a type of salute for a man who I guess would get there in the end.

Saturday 20 August

The second postscript permitted after our World Cup victory had brought history to an end would have to be the day of my wedding to Rebecca. In one sense, the role reversal felt strange, with me in the place of the bridegroom instead of the priest. I recalled the story of an obnoxious curate who wrote and asked his bishop for permission to officiate at his own wedding.

'I have carefully consulted Church Law,' the bishop wrote back, 'and I'm afraid that what you ask is not permitted. But while you are not allowed to marry yourself, it seems that Church Law contains no objection to burying yourself, if you wish.'

My friend Stamford Chestnut, the Rector of Charm-on-Spalding-Moor, was to take the service, with strict instructions from me not to mention either pigs or hairdressing should he feel moved to deliver a homily. For the second time in a fortnight, Geoff Goodmanham acted as best man. He sat beside me now, calm, reassuring me. I kept getting out of my seat and checking things, whether Doris Harsley had the right music, whether the registers were correctly completed, whether Sam Harsley had lit the candles, until Stamford Chestnut gave me a piece of his mind. 'For goodness sake, David, stop fretting about and sit down. I'm in charge today, not you. You just concentrate on not fluffing your marriage vows!' I suppose a bridegroom on his wedding day could have no better maxim than that.

The service went like a dream. As Pam had done a fortnight before, Rebecca walked to the church, with Emma and Sally

Broadhurst following behind her, easily pressed into being bridesmaids again. I turned and watched her as she walked up the aisle, confident, stunningly beautiful, her father clutching her arm for support as he prepared to give away his pride and joy.

We had learnt our wedding vows off by heart, so we didn't need the usual prompting, in a sense marrying ourselves despite the bishop's strictures in my story. We knelt together underneath the chancel arch, its ancient Norman zigzags absolutely covered with flowers with which the villagers had decorated every nook and cranny of the church. Stamford wrapped his white stole around our joined hands and proclaimed, 'I pronounce that they be man and wife together, in the name of the Father, and of the Son, and of the Holy Ghost, Amen.' I noticed his voice falter, I saw that he too had tears in his eyes.

He preached a strange little sermon. 'I'd like to tell you, my friends, about Martin Luther, champion of the Reformation, who moved on from being a celibate monk to a husband and father of six children,' he began. I heard Ivy Weighton give a sharp intake of breath at the number six.

Stamford's theory was that the experience

of marriage and fatherhood was a school for character for Luther, and fashioned him into a true priest, more than any learning and training could have done. He closed his talk with a touching story which made the hairs rise on the back of my neck, because there were eerie echoes of Rebecca's situation.

'When Luther's daughter, Magdalena, was fourteen years old, she lay upon her deathbed, while her father prayed beside her, "O God, I love her so, but thy will be done". He then addressed his dying little girl, "Magdalenchen, you would like to stay with your father here, and you would be glad to go to your father in heaven?"'

'"Yes, dear father, as God wills," she replied, and with that gave up the ghost as her sorrowing father held her in his arms, blessed more than any celibate prince-bishop, his distraught wife weeping beside him. *Du liebes Lenchen*," he preached at her funeral, "you will rise and shine like the stars and the sun. How strange it is to know that you are at peace and all is well, and yet to be so sorrowful."

'To that immense joy, and the sorrow which will only sharpen it, we commit David and Rebecca this day,' Stamford concluded.

We had another eerie experience at the reception, held in a marquee which had been erected in the stackyard of the Weightons' farm. The stackyard had been brushed reasonably clean for the occasion, although the entrance to the marquee was flanked by half a dozen guests, surreptitiously wiping their posh-shoed feet on the grass verge, because they had trodden in something nasty within. They made a quaint guard of honour as we processed into the reception.

Rebecca and I had insisted on outside caterers providing and serving the fare, which we helped fund ourselves. 'On this day of all days, you deserve a day off, Mum,' Rebecca had insisted, saving our eighty guests from mass food poisoning.

But not quite, since Grandma Weighton had insisted on baking the wedding cake.

Rebecca and I could have done with a chainsaw to cut the first slice, but we succeeded at the third attempt, having bent two knives in the process. The cake was then whisked away by the caterers before being served to the guests. Those in the know carefully scrutinized their piece, picking out bits of wax before popping it into their mouth, looking like hospital patients having to swallow a bitter pill. Those who weren't in the know gleefully bit off a chunk, and then looked as if they wished they hadn't, as they rolled the cake morsel around their mouth, trying to place the flavour.

'What's a matter with you, Josh?' I over-heard my great-aunt Ethel ask her husband. 'You look as if you're sucking a lemon!'

'No, it's not that, duck,' came his mumbled reply. 'I was just wondering whether one of my fillings had come loose, or whether this hard bit was in the cake to begin with. It's got a queer taste, almost waxy...'

Peter Broadhurst rolled up his cake into a tight little ball, which he proceeded to bowl overarm at the table opposite him. There was the sound of a plate shattering, followed by a sharp look from his father. 'Now then, Pet-er,' Bill Everingham piped up, very good-naturedly, considering it had been his bread plate that had been the unfortunate victim of the missile. 'You'll have to bowl bet-ter than that if you're go-in' to make Withs' crick-et team. Mind you, cork-ie you'll use will be quite a bit soft-er.'

Flo and Edna were sitting at a table near to ours, with Becky Ludlow and two of my cousins. In the poor lighting within the marquee, Edna was about as blind as her sister, so my cousins willingly helped them by cutting up their food and describing precisely what the delicacies were. 'Now this is nice, it's chicken vol-au-vent,' I overheard one say.

'Yes, you try a bit, Flo,' Mrs Ludlow agreed encouragingly. 'You can't beat a few chicken vents, you really can't.'

'And what about this special sausage? It's a Frankfurter, I think,' my other cousin suggested.

'Oh go on, Edna,' Mrs Ludlow cajoled. 'I just love getting a nice Frank Fitter in between my teeth.' I was only grateful that for sweet we had opted for raspberry pavlova and had wisely avoided sillybugger trifle.

When it came to the cake course, neither Flo nor Edna could be prevailed upon to eat even a crumb. 'Oh come on,' I heard my cousin say encouragingly, 'I understand it's been specially baked by the bride's grandmother. What a talented lady she must be.'

'That's why we don't want any of it,' Flo bluntly replied.

'Now don't be like that,' my cousin persisted. 'We mustn't risk causing offence.

Just try a little bit.' She broke off a piece and put it to Flo's mouth, but her lips remained tightly and obstinately sealed.

To prevent the whole episode degenerating into a force-feeding session which even the suffragettes would have blanched at, I rose from high table and walked over to my cousins. 'I think Flo and Edna have probably had enough,' I advised them. 'They don't get out much these days, so their appetites are rather small. We'll wrap the cake up in their serviettes so they can take it home with them.'

'And feed it to t' cat!' I heard Flo mutter.

'Ee, Vicar, it's good of you to pop over,' Edna enthused, fortunately drowning out her sister's sour comment. 'We're right enjoying ourselves. What a lovely wedding – Miss Weighton's voice was as clear as a bell. Yours was too, although you're used to speakin' up. She's a lovely girl your wife, a lovely girl. I used to travel on t' bus with her when she was a schoolgirl, gave her a bit o' protection when secondary mod kids went wild as they were wont to do. But she had a lovely forgiving and loving nature. You're a lucky man and she's a lucky woman. God bless you both, God bless you both.'

'God bless you as well, Edna,' I replied. 'I

see Hinderwells are getting on really well with the renovation. You'll soon be in your new home.'

'Ay, I'm so grateful for that, so very grateful,' she exclaimed. 'And we're right pleased that Becky here is going to be our new neighbour when both of the houses are done up. It makes our house cold with no one living next door, so to have anyone occupying it would have been good news. It'll be doubly good having someone like Becky.'

'Yes, and I won't say I won't be glad to see the back of that house o' mine in Eastwith,' Mrs Ludlow declared. 'Despite all the memories, I can't wait for the day when I leave it. I've always hated the place, always.'

'Who will you put in the new bungalow when it's built?' Flo asked, as blunt as ever. 'Make sure it's someone we can get on with.'

'That narrows it down to a short-list of none in your case,' I thought. 'There are a few people who are a possibility,' was my official reply. I thought of old Martin if he needed to shake off his enema-obsessed nurse. And then there was Captain Dunnington if their large house got too much to handle. 'Although perhaps we'll leave it empty, just in case you and your sister fall out and need separate accommodation!' I joked, as I made my way back to my place.

'Well, I never!' Flo blurted out. 'How rude can you get?' Edna just laughed.

The wedding speeches went off OK. Despite my experience of preaching, I was extremely nervous, and gabbled on about the history of my wife's name, talking about the first ever Rebecca in the Book of Genesis, another farmer's daughter, another beautiful girl, who had been wooed by Isaac, Abraham's son. 'Well fancy that, fancy that,' Becky Ludlow piped up. 'I never realized my name was so hysterical.'

And the eerie experience? Geoff Goodmanham read out the cards and telegrams, the usual amalgam of jolly best wishes and raunchy messages from college friends. And then his face took on a serious expression. 'This letter is from a solicitor in York,' he said, holding up an official-looking document. 'He read about your forthcoming marriage in the local paper...'

I shuddered as I recalled the headline which had appeared in the *Evening Press* last week, 'Head teacher Geoff looks on as Dave and Rebecca tie the knot!'

'...and forwarded the enclosed letter.

Apparently he was the legal executor for someone who left him instructions that this letter was to be read out at Rebecca's wedding. That certain someone we all knew very well. His name was Hans.'

An expectant hush descended upon the marquee. Even the cattle in the nearby barn stopped their mooing and pricked up their ears. Rebecca's ruddy complexion turned pale, her mother turned ashen and I could see her hands shaking as Geoff opened the envelope and began to read Hans' words from the other side of the grave.

'"My dear Rebecca,"' Geoff began. '"That you are this letter having read to you..." I'm sorry, but that's how it's put,' Geoff broke off. 'It's obviously genuine Hans, complete with the broken English we all knew and loved!'

He began again, his face deadpan. '"That you are this letter having read to you, means that I am not able to be with you on this your greatest day. And for that I am very sorry. Sorry because your family have been always so generous and very kind to me, and I would have liked very much to have shared this celebration with them. You have all treated me as one of your family since twenty-five years, taking me in when no one else wanted to know me and making your home my home.

'"*Meine Liebling* Rebecca, your beautiful mother and hardworking father will be so deeply proud of you on this your wedding day. I have loved you since you were tiny, treating you as the daughter I never had, and you returned my affection, treating me like a second father. I am so proud of you, so proud that you mastered the language of my birth, so proud that you now teach that language to a world which has at last found fragile peace. I pray that God may bless you every day of your marriage and that your happiness and love may abound. I envy the fellow who the good fortune has to be your husband, and charge him to care for you, otherwise he will have to answer to the man from the land of 'vere the vampires come vrom'!"'

Geoff folded up the letter and solemnly gave it to Rebecca. 'It's simply signed "with all my love, Hans",' he concluded.

The whole reception fell into an awe-filled silence. A tear trickled down Rebecca's face as she re-read Hans' letter to her, an immensely well-written and tactful piece of work. Ivy's colour returned and she looked immensely happy, reassured by Hans' voice from the grave.

The silence was broken by Doris Harsley. 'Well at least he said "With all my love" and not "Bugger off then",' she quipped. 'That would have made a fine message for a girl on her wedding day.' People who moments before had been on the edge of tears burst into peals of laughter, as poignancy was seasoned with humour.

I took the opportunity of putting my arm around Rebecca and kissed her lightly on the cheek. 'God bless us both,' I whispered.

'He'd better,' Rebecca whispered back. 'Or he'll have the man vrom vere the vampires come vrom to reckon with!'

The publishers hope that this book has given you enjoyable reading. Large Print Books are especially designed to be as easy to see and hold as possible. If you wish a complete list of our books please ask at your local library or write directly to:

Magna Large Print Books
Magna House, Long Preston,
Skipton, North Yorkshire.
BD23 4ND